WHAT MOTIVATES BUREAUCRATS?

Power, Conflict, and Democracy:
American Politics Into the Twenty-first Century
Robert Y. Shapiro, Editor

This series focuses on how the will of the people and the public interest are promoted, encouraged, or thwarted. It aims to question not only the direction American politics will take as it enters the twenty-first century but also the direction American politics has already taken.

The series addresses the role of interest groups and social and political movements; openness in American politics; important developments in institutions such as the executive, legislative, and judicial branches at all levels of government as well as the bureaucracies thus created; the changing behavior of politicians and political parties; the role of public opinion; and the functioning of mass media. Because problems drive politics, the series also examines important policy issues in both domestic and foreign affairs.

The series welcomes all theoretical perspectives, methodologies, and types of evidence that answer important questions about trends in American politics.

WHAT MOTIVATES BUREAUCRATS?

POLITICS AND ADMINISTRATION DURING THE REAGAN YEARS

Marissa Martino Golden

COLUMBIA UNIVERSITY PRESS
NEW YORK

Columbia University Press
Publishers Since 1893
New York   Chichester, West Sussex

Portions of chapters 2, 3, and 5 appeared in the *Journal of Public Administration Research and Theory* 2 (January 1992) and are reprinted here with permission.

Photographic material was provided by Spencer E. Golden.

Library of Congress Cataloging-in-Publication Data
Golden, Marissa Martino.
    What motivates bureaucrats? Politics and administration during the Reagan
    years / Marissa Martino Golden.
        p. cm. — (Power, conflict, and democracy)
    Includes bibliographical references and index.
    ISBN 0-231-10696-3 (cloth : alk. paper) — ISBN 0-231-10697-1 (pbk. : alk. paper)
        1. Government executives—United States. 2. United States—Politics and
    government—1981–1989. I. Title. II. Series.

JK723.E9 G65 2000
352.2′93′097309048—dc21

                                                                        00-027260

This book is dedicated
to my mother, Jane Martino,
to the memory of my father, Eugene Martino,
and to our family's newest member, Gina Rebecca

CONTENTS

ACKNOWLEDGMENTS

This book has been a long time coming, and as a result I am indebted to a number of people and institutions who have inspired, facilitated, cajoled, and supported me at various stages of the project.

The project began when I was a graduate student in the Department of Political Science at the University of California, Berkeley, where I benefited from the wisdom of so many people that I cannot begin to thank them all. But David Leonard, Herb McClosky, Nelson Polsby, and Judith Gruber must be singled out as role models and friends—David for getting me hooked on the field of public administration in the first place, Herb for encouraging me to see things from a behavioralist's perspective and for providing the welcome diversions of Pad Thai and sports talk, and Judy and Nelson for being two of the best dissertation advisors imaginable. Nelson's consistent praise of my work gave me the confidence to keep going during both the dissertation and book phases of this project. And Judy's keen insight and sharp editorial eye improved this work immeasurably, and she never once complained when I continued to send her drafts to read long after I had left Berkeley. If I can be even half the scholar, mentor, and friend that she is, my career will have been a success.

At Berkeley, I also enjoyed the camaraderie of the Institute for Governmental Studies, the Survey Research Center, and a dissertation writing group that included Taylor Dark, John Gerring, Chris Muste, Duane Oldfield, Beth Reingold, and Craig Thomas. I thank these individuals for their gentle criticism and helpful suggestions.

The research itself would not have been possible without the "cooperation" of the career civil servants who graciously agreed to participate in my study. They gave willingly of their time and left me with tremendous respect for their dedication and commitment to public service.

During my time at the University of Pennsylvania, I had the good fortune to meet Paul Light, who read my manuscript in its entirety, and to hang out with a great bunch of graduate students and junior colleagues—Jose Cheibub, Steven Cook, Steve Fish, Joe Glicksberg, Marie Gottschalk, Kerry Haynie, and Rudra Sil—who offered much-appreciated encouragement at critical junctures. Subsequently, the Bryn Mawr College Department of Political Science provided me with a new home, a fresh start, renewed self-confidence, and an exceedingly collegial and congenial environment. I also thank Mina Silberberg and Julie Hagen for their editorial help, Joe Mink, Sam Algozin, and Mark Colvson for their assistance with the references, Harriet Newburger for her comments on chapter 7, and, most of all, Amy Slaton who kept me on a schedule when I procrastinated, and encouraged me when I was plagued with doubt.

Finally, I am particularly grateful to the reviewers at both Columbia University Press and the Brookings Institution Press. Although I am still not sure that their comments are addressed adequately in this book, there is no doubt that they forced me to rethink my argument, and that this book is better as a result. I also thank Marjorie Wexler, my copyeditor at Columbia University Press, who was a pleasure to work with.

But my greatest debt of gratitude is to my husband, Spencer Golden. Without his love and support this book would never have been completed, and for that, and for the joy he has brought to my life, I cannot thank him enough.

CHAPTER 1

BUREAUCRATIC RESPONSIVENESS AND THE ADMINISTRATIVE PRESIDENCY

> Every once in a while, somebody has to get the bureaucracy by the neck and shake it loose and say, stop doing what you're doing.
> —Ronald Reagan (1989:392)

> We know more about abstract agents dealing with abstract principals than we do about real bureaucrats dealing with real politicians.
> —James March (1997:693)

> My remarks today . . . will deal with human motivation, and especially what motivates us in our careers in organizations.
> —Herbert Simon (1997:3)

Imagine that you are a career civil servant, a GS-15, and that you work for the Environmental Protection Agency (EPA). You have spent your career at the EPA enforcing laws designed to reduce pollution. Along comes a president who is more concerned with reducing the regulatory burden on industry than with reducing pollution, who confuses nitrogen oxide (a harmless substance) with nitrogen dioxide (a pollutant), and who states that Mount Saint Helens is a greater source of pollution than automobiles. Not only does he advocate policy change and appoint a new agency administrator, but in turn, that new administrator shares his policy views and works with the Office of Management and Budget (OMB) to cut your agency's budget and curtail the issuance of new regulations. In short, all of a sudden, outsiders are not only telling you how to do your job but also trying to reorient your agency's mission.

Two questions arise: What would you do, and why? These are the questions that motivated me to undertake the research for this book and that are answered in the following pages. The fact that thousands of career civil servants at the EPA and other federal agencies found themselves in just that situation during the Reagan years and that thousands more may find themselves in comparable situations in the future makes the answers to these questions particularly important to those of us concerned with the role of the unelected career civil service in the American political system.

This book has a dual mission. The first is to tell a story, the story of the bureaucrat just described. In what follows, I tell the story of how one set of political actors (career civil servants) reacted to one specific set of circumstances (Ronald Reagan's administrative presidency).[1] It is the story of how the upper-level career civil servants (the GS-13s, 15s, and SESers) at the EPA, as well as at the Justice Department's Civil Rights Division (CRD), the Agriculture Department's Food and Nutrition Service (FNS), and the Department of Transportation's National Highway Traffic Safety Administration (NHTSA), reacted to a president who had a very different vision of policy than did his predecessors, and who employed an administrative strategy to bring agency policy in line with his vision and the bureaucracy to heel.

Telling this story allows us to peer inside the windows of some of the buildings—the Justice Department Building, the Nassif Building, the Park Office Center Annex, and the Waterside Mall—that house our federal agencies, thereby putting a human face on the abstract concepts of principal-agent theory. This story needs to be told so that we have a more realistic and less abstract picture of career civil servants and appointee-career relations and of how the two combine to enhance or detract from bureaucratic responsiveness to elected leadership.

The second mission is to improve our understanding of bureaucratic behavior. Here I offer an explanation for the behavior that I found, an explanation that I believe has applicability well beyond the Reagan years. At its core is an emphasis on the management strategies of presidential appointees, civil servants' role perception and profession-based norms, and agency context as the critical motivating factors of bureaucratic behavior. I argue that these factors explain why the bureaucracy is controllable, as well as highlighting the limits of that control.

We know a lot about what motivates members of Congress (see, e.g., Fenno 1973; Mayhew 1974). But federal agencies make policy too. And we know much less about what motivates the civil servants in them, what that tells us about how they should be managed, and how that affects the kinds of policies that federal agencies produce. This book is an attempt to increase our understanding in this regard.

In short, this book is about upper-echelon career bureaucrats—the people who manage federal agencies and who develop and implement public policy—and how they responded to Ronald Reagan's application of the administrative presidency to their agencies during the 1980s. This episode warrants study because it challenged previous theories about the career bureaucracy—theories that held that bureaucrats were insufficiently responsive to their boss in the White House and would use their power to resist his control efforts.

The argument presented in this book is not that bureaucrats are entirely responsive nor that they are entirely resistant to presidential control efforts. Instead, I draw attention to a set of factors that I believe help us understand *both* bureaucratic responsiveness *and* resistance. These factors enable us to integrate rational choice notions of bureaucratic self-interest and principal-agent preferences for top-down control with public administration's ideas about bureaucrats' role perception and its emphasis on the importance of the internal dynamics and socializing experiences of federal agencies. In other words, these factors acknowledge the roles played by the actions of political principals, the historical legacies of federal agencies, and the personal attitudes and beliefs of the civil servants themselves in shaping bureaucratic behavior in the American political system. The book presents evidence drawn from interviews and case studies that provides empirical support for my claim that these factors matter and that demonstrates how and why they matter. The book's primary contributions thus lie in painting a comprehensive picture of bureaucratic life under the conditions of the administrative presidency (how real bureaucrats deal with real politicians), in providing empirical support for the set of factors that I argue shape that life (what motivates us in our careers in organizations), and in providing a framework that enables us to contemplate the normative and prescriptive implications of these findings.

EARLY VIEWS OF BUREAUCRATIC RESPONSIVENESS

Scholars of public administration have long been concerned with the issue of bureaucratic responsiveness to the president. And, at least since the administration of Franklin Delano Roosevelt, presidents and their advisers have shared this concern.

The source of their concern is the fact that since the Pendleton Act of 1883, the federal bureaucracy in the United States has been peopled primarily with career civil servants who are neither elected by the citizenry nor appointed by the president. This fact is viewed as acceptable as long as these unelected "agents" are responsive to elected officials such as Congress and the president—in other words, as long as they follow the orders and obey the directives of their elected and constitutionally designated principals. Moreover, scholars have traditionally placed special weight on bureaucratic responsiveness to the president over and above that accorded to Congress (Kaufman 1956; Moe 1987, 1995).[2] This is due in part to the president's constitutional charge to "take care that the laws be faithfully executed" and in part to the fact that he is the only nationally elected public official (Fesler and Kettl 1996; Fried 1976; Rohr 1986; Woll 1977).

In the years immediately following the passage of the Pendleton Act, scholars and presidents believed that career civil servants could be trusted to neutrally implement the president's policies (Wilson 1887). They believed that politics could be separated from administration and that the job of the civil service was limited to carrying out previously specified tasks in the most efficient manner possible (Wilson 1887). As a result, during the Progressive Era, neither scholars nor presidents spent much time worrying about responsiveness (Kaufman 1956; Mosher 1968).

But over time, both scholars and presidents came to hold the view that bureaucrats exercised discretion in ways that undermined the goals and directives of their elected superior in the White House. With the development of the New Deal and an expanded role for the federal bureaucracy, they came to believe that the bureaucracy had the upper hand in this relationship. They argued that due to a host of factors, presidents were mere "dilettantes" in the face of bureaucracy, rather than its masters (Weber 1946). Among the many factors believed to serve as sources of bureaucratic strength and detriments to bureaucratic responsiveness were bureaucratic ties with interest groups and congressional committees (iron triangles), bureaucratic expertise, monopoly of information and informational asymmetries, bureaucratic rigidity and rule obeisance, bureaucrats' self-interested preferences for shirking and budget maximizing, the differing time frames and "clashing beliefs" between career civil servants and political appointees, appointees "marrying the natives," and the number of hours and task demands in the president's day (Rourke 1984; Meier 1980, 1993; Weber 1946; Ross 1973; Spadaro 1973; Merton 1968; Niskanen 1971; Meller 1966; Heclo 1977; Light 1987; Behn 1989; Aberbach and Rockman 1976; Seidman 1975; Wilson 1977; Pious 1979; Riley 1987). In other words, beginning with the New Deal era in Washington and the behavioral era in the social sciences, scholars identified a variety of factors that led them to believe that the career bureaucracy was insufficiently responsive to elected presidents.[3]

At the same time, presidents echoed and expanded on this scholarly view. Most famously, Franklin Roosevelt is alleged to have remarked (Neustadt 1990:37),

> The Treasury is so large and far-flung and ingrained in its practices that I find it impossible to get the action and results I want—even with Henry

[Morgenthau] there. But the Treasury is not to be compared with the State Department. You should go through the experience of trying to get any changes in the thinking, policy and actions of the career diplomats and then you'd know what a real problem was. But the Treasury and State Departments together are nothing compared to the Na-a-vy. The admirals are really something to cope with—and I should know. To change anything in the Na-a-vy is like punching a feather bed. You punch it with your right and you punch it with your left until you are finally exhausted and then you find the damn bed just as it was before you started punching.

Among the many presidential aides to express the president's point of view was Joseph Califano (1975:23), President Lyndon Johnson's secretary of Health, Education and Welfare (now Health and Human Services), who wrote, "More often than not these agencies operate as independent fiefdoms, responsive to their own constituencies, pet theories, and the congressional committees to which they look for oversight, rather than to presidential leadership and the broad national interest."

Such was the situation entering the 1980s—presidents railed against an out-of-control bureaucracy, and scholars (presidency scholars, public administrationists, sociologists, and economic theorists alike) provided theoretical justification for their laments. But then along came Ronald Reagan riding into Washington on an antigovernment, antibureaucracy platform. Reagan's (1989:392) statement that "every once in a while, somebody has to get the bureaucracy by the neck and shake it loose and say, stop doing what you're doing" was the presidential equivalent of "I'm mad as hell, and I'm not going to take it anymore." Building on a strategy initially designed and developed by President Richard Nixon, Reagan brought to full flower a strategy that Richard Nathan has dubbed "the administrative presidency" (Durant 1992; Nathan 1975, 1983a; Seyb 1992; Waterman 1989).

THE ADMINISTRATIVE PRESIDENCY

The administrative presidency is a management strategy designed to ensure bureaucratic responsiveness to the president. It is intended to help presidents achieve their policy goals administratively through the bureaucracy rather than legislatively through Congress, and to bring the bureaucracy to heel (Durant 1992; Nathan 1983a). It consists of a set of tools whose purpose is to rein in the bureaucracy, overcome the bureaucratic advantages just identified, and enable presidents to achieve their policy objectives without requiring congressional consent (Rubin 1985; Sanders 1988). In short, this strategy was explicitly devised by Nixon and adopted by Reagan to overcome the power deficit perceived by both scholars and presidents, to enhance presidential control over the "fourth branch" and its personnel, and to create a more responsive bureaucracy.[4]

To this end, the administrative presidency utilizes a set of tools, perhaps more aptly described as an arsenal of weapons.[5] At their core are strategic appointments (Durant 1992; Ingraham 1995; Michaels 1997; Nathan 1983a; Wood and Waterman 1991). Whereas earlier presidents typically appointed individuals who had ties to agency clients and interest groups and whose loyalties were thus divided, administrative presidents select their appointees strategically, based on their ideological policy congruence with the president. This tool is designed to avoid the traditional problem of appointees who "marry the natives." Examples of this approach include Nixon's replacement of George Romney with James Lynn at the Department of Housing and Urban Development and Reagan's appointment of committed conservatives such as James Watt, William Bradford Reynolds, and Clarence Thomas at the Department of the Interior, Civil Rights Division, and Equal Employment Opportunity Commission (EEOC), respectively (Lynn 1984; Maranto 1993b; Waterman 1989).

In addition, the administrative presidency is distinguished by its use of this appointment strategy at all levels of the organization. That is, administrative presidents make strategic appointments not only at the cabinet level but also at the subcabinet level and below—as far down into the bowels of the agency as the law will allow (Durant 1992; Ingraham 1995). To do this, presidents capitalize on two institutions: Schedule C appointments and the Senior Executive Service (SES). The Civil Service Reform Act (CRSA) of 1978, which created the Senior Executive Service at the top of the civil service hierarchy, allows up to 10 percent of the SES to be composed of noncareer appointees. Together with Schedule C, a special class of appointees established by President Dwight Eisenhower, presidents are able to make more than 2,300 lower-level appointments (Ingraham 1987; West 1995). The keys to this tool are that appointments are made at all levels of the agency, and that the appointees are selected according to the same ideological criteria as those for cabinet-level strategic appointees. At the Civil Rights Division during the Reagan administration, for example, potential appointees to both the Schedule C and the noncareer SES were given "ideological litmus tests," and their résumés were scanned for evidence of membership in conservative organizations such as the Federalist Society (Holt 1998; Maranto 1993b; Warshaw 1996). This tool—the appointment of large numbers of lower-level strategic appointees—enables presidents to better monitor the activities of career civil servants, as well as to assign line functions to trusted loyalists.

Strategic appointments are, however, just one tool in the administrative president's arsenal. The administrative presidency also uses the Office of Management and Budget to bring the bureaucracy to heel. When used strategically, the OMB makes all the final budgetary decisions and prevents federal agencies from having recourse to Congress. As Waterman (1989:38) has written,

> By requiring all departments and agencies to submit their proposed budgets to OMB, the Nixon and Reagan administrations gained greater influence over the budgetary process. In the case of the Reagan administration, OMB went so far as to inform various agencies of the exact amount of funding they would receive and how much they had to cut from their proposed budgets. OMB also included detailed plans regarding the number of layoffs for each department and proposals for the reorganization of functional units. By providing a point of central clearance for all executive branch budgetary requests, OMB has reduced the ability of individual agencies to make an end run around the president and request more money from Congress.

This tool—centralized, top-down budgeting—clearly poses a threat to the alleged bureaucratic goal of "budget maximizing" (Fiorina and Noll 1978; Niskanen 1971).

The OMB houses another of the administrative presidency's weapons: the Office of Information and Regulatory Affairs (OIRA). The administrative presidency employs this unit to conduct central clearance, regulatory review, and cost-benefit analysis (West 1995). This capacity is among the administrative presidency's most potent tools (Benda and Levine 1988; Goodman and Wrightson 1987; Harris and Milkis 1989). It enables the OMB to review all agency proposals, be they regulatory or legislative, in order to assess their consistency with the president's policy agenda and regulatory program. In addition, both Reagan and Bush used an entity located in the vice president's office—and called at various times the Vice President's Task Force on Regulatory Relief, the Vice President's Council on Competitiveness, and the Quayle Council—to conduct similar reviews, also with the purpose of ensuring policy consistency (Percival 1991; Portney and Berry 1993; U.S. Vice-Presidential Task Force on Regulatory Relief 1981). As James Miller, Reagan's first director of OIRA (quoted in Ball 1984:72) stated,

> Among the people whose behavior we are trying to influence are the GS-13s and 14s who draft the rules. The Executive Order [EO 12291] says to them:

even if you get a nonconforming proposal past your agency heads, even if you've captured or just plain fooled them, that proposal is likely to be caught at OIRA and there's no chance in Hades of capturing those people.

Thus, regulatory review, whether conducted in the OMB or in the vice president's office, is designed to ensure that agency regulations and legislative proposals conform to the president's policy goals, and to serve as a check on the activities of career bureaucrats whose policy goals may differ from the president's.

Finally, the administrative presidency avails itself of micromanagement techniques, including reorganization and personnel management (Waterman 1989). This includes taking advantage of loopholes in the Civil Service Reform Act of 1978 to transfer and demote career civil servants who are viewed as noncompliant, and employing "hit lists" to single out other noncompliant personnel (Ingraham 1995; Lash et al. 1984; Waterman 1989). It also includes what Benda and Levine (1988) and Ingraham (1995) call "jigsaw puzzle management." Jigsaw puzzle management enhances appointees' ability to control their career subordinates by employing lower-level appointees to perform line functions traditionally performed by career personnel, thus bypassing the potentially recalcitrant careerists. In addition, jigsaw puzzle management enables appointees to allow civil servants to perform specific tasks while at the same time consciously keeping them in the dark as to the overall strategy being pursued.

In sum, the tools of the administrative presidency—increasing the number, location, and strategic nature of political appointees, budgetary and regulatory review, reorganization, and micromanagement and personnel strategies—were designed to combat the traditional sources of bureaucratic power, obtain a more compliant and more responsive bureaucracy, and help presidents achieve their policy goals. President Reagan seized upon this arsenal and deployed it in an unprecedented attempt to control the bureaucracy (Aberbach and Rockman 1990; Benda and Levine 1988; Durant 1992; Nathan 1983; Rockman 1993; Sanders 1988).

ASSESSING THE ADMINISTRATIVE PRESIDENCY AND REAPPRAISING RESPONSIVENESS

Ronald Reagan's adoption and deployment of the administrative presidency raised new questions for scholars and spawned new debates among them. During the Reagan years and into the 1990s, debate raged about the effectiveness of the administrative presidency (Did it enhance bureaucratic responsiveness? Did it change policy in the direction desired by the president?), its implications for our understanding of bureaucratic motives and power, and its normative utility (Was the administrative presidency a "good" thing?). Rational choice theorists hailed the administrative presidency as evidence of the utility of contractual arrangements, incentives, and "sticks" to overcome the presidents' informational asymmetries and hold agencies accountable (see, e.g., Moe 1985b, 1995). Quantitatively inclined political scientists argued that the Reagan years provided empirical proof that policy does change in the direction desired by elected principals (see, e.g., Wood and Waterman 1991, 1994). And public administrationists expressed concern about the increased number of appointees and their effect on the morale and capacity of the career civil service (see, e.g., Aberbach and Rockman 1988; Ban 1987; Ban and Ingraham 1990; Ingraham 1987; Rourke 1991a, 1992a; Volcker 1990). These questions, though spawned by Reagan's watershed presidency, relate in significant ways to enduring questions about the role of the career civil service in the American political system. (For a discussion of the "big questions" in public management, see Behn 1995.)

This book addresses five of these questions. First, did Reagan's administrative presidency increase bureaucratic responsiveness? To date, this question has been addressed mainly by employing quantitative data at the aggregate level (but see Ingraham 1991; O'Leary 1995). Here, political scientists have attempted to measure the extent to which policy changed in the direction desired by the president (see, e.g., Wood and Waterman 1991, 1994). Much of the evidence seems to indicate that the tools of the administrative presidency, such as Reagan's appointment of Anne Gorsuch at the EPA, did result in policy changing in the desired direction (Wood and Waterman 1991, 1994). This leads Wood and Waterman (1991, 1994) to conclude that responsiveness is a nonissue in the post-Reagan era (see also Jaffe 1998). Some research argues, however, that these policy achievements were not all they were advertised to be and that the administrative presidency actually failed to achieve the president's policy goals (see, e.g., Durant 1992).

In this book, I take a different approach. I am interested in the responsiveness of a particular set of political actors (career civil servants) to a specific principal (the president), not whether policy responded to the president's agenda. Thus, I examine how bureaucrats actually behaved in response to Reagan's administrative presidency. For example, I examine Gorsuch's impact on the civil servants at the EPA, rather than using her arrival and departure as data points. This approach does not allow me to examine the extent to which policy changed or to make a statement about responsiveness in terms of policy outputs or outcomes. But it does enable me to gain insight into how the administrative presidency and, in particular, presidential appointees affected the behavior of the career civil servants they were intended to control. This, in turn, improves our understanding of the extent to which unelected civil servants can be counted on to take care that the laws are executed in a manner faithful to the president.

A second puzzle raised by Reagan's use of the administrative presidency is, What happened to the bureaucratic power advantage identified by pre-Reagan social scientists and presidents? How was Reagan able to overcome his perceived power deficit? A number of post-Reagan scholars have provided useful accounts of macrolevel changes that have facilitated this shift in the balance of power from bureaucrats to presidents. Moe (1985b), Rourke (1987, 1991a), and Aberbach and Rockman (1991) have all identified important institutional changes that have diminished the role of the bureaucracy in the contemporary political system. Among these developments are the demise of iron triangles, the rise of divided government, and the administrative presidency itself.

I focus on the microlevel, on how these institutional changes affected the daily lives of career civil servants and their relations with their political principals.[6] In turn, this enables us to better understand the power dynamics that affect bureaucratic responsiveness inside federal agencies. The framework presented in chapter 2 and the case studies that follow provide a lens through which to examine what happened to the informational asymmetries, captured appointees, and budget-maximizing bureaucrats that allegedly characterized the pre-Reagan bureaucracy, and to examine the role played by the administrative presidency itself in altering the balance of power between these two sets of actors. This improves our understanding of what caused these features to be so "overtowering" in the first place and how and why they were vulnerable to the challenge posed by the administrative presidency.

Reagan's use of the administrative presidency provoked a third, normative, debate concerning the "proper" role of the career civil service in the American political system. Scholars such as Nathan (1983, 1985, 1986) and Moe (1985b), on the one hand, reacted to the administrative presidency by singing its praises and advocating the type of top-down control that prevailed during the Reagan years. Their assessment results from the fact that their primary, if not exclusive, concern is with bureaucratic responsiveness to the president. Public administrationists, on the other hand, have had a more guarded reaction to the administrative presidency (see, e.g., Aberbach and Rockman 1988; Durant 1992; Ingraham 1987; Rourke 1991a, 1992b; Waterman 1989). This is because they place greater emphasis on other goals that we set for the bureaucracy, including competence and effectiveness. As Rourke (1992a:15) has written, "This discussion has sought to draw attention to the somewhat different, though no less alarming, fact that the policymaking process in the United States may also suffer when the voice of professionals is too weak rather than too strong in the development of national policy."

Normative issues involve value judgments and thus cannot be resolved with empirical evidence. Nonetheless, I believe that examining Reagan's application of the administrative presidency and how upper-level career civil servants reacted to it can shed light on this debate, because doing so highlights some of the trade-offs and consequences resulting from the methods used by the Reagan administration to increase bureaucratic responsiveness. In particular, such an examination draws attention to the potentially positive role played by bureaucratic voice, "loyalty that argues back," and "speaking truth to power," in attaining the goals of deliberative democracy, and it demonstrates how the administrative presidency, coupled with civil servants' preexisting inclination to cooperate, inhibits these bureaucratic functions.[7]

The fourth debate concerns the issue of what motivates career civil servants in the first place.[8] In my view, it is not possible to assess the administrative presidency and its impact on bureaucratic responsiveness without also addressing this issue. The reason is that the administrative presidency makes certain assumptions about the motives of career bureaucrats that need to be examined in any assessment of the strategy itself. Are career civil servants motivated by "inner checks" such as professionalism, role perception, and agency socialization (Friedrich 1940; Gaus 1936; Kaufman 1960; Pfiffner 1987; Rourke 1992a)? Or are they motivated solely by self-interest (which can be manipulated by presidential management strategies, contractual arrangements, and monitoring devices) (Heap et al. 1992; Niskanen 1971; Tullock 1965)? Rational choice theorists emphasize the self-interested, utility-maximizing nature of career bureaucrats (and everyone else, for that matter), whereas public administrationists tend to focus on the norms and ethos of civil servants, their professions, and their agencies (DiIulio 1994; Eisner 1991; Heap et al. 1992; Kaufman 1960; Niskanen 1971; Perry and Wise 1990; Pfiffner 1987, 1988; Pruitt 1979; Rourke 1992a; Wilson 1989).

This debate about motives is reminiscent of two earlier debates in public administration, one between scientific management and the human relations school, and the other between Carl Friedrich (1940) and Herman Finer (1941) on the subject of bureaucratic accountability. The scientific management/human relations debate (also referred to as theory x and theory y) took place between the followers of Frederick Taylor (1911), who believed that workers were best motivated by "sticks" and financial incentives, and the followers of Elton Mayo (1945), who believed that workers worked best when they received positive reinforcement (in the form of job satisfaction and self-actualization) for their labors (McGregor 1960; Scott 1981). Friedrich (1940) believed that career civil servants could be trusted because of their professionalism and obligation to serve the public interest, whereas Finer (1941) felt that top-down external checks (such as the administrative presidency) were necessary to ensure that bureaucrats were held sufficiently accountable.

I do not claim to have resolved these debates over whether career civil servants are best characterized as *homo economicus* or *homo sociologicus* (or *homo politicus*) or to answer the philosophical question of human motivation (see, e.g., Heap et al. 1992; Maslow 1943; Simon 1976). But I do present empirical evidence of self-interested, public-spirited, *and* sociologically driven behavior that illuminates this debate. I do so by treating the motivational factors suggested in both the rational choice and public administration literatures as hypotheses and seeking evidence of their presence or absence as motivating forces for the civil servants I studied.[9] As Mansbridge (1990:11–12) has written about self-interest more generally, "What we need to study is when we can expect self-interested motivation, what forms self-interest will take, when we can expect non-self-interested motivation, what forms (good and bad) it will take, and crucially, which contexts promote which kinds of motives."

The next chapter discusses the specific factors that I believe warrant scrutiny as potential motivating forces underlying bureaucratic behavior. The competing literatures just mentioned suggest the importance of examining three sets of variables: the resources of appointed principals (the means at their disposal to coerce bureaucrats and prevent shirking and sabotage), the internal workings of agencies (the ways in which agency esprit, historical legacies, and profession-based norms affect bureaucratic reactions to top-down control), and the individual motives (both self-interested and public spirited) of the bureaucrats themselves.[10]

Finally, in my view, all four of these debates are in essence debates about management and, with the possible exception of the debate between the scientific management and human relations schools, about *public* management.[11] All these debates raise the question of how we can most effectively manage the unelected "fourth branch" to ensure that it is sufficiently responsive to elected officials (as well as best able to achieve the other goals that we set for it). In order to answer this question, we need to know more about how career civil servants react to various approaches to management. Reagan's administrative presidency provides a prime opportunity in this regard. This is because Reagan employed the approach advocated by Taylor (1911), Finer (1941), and principal-agent and other economic theorists to an unprecedented degree, thus providing us with a laboratory setting in which to examine bureaucratic responsiveness under conditions of top-down control during one of the most contentious moments in American bureaucratic history.[12] Such an examination cannot answer all our questions about public management, nor can it definitively resolve all the debates discussed here. But it does suggest that theory x approaches to management, although quite effective at increasing presidential control, entail certain costs and may not be the *only* "best way."

THE ARGUMENT

This review of the debates spawned by Reagan's administrative presidency foreshadows the arguments presented in this book. First, I argue that the career civil service is neither entirely responsive nor entirely resistant, but rather that bureaucratic behavior under the conditions of the administrative presidency is a mixture of both, albeit—at least at the upper levels of the civil service—considerably more responsive than resistant. This "neither/nor" finding, although not as satisfying as an "either/or" argument, better describes the realities of bureaucratic life in the United States and better positions us to assess presidential management strategies.

Second, I provide an explanation for this mixed bag of bureaucratic behavior by drawing attention to the conditions that promote responsiveness and those that promote resistance. These conditions include Reagan's application of the tools of the administrative presidency, bureaucratic self-interest, role perception, and agency context. These factors illuminate the perennial question of what motivates bureaucrats (see Behn 1995 for a discussion of the importance of this question). Here, I also make a "neither/nor" argument, contending that upper-level career civil servants in the United States are motivated by *both* self-interest and altruism and that their behavior is also colored by their agency setting and, to a lesser extent, their personal political beliefs. I further argue that even when self-interest is present, under the conditions of an administrative presidency it is more likely to lead to cooperative than to resistant behavior. Again, this explanation is not as parsimonious as that offered by rational choice theorists, but, in my view, it better captures those factors that actually motivate upper-echelon civil servants. Moreover, identifying the factors that motivate civil servants provides us with greater insight into how to manage them.

Third, the portrait of bureaucratic behavior presented in this book enables me to reassess the differing conceptions of bureaucratic and presidential power. As numerous scholars have noted, power is an elusive concept and notoriously difficult to measure (Berry 1989; Dahl 1957). As a result, I do not purport to make a definitive statement about who holds the reins of power in the American political system. But I can and do demonstrate *how*, at the microlevel inside federal agencies, the administrative presidency tips the balance of power away from the bureaucracy and toward the presidency (see also Moe 1985b, 1995).

Fourth, I assess both the administrative presidency and the issue of responsiveness in a normative context. Here, I more explicitly align myself with the public administration side of the debate. However, I attempt to more adequately address the complaint that defenders of bureaucracy have failed to provide an adequate defense for the role of the career civil service (Jaffe 1998). In the book's last chapter, I use recent work from the field of deliberative democracy to highlight the value of bureaucratic input in democratic deliberation and decision making. This is not to say that I think we can "trust" the bureaucracy (Light 1997). But it is to say that I think we need to find a way to control the bureaucracy without detracting from the deliberative process by which we make policy decisions, and that I believe that the career civil service has a valuable role to play in that process.

Finally, I consider the implications of my findings for public management. Here I argue that there is no "one best way" to manage the career civil service. But I do suggest that although the tools of the administrative presidency turn out to be quite effective at "taming" the bureaucracy and bringing it to heel, there are other (more sociological) means available to presidents—including cultivating careerists' role perception, exercising leadership, and capitalizing on the socializing forces at work in federal agencies—that potentially enable them to strike a better balance between their desire for responsiveness and the polity's need for deliberative democracy.

All these arguments are based on the empirical evidence presented in chapters 3 through 6. Before we can proceed to those case studies, however, we need a framework in which to examine bureaucratic responsiveness and a method for doing so. And we need to identify and define those factors that potentially explain the extent to which upper-level career civil servants are responsive to their presidential principals. These are the tasks of chapter 2.

Debate continues to rage over the extent to which career civil servants can be trusted and the role that they ought to play in the policy process (Light 1997).

This book is predicated on the assumption that such questions can be answered only by a careful analysis of actual bureaucratic behavior and by a middle-range theory that acknowledges the complex and varied sources of that behavior. The chapters that follow represent an attempt to further our understanding in both these regards. The portrait that emerges neither "hallows" nor "hollows" the upper-level career civil servants who are the locus of my study but, rather, depicts those features of bureaucratic life that are of enduring concern in a democratic polity.[13]

CHAPTER 2

A FRAMEWORK FOR ANALYSIS

As I stated in chapter 1, the aim of this book is twofold: to capture the drama of bureaucratic life during the Reagan years and to use that drama to illuminate the causes and consequences of bureaucratic responsiveness and resistance. Its goals are both to describe bureaucratic behavior during Reagan's administrative presidency and to use that description to improve our understanding of such behavior. This chapter lays out the conceptual framework that I developed to identify the "response options" available to career civil servants during the Reagan years, introduces the factors that enable us to explain why they responded the way they did, and presents the research design that I employed in the study.

STUDYING BUREAUCRATIC BEHAVIOR: EXIT, VOICE, LOYALTY, AND NEGLECT

The framework that I devised operationalizes the study's dependent variable, the bureaucratic response to Ronald Reagan's implementation of the administrative presidency. My goal was to develop a framework that would include any and all possible responses to the administrative, managerial, and policy changes brought about by Reagan's presidency.

It was in this context that the work of A. O. Hirschman was a source of inspiration. In his *Exit, Voice, and Loyalty: Responses to Decline in Firms, Organizations and States* (1970), Hirschman studied phenomena quite different from the one with which I am concerned here. However, I found that the images evoked by the title of his book captured what I wanted to measure, the resistance (exit and voice) and cooperation (loyalty) of career civil servants. As a result, I developed a framework that invariably calls to mind Hirschman's work. I therefore must emphasize that although I have borrowed liberally from, and been influenced by, Hirschman's work, I am neither testing nor critiquing his theory. I am, however, adopting his language or, more precisely, the images that his language evokes, to describe both bureaucratic resistance and bureaucratic cooperation. Following Hirschman (and others who have modified his framework), I sorted the bureaucratic responses into four categories: exit, voice, loyalty, and neglect.[1]

EXIT

Exit is the easiest category to define. Civil servants were exiters if they left their agency during the time period under study. The possible reasons for exit are diverse but relevant. Did they exit in protest (Weisband and Franck 1975)? Did they resign because of a policy disagreement with the presidential administration (Holt 1998)? Were they fired because their political beliefs were out of step with the administration? Or did they leave for reasons that do not bear directly on the issue of bureaucratic responsiveness to the presidency, such as leaving for a higher-paying job? In later chapters, I discuss and analyze the extent of turnover, the type of individuals exiting, and the reasons for their exit in each of the four agencies studied.

VOICE

Voice is a richer and broader category. Voice covers any type of resistance other than exit undertaken by agency careerists; in other words, it is any expression of dissatisfaction or resistance from within (Hirschman 1970; Kato 1998; Oldfield 1996). The bureaucratic politics literature describes the many guises that bureaucratic resistance can take. Those most frequently alluded to in the literature are sabotage, the deliberate slowdown of agency activity (sometimes referred to as foot-dragging), "guerilla warfare," leaking, and whistle-blowing (see, e.g., Allison 1971; Brehm and Gates 1997; Glazer and Glazer 1989; Heclo 1977; Johnson and Kraft 1990; Neustadt 1990; O'Leary 1994, 1995; Pious 1979; Riley 1987; Waterman 1989). I have also included a subcategory labeled "voice by argumentation" (Heclo 1977; Pfiffner 1987), which includes any behavior—verbal or written—by which career civil servants express dissenting views, or present their objections to policy change, to appointed superiors in their agency, at the Office of Management and Budget (OMB), or at the Office of Information and Regulatory Affairs (OIRA). Finally, I added a "collective" subcategory for the alleged "banding together" of career civil servants to "function as a resistance movement" (see, e.g., Schlesinger, quoted in Pious 1979:211). In the case studies, I provide instances of each of these types of resistance and assess their prevalence.

LOYALTY

Loyalty is behavior that is responsive rather than resistant to elected officials. Loyal civil servants comply with the directives of presidents and their designated deputies and actively and responsibly implement the administration's policies. My framework encompasses two possible reasons for loyalty. One is based on the image of the loyal British civil servant, "on tap but never on top" (Campbell and Wilson 1995; Coxall and Robins 1989). In this model, civil servants dutifully serve whichever party wins at the polls, hold no partisan views or personal preferences of their own, and "work with equal enthusiasm for any duly constituted government" (Campbell and Wilson 1995:15; see also Gordon 1971). Although scholars (see, e.g., Campbell and Wilson 1995) agree that this model no longer accurately reflects reality, even in Great Britain (if it ever did), it remains an "ideal type" with which to compare our own civil servants. In the American context, this translates into bureaucratic cooperation based on a conscious conviction that bureaucrats should adhere to a civil service ethic. By this I mean that a bureaucrat's actions are based on an understanding of the civil servant's "proper" role in a democracy.

However, there is a second possibility. Civil servants might act loyally because they share the president's policy beliefs. Civil servants may be loyal to a president's ideology and policy agenda. They may "share the principal's preferences" (Brehm and Gates 1997:20). Some agencies may lack the "clashing beliefs" between careerists and appointees found in Aberbach and Rockman's early work; in fact, their more recent research supports this type of loyalty (Aberbach and Rockman 1976, 1990, 1995a). In other words, civil servants may not have been dissatisfied with either the Reagan administration's policies or its management techniques and may therefore have complied because they supported the changes they were being asked to make.

The causes of loyal behavior are discussed in greater detail later. For now, it is sufficient to note that loyalty is one of two categories intended to capture behavior in which career civil servants cooperate with the president and his appointees, faithfully implement presidential policy directives, and embrace policy change (for an example of this type of loyalty, see Ingraham 1991).

NEGLECT

Neglect is the second such category. Neglect refers to bureaucratic attitudes and behavior not otherwise covered by the exit, voice, loyalty framework (Farrell 1983; Holt 1998; Lowery and Rusbult 1986; Withey and Cooper 1989). As in the case of loyalty, neglectful behavior is cooperative. But it differs from loyalty in its cause and motivation. In essence, neglect is cooperative behavior motivated by reasons other than loyalty. One cause for cooperative behavior stemming from neglect is policy ambivalence. Here, cooperation results from civil servants' lack of strong policy or ideological convictions. In this case, cooperation in the form of neglect is the default behavior. A second source of neglect is cooperative behavior that results from the constraints and incentives imposed on civil servants by political appointees. Here, compliance is either strategic or coerced. It is classified as neglectful because without the proactive element of loyalty, it is cooperation by default.

Neglect can be distinguished from the other categories of behavior in a number of ways. First, it differs from loyalty because although the behavior is cooperative, it lacks the criteria that define loyalty. It does not assume policy agreement. More important, it does not require that civil servants have a consciously developed sense of their role in the democratic process. Second, it differs from voice. It is not passive resistance; in fact, it is not resistant at all. Thus, it is distinct from foot-dragging or the deliberate slowdown of agency activity. Such behaviors are categorized as subparts of voice, not neglect.

The theoretical roots of neglectful behavior lie in the notion that bureaucrats are inclined to follow the path of least resistance. Resistance requires considerable expenditure of effort and energy, whereas neglect is the result of bureaucrats' desire to make as few waves as possible and to avoid conflict and confrontation.

The exit, voice, loyalty, and neglect framework (EVLN) is a theoretical lens, not a hard-and-fast schematic. It is designed to examine the response options available to, and exhibited by, upper-level career civil servants during the Reagan administration and to capture the flavor, nuance, and complexity of that behavior. As will become evident in subsequent chapters, bureaucrats engaged in a range of behaviors during the Reagan years, and the EVLN framework proved particularly helpful in identifying them.

Explaining Bureaucratic Behavior: Civil Servants, Their Agencies, and Their Principals

In the following case studies, we will see both responsive and resistant behavior. Indeed, I argue that "neither/nor" better describes the realities of bureaucratic life than do arguments that bureaucratic behavior is either all-resistant or all-responsive. But what fosters or inhibits responsiveness, and what encourages or hinders resistance? In this section, I present the sets of factors that I argue enable us to account for the variation in bureaucratic behavior revealed by the EVLN framework.

I contend that three sets of factors help explain how bureaucrats react to presidential control efforts. The first set of factors—self-interest and role perception—operate at the individual level. The second set focuses on the various facets of agency context—the agency's history, culture, and professional norms—that shape how individual civil servants perceive their options. The final set—encompassing the components of the administrative presidency—enables us to examine the extent to which the actions of political principals shape the behavior of their bureaucratic subordinates and whether or not these actions are more likely to promote responsiveness or provoke resistance.

Since my argument supporting this particular set of factors is primarily inductive, I will discuss cause and effect in more detail after I have presented my empirical evidence. Here, I will summarize the key factors that I will explore in greater depth later, and the key findings that I will present in greater detail in the case study chapters of this book.

Individual-Level Explanations: Self-Interest and Role Perception

In the literature on bureaucracy, there currently is considerable debate between scholars (particularly rational choice theorists) who explain bureaucratic behavior deductively and believe that bureaucrats are self-interested utility maximizers, and those (more closely identified with the fields of public administration and public management) who emphasize the roles of altruism, public spirit, role perception, and principle as the main determinants of bureaucratic behavior.

The first group, the rational choice theorists, argue that political man is comparable to economic man and that, as a result, political actors, whether political parties, members of Congress, or bureaucrats, seek to maximize their utility (Downs 1957; Fiorina 1977; Mayhew 1974; Niskanen 1971, 1991, 1994). That is, decisions about how to behave involve a calculation of one's self-interest. According to this view, the behavior of even those at the highest ranks of the civil service is best explained by their concern for their own personal well-being (Tullock 1965). More specifically, self-interest calculations lead bureaucrats to seek to maximize their agency's budget or, in some cases, to maximize their job security or on-the-job leisure (Downs 1967; Niskanen 1971, 1991).[2] Moreover, both bureaucratic self-interest in general and budget maximizing in particular lead to conflict between bureaucrats and their elected and appointed bosses (Kiewiet and McCubbins 1991; Niskanen 1991).[3] In turn, this conflict explains "the unresponsiveness that nearly everyone has criticized in bureaucracies" (Kettl 1993:419; see also Niskanen 1991).[4] Although more recent research by these scholars has been used to demonstrate bureaucratic responsiveness (see, e.g., Kettl 1993; Wood and Waterman 1991), the focus on self-interest as the primary determinant of behavior remains the core of this literature, and rational choice theorists continue to disparage all hope of motivating employees through appeals to altruism or the public good (Light 1997).

The second group seeks to draw attention to altruism, the alter ego of self-interest (see, e.g., Brehm and Gates 1997; DiIulio 1994; Kelman 1987a,b; Monroe 1998; Pfiffner 1987, 1988; Rom 1996). Called variously *altruism, public spirit, role perception,* and *principle,* the central idea underlying this school of thought is that "even in the bowels of government agencies, there is more self-sacrifice and less self-interest than rational choice theory allows" and that "rather than being motivated solely by self-interest," most government officials—including career bureaucrats—are "influenced in large part by public spirit" (DiIulio 1994:316; Rom 1996:14). In essence, according to this view, career civil servants (as well as other political actors) want to "do the right thing." This theory suggests that it may be possible to motivate civil servants by appealing to their sense of duty, and that these non-self-interested motivations are reasons to expect career civil servants to behave responsively, cooperatively, and compliantly (see, e.g., Bendix 1949; Derthick and Quirk 1985). None of the scholars in this group dispute the existence of self-interest as a motivating force in bureaucratic life (Mansbridge 1990). But they do seek to draw attention to the limits of accounts that rely solely on self-interest and to suggest the need to explore other factors that may motivate career civil servants.[5]

To weigh the competing claims of these two schools of thought, I included two factors in my explanatory framework. The first, self-interest, acknowledges that self-interest invariably plays some role in human behavior in general and bureaucratic behavior in particular. But it differs from the rational choice literature in two important respects. First, it is an empirical category. My framework makes no a priori assumptions about behavior but, rather, enables me to identify instances of self-interested behavior in my data (discussed later in this chapter). Second, my framework moves beyond the either/or dichotomy of rational choice theorists and their critics. Instead, following Mansbridge (1990:11–12), my goal is to identify "when we can expect self-interested motivation, what forms self-interest will take, when we can expect non-self-interested motivation, what forms (both good and bad) it will take, and crucially, which contexts provide which kinds of motives." In other words, my framework allows for the possibility that self-interest may vary (with respect to both its prevalence and the type of behavior it leads to) and seeks to identify those conditions that promote or discourage self-interested behavior. In particular, I focus on the roles played by agency context and the administrative presidency itself in shaping both the extent and the direction of self-interested behavior.

The second individual-level factor is role perception (Pfiffner 1987, 1988). Including role perception in my explanatory framework allows for the possibility that the behavior of upper-level career civil servants may be shaped by non-self-interested motives. Role perception is the most relevant of the various facets of altruism because it focuses on how civil servants perceive their roles as civil servants and how that perception shapes their behavior. In other words, the concept of role perception provides a possible explanation for the presence of cooperation in federal agencies, namely, that civil servants are socialized into understanding their role as unelected officials in a democratic political system (Bendix 1949). As Pfiffner (1988:102) has written, "First of all, they [career bureaucrats] realize that a new president was elected by the voters and has a legitimate mandate to implement his programs and priorities. . . . As one said: 'Of course there will be changes around here—there's been an election and nobody elected me.'" The concept of role perception is thus meant to capture a civil service ethic, code of conduct, and sense of duty that lead career civil servants to be responsive to their presidential principals (Bendix 1949; Derthick and Quirk 1985; Friedrich 1940).[6] Its presence was ascertained through the interviews I conducted with career civil servants, discussed in greater detail later in this chapter.

Including these two individual-level explanatory factors in my framework yields some interesting findings and a puzzling dilemma. First, my research provides support for the presence of both self-interested and role perception–based behavior, but it also demonstrates the limits of either as the sole explanation for bureaucratic responsiveness or resistance during the Reagan years. Second, my research reveals that each motive produced a variety of behavior but that, at least during the Reagan years, both produced more responsiveness than resistance. Third, examining these two findings in tandem—the presence of both motives and the fact that both motives can produce cooperative behavior—brings to the fore the dilemma we face in choosing between competing control strategies (see Gormley 1989).

With respect to self-interest, the case studies presented in this book provide considerable support for the self-interest concept. Career civil servants frequently acted in ways that served their own self-interest. However, my research also found that civil servants also acted in ways that belied their self-interest. As we will see, engaging in behaviors such as exiting or using voice by argumentation often had costs (such as unemployment) that seemingly reduced rather than maximized a civil servant's utility. Moreover, even when self-interest was present, self-interest calculations led to a wide range of behaviors, most commonly including complying with the directives of political principals, frequently including neglectful behavior, and only rarely including budget-maximizing (or even budget-enhancing) behavior. Overall, the self-interest motive increased bureaucratic compliance during the Reagan years. Finally, self-interest calculations were influenced in significant ways by other factors, particularly the tools of the administrative presidency itself, thus lending credence to the arguments of those who emphasize the importance of incentives and sanctions in shaping the behavior of individuals in organizations (Kiewiet and McCubbins 1991; Moe 1985b; Wood and Waterman 1991, 1994). That is, in keeping with much of the recent research on principal-agent theory (see, e.g., Wood and Waterman 1991, 1994), I found that Reagan's administrative presidency structured incentives in a way that altered bureaucrats' self-interest calculations and led to a great deal of bureaucratic compliance. Thus, as I will demonstrate in the case studies, self-interest is neither unidimensional, unidirectional, nor omnipresent. But it is an important component of any account of bureaucratic behavior under an administrative presidency.

With respect to role perception, I found that the career civil servants I studied shared a common conception of their proper role and adhered to a civil service ethic regarding that role. Careerists expressed quite eloquently and consistently their view that their actions during the Reagan years were limited by their nonelected status, by the fact that they were and should be hierarchically subordinate to the appointed officials in their agencies, and by the legitimacy of those with an electoral mandate. In short, civil servants' personal attitudes toward their role in a democracy produced behavior that could not be explained by self-interest. At least in the case of upper-echelon career civil servants, the way they perceived their role in the larger political system served as a foil to their self-interest. Moreover, the presence of this code of conduct regarding the job and role of the nonelected civil servant suppressed bureaucratic resistance and produced loyally cooperative behavior. The civil servants I interviewed not only wanted to "do the right thing," but they also believed that loyalty to presidential leadership *was* "the right thing." Role perception thus accounts, in large measure, for the high levels of bureaucratic responsiveness that I found. These findings, which are in keeping with much of the recent research in public management, suggest that self-interest is only part of the story; they also "call assumptions of universal bureaucratic resistance and adherence to the status quo into serious question" (Ingraham 1991:192; see also Derthick and Quirk 1985; Pfiffner 1987).

These findings regarding self-interest and role perception present an interesting dilemma for both presidents and scholars. This dilemma becomes apparent when these two competing explanations for responsiveness are compared. In keeping with much of the recent research on principal-agent theory (see, e.g., Wood and Waterman 1991, 1994), I found that Reagan's administrative presidency structured incentives in a way that altered bureaucrats' self-interest calculations and led to a great deal of compliance. But, in keeping with much of the recent research in public management (see, e.g., Derthick and Quirk 1985; Ingraham 1991; Pfiffner 1987), I also found that bureaucrats' role perception *also* fostered responsiveness. The dilemma, therefore, is this: Should presidents and other public managers adopt the methods advocated by the economically oriented principal-agent theorists? After all, my evidence shows that the tools of the administrative presidency were quite successful at altering how bureaucrats perceived their self-interest and thereby at controlling bureaucratic behavior. Or should they employ the more sociological style championed by public management scholars that recommends relying more heavily on civil servants' role perception and sense of duty to ensure responsiveness to elected and appointed principals?

At this point, we could prescribe either control strategy. The next task thus becomes to find a way to move beyond this either/or thicket. The way that I do so in this book is to expand the range of factors I consider as potential explanations for bureaucratic behavior. By including additional factors in my explanatory framework, other sources of responsiveness and other means of attaining such responsiveness are revealed. This recasts the dilemma by suggesting that the range of bureaucratic motives and the choice of control strategies are not limited solely to the motives and options discussed here.

AGENCY-LEVEL FACTORS

It should be clear from the preceding discussion that self-interest and role perception offer necessary but not sufficient explanations of bureaucratic behavior. First, both factors tended to produce responsive behavior during the Reagan years, but we know that not all bureaucrats were responsive all the time. In fact, the EVLN framework reveals the presence of both exit and voice during this time period—behavior that cannot be explained by either self-interest or role perception. Second, although our discussion of self-interest took into account the role played by the administrative presidency, neither self-interest nor role perception acknowledges that civil servants are members of organizations—in this case, federal agencies—and the effect that such membership might have on their reactions to Reagan's administrative presidency. Thus, despite the importance that I attribute to individual-level factors, I also argue that a great deal of bureaucratic behavior can be explained by the agency setting in which civil servants find themselves.

An extensive body of literature examining the role of agency culture supports this contention (see, e.g., Eisner 1991; Eisner and Meier 1990; Kaufman 1960; Khademian 1996; Marcus 1980; McCurdy 1993; Pruitt 1979; Selznick 1957; Wilson 1989). This research demonstrates that the norms, beliefs, practices, and values shared by members of an organization shape both their behavior and their decisions, and that as a result, understanding an organization's culture is "an indispensable tool for predicting the reaction of employees to a new policy or a changing situation" (McCurdy 1993:4). As McCurdy (1993:5) has observed, "For people who study such things, organizational culture is a powerful means for predicting how members behave."

The theoretical underpinnings of agency context are illustrated by Miles's law, which states that "where you stand depends on where you sit." By this, Miles (1978) was suggesting that bureaucrats' attitudes and behavior (where they stand) are influenced by organizational context (where they sit). In other words, the civil servants in an agency, through a mix of self-selection and socialization, tend to acquire "a distinctive way of seeing and responding to the world" (Wilson 1989:93). For example, Meier and Nigro (1976) found that civil servants' political attitudes were better explained by agency membership than by individual-level attributes such as race or class.

It follows that civil servants in different agencies might take different stands toward the Reagan administration's infringements on their turf. This leads to the hypothesis that behavior will vary by agency and that bureaucrats in different agencies will react differently to the Reagan administration's application of the administrative presidency to their agency.

This emphasis on agency context is not meant to imply that all agencies are different and that therefore all bureaucratic behavior is different.[7] Rather, it is an attempt to examine the effect that agency-level factors have on how civil servants respond to presidential control efforts. The literature on federal agencies, as well as the research presented here, suggests that four agency-level factors—ideology, dominant agency profession, agency history, and esprit de corps—are significant.

CAREERIST IDEOLOGY

As pointed out in chapter 1, Republican presidents—Nixon and Reagan in particular—have brought to office the view that "liberal bureaucrats" will sabotage their policy plans. Survey researchers such as Aberbach and Rockman (1976, 1990) have found that careerist attitudes differed from those of appointees on a range of issues during both the Nixon and Reagan administrations (see also Cole and Caputo 1979; Maranto 1991, 1993c). Moreover, they found that these attitudes varied across agencies, with civil servants in "social service" agencies (HEW, HUD, OEO) expressing more liberal views than those in "other" agencies (Aberbach and Rockman 1976).

These studies, however, were primarily attitudinal and did not include an examination of whether or not, and the extent to which, those attitudes affected behavior. In addition, Aberbach and Rockman (1990, 1995a) noticed a shift in the political attitudes of high-ranking career civil servants between the Nixon and Reagan administrations (see also Aberbach 1991). Beginning in 1986 and becoming more pronounced by 1990, they found a significant drop in the number of self-identified Democrats and a corresponding rise in the number of Independents and Republicans. At the same time, they found that Reagan appointees were more ideologically conservative than their Nixon-era predecessors.

As Pfiffner (1988:103) has noted, "What counts is how these officials behave in the context of their jobs"—that is, the extent to which they act on their personal political attitudes in their work setting. My research focuses on the link between ideological predispositions and bureaucratic behavior as well as the role of agency context in promoting or discouraging ideological resistance. Based on Aberbach and Rockman's findings regarding attitudinal differences across agencies, I hypothesize that only some agencies will share enough of an internal ideological consensus to produce resistant behavior. Furthermore, where this consensus is present, exit and voice will be much more common than in agencies that lack an agencywide "liberal bias."

DOMINANT AGENCY PROFESSION

The importance of professional norms and their effect on decision making is well established (see, e.g., Eisner 1991; Eisner and Meier 1990; Katzmann 1980; Mosher 1968; Pruitt 1979; Rourke 1992a; Wilson 1989). For example, the preference of National Highway Traffic Safety Administration (NHTSA) engineers for "changing the automobile rather than the driver or the highway" led NHTSA to adopt regulations requiring cars to come equipped with seat belts and air bags (Wilson 1989:62; see also Pruitt 1979). And attorneys in the Antitrust Division of the Justice Department have historically favored cases different from those selected by staff economists (Eisner and Meier 1990).

It follows that the profession of careerists in an agency will also influence their reaction to presidential control efforts. Certain careers, such as law, encourage the development of many of the same qualities useful for resistance. Attorneys are accustomed to presenting arguments as part of their everyday work and hence are more likely to feel confident using voice in this, more political, context (Golden 1992). Other professions, particularly scientific ones, may produce a less adversarial professional norm (Golden 1992). Without experience in, or orientation toward, voice, these professionals may be more hesitant to use it in the context of presidential control efforts. In addition, the profession of careerists may narrow their alternative job prospects and hence their ability to use exit as a resistance tactic. Civil servants in agencies that house individuals from multiple professions, such as Eisner and Meier's (1990) Antitrust Division, also may react differently from those agencies, such as the Forest Service, in which one profession dominates (Wilson 1989; see also Kaufman 1960).

AGENCY HISTORY

Agency culture refers, in part, to the shared learning experiences of organizational members (Schein 1992). Learning is shared when organizational members have a history of shared experiences. This "history of shared experiences" is thus a prerequisite to the development of an agency's culture (Schein 1992:10). To Trice and Beyer (1993:6), "a particular culture will be based in the unique history of a particular group of people coping with a unique set of physical, social, political, and economic circumstances." This is particularly relevant in the setting of public bureaucracies.

Behind all agencies are the events recorded in the agency's institutional memory. For example, although no current careerists worked in the Forest Service during the reign of Gifford Pinchot, his impact on the development of the Forest Service is legendary and provided future generations of foresters with a strong sense of identity. Likewise, NASA was fundamentally changed by the explosion of the *Challenger,* an event that made the agency "gun-shy" in a way that it had not been before the explosion (McCurdy 1993). In other words, these experiences become frames of reference through which members of an organization process new information.

By including an agency's historical legacy in our framework, we are able to examine the extent to which careerists' responses to the Reagan administration were colored by their agency's institutional memory of previous experiences and their agency's prior encounters with its external environment. As we will see in the chapters that follow, careerists in agencies that had a history of positive experiences were more likely to use voice than those in agencies whose histories had been marred by agency setbacks. I argue, and the case studies provide empirical support, that the existence of shared history and learning and the nature of those historical events and experiences played a significant role in shaping reactions to Reagan's administrative presidency. The nature of these pre-Reagan experiences and the legacy they left behind are therefore integral parts of the explanatory framework presented in this work.

AGENCY ESPRIT DE CORPS

Agency esprit de corps has been used to explain the power of agencies (Meier 1980, 1993; Rourke 1984).[8] Esprit refers to the spirit of an agency; the camaraderie, commitment, and cohesion of its members; and their psychological ties to the agency (Meier 1993; Romzek 1990, 1992; Romzek and Hendricks 1982; Rourke 1984). Esprit is thought to be important because it invigorates an agency, motivates its members, and enhances its ability to recruit new members (Meier 1993; Rourke 1984). In this study, esprit is applied to agency reactions to presidential control. My hypothesis is that careerists in an agency that has a sense of esprit, whose members share a strong commitment to the agency's mission, and that features a great deal of agency cohesion and camaraderie will be more loyal to their agency and less loyal to the president and therefore more likely to resist and less likely to cooperate with presidential change agents. Moreover, since these careerists share their feelings about the agency, they will be more likely to engage in collective resistance. In an agency lacking such esprit, individuals or groups will be less likely to mobilize in opposition to budget cuts or policy redirection and more likely to exhibit neglectful behavior. Thus, taking into account careerists' attitudes toward their agency helps us understand their behavior.

This section has presented the theoretical claims underlying my argument regarding the importance of agency context. Without going into detail here, a number of these claims are demonstrated in the case studies presented in chapters 3 through 6. As those case studies reveal, civil servants are, to a great extent, creatures of their agencies, and their experiences in those agencies have a significant effect on their behavior vis-à-vis their political principals. Agency-level factors were particularly helpful in explaining those instances in which civil servants did or did not use exit and voice. Civil servants in some agencies were more hesitant to use these response options than were civil servants in other agencies, and this hesitance can be traced to the various facets of their agency's culture presented here. Moreover, some agencies were more vulnerable to the tools of the administrative presidency than others, and again, this vulnerability (manifested in neglectfully cooperative behavior) can also be traced to the characteristics of their agencies. Overall, agencies with greater cohesion and homogeneity (both professionally and ideologically) and those with more "successful" historical experiences were more likely to exercise exit and voice, whereas more diverse and less historically successful agencies were more likely to exhibit neglectful behavior in response to Reagan's administrative presidency.

The implications of including agency context in our explanatory framework are therefore threefold. First, as the case material will make clear, this argument does not lead to the conclusion that all agencies are different. Rather, it means that because of a confluence of characteristics, some agencies are more likely to resist presidential control efforts, whereas other agencies—lacking these characteristics—are more susceptible to presidential control. Second, from the president's point of view, agencies with "weaker" cultures are more amenable to presidential control, and agencies with "stronger" cultures are more difficult to control. Thus, at a minimum, it is useful for would-be principals to ascertain what type of agency they will face. But third, examining the effect that agency context has on bureaucratic behavior also reveals the potential downside of more passive agency cultures and the potential value of more assertive ones. In other words, although on the surface it may seem to be in a president's best interest to have an executive branch composed of agencies whose ideological and professional compositions and historical legacies make them more amenable to control, the case studies reveal the value of agencies whose cultures empower civil servants to "argue back" and "speak truth to power." Accordingly, increasing our understanding of agency culture not only enables us to more fully explain bureaucratic behavior but also highlights the positive contributions that agencies with "stronger" cultures can bring to the policy process.

The Administrative Presidency: The Role of Political Principals

Upper-level civil servants do not act entirely in isolation, protected from other political actors by metaphorical moats around their agencies. Rather, bureaucratic behavior is partly a function of the actions of other actors in the political system and the extent to which federal agencies are buffered from those actors. The final factor in my explanatory framework is, therefore, the role of the administrative presidency itself in determining the extent to which civil servants exercise exit, voice, loyalty, or neglect.[9]

As I pointed out in chapter 1, much of the literature lamenting the lack of responsiveness by career civil servants was written before the development of the administrative presidency (see, e.g., Heclo 1977; Neustadt 1960; Pious 1979; Weber 1946). This literature described federal agencies as independent fiefdoms, impervious to presidential control (Califano 1975). But President Reagan was different from his predecessors and used the tools of the administrative presidency to a greater extent than any president before or since (Durant 1992; Moe 1985b). It follows that his use of these tools may have altered bureaucratic behavior. Indeed, as is clear from Reagan's (1989:362) remark that "every once in a while, somebody has to get the bureaucracy by the neck . . . and say, stop doing what you're doing," that was his intent. Therefore, in order to determine the extent to which Reagan's use of the administrative presidency did in fact alter bureaucratic behavior, we must include the administrative presidency itself in our account of bureaucratic behavior during the Reagan years.

In addition, including the administrative presidency in our framework enables us to evaluate how much influence political principals—in this case, presidential appointees—actually have or can have over their bureaucratic agents, and why. To what extent can political principals design systems that enable them to monitor bureaucratic behavior and overcome the informational asymmetries and other obstacles that they are alleged to have faced? The answer to this question is important to principal-agent theorists because they are concerned with issues of institutional design (see, e.g., Kiewiet and McCubbins 1991; Miller 1992). But it is also important to public administrationists because they are concerned with the normative implications of relying on this particular factor as the primary means of achieving bureaucratic responsiveness (see, e.g., Aberbach and Rockman 1988; Ingraham 1987; Rourke 1991a, 1992b).

To assess the impact of the administrative presidency on bureaucratic behavior, it is necessary to "unpack" the administrative presidency and to identify how and why it works its magic and which tools and what facets of the administrative strategy are the driving forces underlying its impact. This book does this through in-depth case studies that examine which tools were applied to each of four agencies, how they were applied, and with what effect.

The evidence presented in those case studies demonstrates the overwhelming impact that the tools of the administrative presidency had on the behavior of upper-echelon career civil servants during the Reagan years. In particular, the management style adopted by strategic appointees and the manner in which they used their supervisory status colored civil servants' perceptions of the behavioral options available to them and constrained those options. In each of the agencies studied, it was clear that the president's appointees—the bureaucrats' principals—had a strong influence on bureaucratic behavior. Although the details of how this worked are presented in subsequent chapters, the two main effects on bureaucratic behavior are summarized here. First, the tools of the administrative presidency made it more difficult for civil servants to resist, even if they had wanted to. In particular, the micromanagement techniques employed by Reagan's strategic appointees—including their use of jigsaw puzzle management—took careerists out of the loop and rendered most types of voice all but impossible. Second, these management techniques changed the way that civil servants calculated their self-interest. Faced with "hit lists," demotion, transfer, and a general atmosphere of fear and distrust, bureaucrats found that their utility was enhanced by cooperation, not resistance. In general, the administrative presidency increased the extent to which career civil servants exhibited neglectful cooperation, diminished the extent to which they used (or were able to use) voice, and, in some cases, hastened their exit. The reasons that the administrative presidency affected bureaucratic behavior in this way were twofold. First, the managerial component of the administrative strategy made it more difficult for civil servants to engage in resistant behavior. And second, it created greater incentives to cooperate, albeit neglectfully.

As a result, during the Reagan years, the power position of the administrative presidency—not the power position of the bureaucracy—was so "overtowering" that almost all bureaucratic behavior was colored by its presence. The higher ranks of the civil service were *not* impervious to presidential influence. In fact, although self-interest, role perception, and agency context all came into play, nothing was as powerful a determinant of bureaucratic behavior as the way in which and extent to which the tools of the administrative presidency were utilized in the civil servant's agency.

This finding has clear implications for those interested in controlling the bureaucracy. Despite this finding, however, examining the administrative presidency alongside the other explanatory factors discussed in this chapter gives rise to the notion that there are alternative means of attaining bureaucratic compliance. Placed in the context of other motivating factors, it becomes clear that the administrative presidency is only one way of solving the motivation-compliance puzzle. Indeed, my explanatory framework suggests that the motivation-compliance puzzle has many pieces and various solutions and that it is only by comparing these different pieces and solutions that empirical, normative, and prescriptive assessments can be made. To facilitate these comparisons, the next four chapters present case studies of four federal agencies during the Reagan years.

RESEARCH DESIGN

WHY REAGAN?

This book focuses on one presidential administration—the eight years of Ronald Reagan's presidency. As I observed in chapter 1, the central assumption of a wide range of literatures, ranging from the presidency literature to rational choice and principal-agent theory, is that bureaucrats continually resist change, are wedded to the status quo, and possess the tools and will to sabotage and derail the president's program. Since I am concerned with examining the nature and extent of this resistant behavior, I selected the case most likely to provoke a resistant response. That case is, without a doubt, the Reagan presidency.

As has been amply documented in the literature (as well as the popular press), Ronald Reagan targeted the bureaucracy, employed all the tools of the administrative presidency, took away bureaucratic discretion and autonomy, slashed agency budgets, presented federal agencies with policy agendas that were a marked departure from the status quo, and engaged in bureaucracy bashing to an unprecedented degree (Durant 1992; Goldenberg 1984; Ingraham 1995; Pfiffner 1987; Rubin 1985). Terry Moe (1985b:235) has written that "more than any other modern president, Ronald Reagan . . . moved with dedication and comprehensiveness to take hold of the administrative machinery of government." In Durant's view (1992:4), Reagan applied the administrative strategy to the pursuit of his policy goals, "to an extent unprecedented in terms of its strategic significance, scope, and philosophical zeal."

In short, I chose the Reagan administration as my focus because it contained all the elements—significant policy departures from the status quo, budget cuts, a conservative presidential administration, loss of bureaucratic autonomy and discretion, and even loss of job security—that theory predicted would produce bureaucratic resistance. The presence of these elements sets the stage for our examination of the bureaucratic response.

CASE SELECTION

To study the bureaucratic response to the Reagan presidency, I conducted in-depth case studies of four federal agencies, the National Highway Traffic Safety Administration (NHTSA), Department of Transportation; the Food and Nutrition Service (FNS), Department of Agriculture; the Civil Rights Division (CRD), Department of Justice; and the Environmental Protection Agency (EPA). I looked at four agencies in this study to avoid the limitations of single-case analysis. If I found civil servants in only one agency to be compliant, the reasons for compliance might be idiosyncratic to that agency. But if civil servants engaged in similar patterns of behavior across agencies, we can have more confidence in the generalizability of my findings.

I selected the four agencies using a variety of criteria. The first criterion, shared by all four agencies, was the presence of presidential initiatives likely to provoke a bureaucratic response. As in the selection of the Reagan presidency itself, my goal was to maximize the likelihood of resistant behavior.

Second, I sought cases that would provide variation in the independent variables discussed earlier in this chapter. Accordingly, the cases differ in the types of control measures used by the Reagan administration, the professional composition of agency personnel, and other dimensions of agency context.

Finally, the cases differ in those traits traditionally thought to distinguish agencies, such as policy domain (regulatory, redistributive, and constituent), the technological complexity of the agency's tasks, and the agency's interest-group environment (Lowi 1964; Meier 1993; Ripley and Franklin 1991; Rourke 1984; Wilson 1989).

In short, all four cases share the characteristics of presidential intervention, presidential policy goals that significantly departed from previous agency policy, and the application of the tools of the administrative presidency. But they differ in the mix of tools used and the nature of policy change sought. Equally important, the agencies vary with respect to agency characteristics.

RESEARCH METHOD

My research relies primarily on seventy in-depth, face-to-face interviews I conducted with current and former career civil servants in the four agencies I was studying. I also conducted seven interviews with outside observers in Congress and the interest-group community, and two interviews with subcabinet political appointees who served in administrations before or after the Reagan administration. These interviews were supplemented by a short questionnaire distributed to interviewees at the conclusion of each interview (see appendix 2). Most of the interviews took place in the interviewees' offices in Washington, D.C., in 1990 and 1991.

I used interviews for a number of reasons. First, since I sought information regarding the behavior and motivations of a group of individuals frequently characterized and stereotyped by others (both other political actors and other academics), it made sense to get the story "from the horse's mouth." I talked to career civil servants because they were the political actors whose behavior and motivations I wanted to learn about.

The flexibility allowed by an interview instrument was a second reason I chose this method. The questions were open-ended, and while interviews were semistructured using a preestablished interview schedule (see appendix 1), I was able to add follow-up questions that followed logically from the interviewees' statements. Third, I wanted to move beyond attitudinal studies and to link attitudes with behavior. This was also easier to do through interviews than with a survey instrument. Moreover, interviews allowed me to cover a large number of topics in depth. On average, the interviews were one hour in duration, although many lasted considerably longer.

Despite my confidence in this method, I took a number of precautions to avoid any potential pitfalls of relying so heavily on self-reported attitudes and behavior. First, I assured all interviewees of anonymity and confidentiality. I emphasized the academic nature of my research, promised that the audience for my research included neither their supervisors nor the *Washington Post*, and told them that they would not be identified in any way (by name or title) in the text. I thus tried to create an environment in which the interviewees would feel that they could be frank and open without any fear of repercussions or reprisals.

Second, I talked to both former and current civil servants in each agency.

Former civil servants were those no longer associated with the agency under study. In all but one case, they were no longer affiliated with the federal government at all. As a result, they were not subject to the inhibitions of those who were still serving in agency positions. The fact that their accounts were consistent with those obtained from current civil servants increased my confidence in the frankness and accuracy of all accounts provided. Similar reassurance in this regard was provided by my interviews with outside observers (e.g., interest-group representatives who monitor the agencies under study). Although I conducted only one or two such interviews for each agency, these accounts served as a further check on the frankness of the interview reports. If I had obtained radically different accounts of events and behavior from these observers, it would have caused me to reconsider my methodology. But that did not happen.

Third, to avoid any potential problems associated with self-reporting, I did not limit my interviews to self-reporting. My questions asked not only about the individual's own attitudes and behavior but also about "civil servants in your agency" and "your colleagues." This provided civil servants with an opportunity to "rat on" their coworkers without having to admit to any misconduct on their own part. In addition, in those agencies for which primary and secondary accounts of events that took place during the time period under study were available (e.g., the EPA and the CRD), I consulted those sources for comparison (see, e.g., Holt 1998; Landsberg 1993, 1997; Selig 1985; Smith 1991).

The responses I obtained from my interviews provide further evidence that the interviews elicited frank accounts of bureaucratic behavior during the Reagan years. There is no other way to account for the careerist who reported to me that he had perjured himself before Congress to protect his appointed boss. Although this was the most extreme case, interviewees often reported behavior that showed them in an unfavorable light, as well as reporting on situations in which their behavior was more flattering. In short, interviewees reported on the good, the bad, and the ugly, thus increasing my confidence that their responses were candid and forthcoming.

As a result of the precautions I took and the responses that the interviews elicited, I am confident that my choice of interview subjects was appropriate to the task and that the findings reported in this study paint an accurate picture of bureaucratic behavior during the Reagan years.

SELECTION OF INTERVIEW SUBJECTS

I selected the interviewees according to several criteria. Given my interest in the higher civil service, I talked only to professionals and managers holding decision-making positions who dealt with policy issues and who worked closely enough with political appointees to be able to offer judgments about those appointees. Although strict GS ranking was not applied, all but two interviewees held the rank of GS-13 or higher, and approximately three-quarters served at the Senior Executive Service (SES) level. In short, the civil servants I interviewed held professional positions vested with authority and discretion.

To qualify to be interviewed, civil servants had to have served in their agency before the Reagan administration and had to have continued to serve for at least part of Reagan's eight years. This was necessary for two reasons. First, it gave the interviewees a point of comparison. Second, and more germane to my theoretical concerns, I wanted to study those for whom Reagan and his policies represented a change. That is, for newcomers to an agency, Reagan represented the status quo rather than a disruption of the status quo. However, since I was also interested in "exit," continuous service throughout the Reagan years was not a selection requirement.

I tried to have a mix of current and former civil servants in my interview sample, both to check their veracity and to include "exiters." I also tried to interview civil servants with different professional backgrounds (e.g., attorneys, economists, engineers, scientists) and different perspectives.[10] I obtained the names and identities of the civil servants I interviewed from two sources: agency telephone directories published by the U.S. Government Printing Office and privately published directories such as the *Federal Executive Directory,* the *Federal Staff Directory,* the *Federal Yellow Book,* the *U.S. Government Manual,* and the *Martindale-Hubbell Law Directory.* Names were selected based on agency and title and were further screened, when possible, to target certain offices within agencies and to include civil servants of various professional backgrounds. After considering these factors, I chose the interviewees at random. Additional interview subjects were added by a method known as snowballing (Cook 1988; Kingdon 1984): When interviewees suggested additional names, I added those individuals to the study.[11]

Former federal career officials were identified mainly through snowballing (Cook 1988; Kingdon 1984). Interviewees and other contacts were asked to name civil servants who had served in their agency before and during the Reagan administration but who were no longer associated with the agency. Directories such as *Martindale-Hubbell* were also helpful in locating former careerists for whom I had names but whose whereabouts were unknown.

The response rate was high (seventy out of seventy-eight civil servants; seventy-nine out of eighty-seven total).[12] There was some drop-off in the number of completed questionnaires (fifty-nine out of seventy). The interviews were relatively evenly distributed among the agencies and between current and former career civil servants. However, fewer interviews were conducted at the smaller agencies (the FNS in particular), and interviews with former agency members were limited by my ability to locate them.[13] Because attorneys were easier to track down than other former civil servants, they tend to be somewhat overrepresented in my sample of former career civil servants. As a result, I conducted fewer interviews with former careerists in agencies with fewer attorneys (again, the FNS in particular).

INTERVIEW SCHEDULE

I asked the respondents a series of open-ended, semistructured questions about the following topics:

- The application of the tools of the administrative presidency in their agency
- The attitudes and behavior of the political appointees in their agency
- Their own and their coworkers' attitudes toward the Reagan appointees in their agency
- Relations between presidential appointees and career civil servants
- Policy disagreements and conflicts between careerists and appointees during the Reagan years (and compared with those experienced during other administrations)
- The attitudes and behavior of agency careerists when such conflicts occurred
- Self-reported bureaucratic behavior in response to the administrative presidency
- The behavior and activities of coworkers, peers, and colleagues
- The range of options that civil servants considered or adopted in response to personal, political, or policy disagreements
- The philosophical views held by civil servants regarding their role in the political system
- The behavior of external actors during this time period and the careerists' views and analysis of this behavior

Many questions invited comparisons with previous administrations (the complete interview schedule is presented in appendix 1).

The supplemental questionnaire (which is supplied in appendix 2) assessed more directly the relative significance of the various tools of the administrative presidency and the relative influence of different political appointees. It also invited comparisons with the Carter administration. Finally, the questionnaire contained standard, commonly used questions about the respondents' personal political beliefs and partisan affiliation.[14]

The next four chapters present the four case studies, and they follow the same basic organizational format. First, each case study describes Reagan's policy agenda for the agency under study and demonstrates how that agenda departed from previous agency policy. This provides the basis for what agency careerists were responding to. Each chapter then outlines Reagan's application of the administrative presidency in the agency. Here, the tools used by the administration in each agency (regulatory review, strategic appointments, etc.) are discussed. Particular attention is paid to the political appointees and their approach to the agency's management, as I found that appointees were the most proximate tool to the career civil servants and the one most relevant to their comments, thoughts, and behavior. These two factors—the president's policy agenda and his application of the administrative presidency strategy—along with a historical overview of each agency, set the stage to turn to the bureaucratic response.

Each chapter then describes the behavior of the career civil servants being studied. This part of each chapter employs the exit, voice, loyalty, and neglect framework discussed earlier in this chapter. Finally, each of the case study chapters concludes with a brief analysis of the chapter's findings.[15]

The bulk of my analysis is reserved for chapter 7. There I return to the set of explanatory factors introduced in this chapter and assess their utility in accounting for the behavior described in the case material. Chapter 7 also returns to the normative and prescriptive issues raised in chapter 1. In this regard, I leave the reader with some thoughts on the *consequences* of the behavior that I found. I argue that both compliance *and* resistance have consequences for both policymaking and administration. In my view, bureaucratic cooperation can lead to an insufficient role for bureaucratic expertise in agency decision making. Bureaucratic silence serves neither presidents nor citizens in a pluralistic political system. Rather, I believe that there is a need to foster deliberative democracy inside federal agencies, and that such deliberation can enhance decision making without diminishing responsiveness.[16] In my view, cultivating a version of deliberative democracy inside federal agencies can help resolve the issue of the appropriate role for the career civil service in the American political system by striking a balance between the need for unelected bureaucrats to be responsive to elected officials and the need for their unique perspective and expertise to be a more integral part of the deci-sion-making process. I hope that by the time the reader reaches the end of this book, he or she will share my concerns about the consequences of exit, voice, loyalty, and neglect for the effective operation of government and will be per-suaded by my prescription.

CHAPTER 3

THE NATIONAL HIGHWAY TRAFFIC SAFETY ADMINISTRATION: CAR NUTS AND CAUTION

       The National Highway Traffic Safety Administration (NHTSA) is famous for its recall of the Ford Pinto, its attempts to mandate seat belts and air bags in automobiles, and its consumer hotline. But to the political scientist, it is a social regulatory agency peopled by career civil servants with expertise in automotive engineering (Harris and Milkis 1989; Pruitt 1979). As such, it provides a laboratory in which we can examine the behavior of these career civil servants and assess the competing ideas about their behavior discussed in the preceding chapter.

       This chapter focuses on the reaction of NHTSA's career civil servants to the Reagan administration and its application of the administrative presidency to their agency. By examining how these careerists reacted, we can begin to answer the questions posed at the outset of this book. First, this chapter provides considerable evidence of bureaucratic compliance and little evidence of bureaucratic recalcitrance. Second, it supports my contention that both agency context and the tools of the administrative presidency played pivotal roles in how bureaucrats reacted to the Reagan administration. There was plenty to react to at NHTSA, including Ray Peck's controversial rescission of the passive restraint rule. But the response of NHTSA's careerists was muted, because of both the agency's culture—specifically its professional and ideological composition and historical legacy—and the manner in which Reagan's strategic appointees employed the tools of the administrative presidency in their agency.

THE AGENCY'S SETTING AND HISTORY

The National Highway Traffic Safety Administration was created in 1966 by the National Traffic and Motor Vehicle Safety Act, largely as a result of the public outcry over two scandals: the dangerous defects in the popular General Motors Corvair, publicized by Ralph Nader in *Unsafe at Any Speed*, and the well-publicized wiretapping and spying subsequently conducted against Nader by General Motors.[1]

NHTSA was born of consensus (Mashaw and Harfst 1990b). The National Traffic and Motor Vehicle Safety Act passed both houses of Congress without a single negative vote. It also had the endorsement and support of President Lyndon Johnson. The enabling statute was passed at a time when Americans, including their elected representatives in Washington, believed in the ability of science and technology to improve the quality (and safety) of life. NHTSA was designed to do for auto safety what NASA had done for space exploration. As one person testified during the congressional hearings, "If we can send a man to the moon and back, why can't we design a safe automobile here on Earth?" (quoted in Mashaw and Harfst 1990b:64).

The National Traffic and Motor Vehicle Safety Act mandated a regulatory approach to auto safety (Mashaw and Harfst 1990b:47). The new agency, initially housed in the Federal Highway Administration (FHA) in the newly created Department of Transportation, was required to set "appropriate federal motor vehicle safety standards." The legislation also included congressionally mandated deadlines for the establishment of such standards, and it empowered the agency to order manufacturers to recall vehicles found to have safety-related defects. In 1974, the National Traffic and Motor Vehicle Safety Act was amended because of dissatisfaction with the agency's performance. The amendments included a provision subjecting the agency's rule-making activity to the legislative veto.

Under the direction of a politically appointed Administrator, NHTSA's 640 careerists are charged with implementing the agency's statutory mandate by issuing regulations, investigating and recalling defective automobiles, and developing programs designed to modify driver behavior.[2] Agency professionals are drawn from the engineering, legal, psychological, highway safety management, and economic professions. Both the agency's attempt to balance its three primary responsibilities (regulation, recalls, and driver behavior modification) and its professional mix of engineers, attorneys, and economists have been sources of considerable tension and conflict in the agency (Mashaw and Harfst 1990b).

The agency had five administrators between its founding in 1966 and Reagan's inauguration in 1981. The agency's first administrator was William Haddon, a physician and epidemiologist who relied heavily on scientific evidence in his decisions. Reflecting the agency's scientific mission, Haddon was retained as NHTSA's administrator even when the occupant of the White House changed from a Democrat to a Republican with Richard Nixon's victory in 1968. During his tenure, NHTSA issued regulations governing a wide range of automotive features, such as brakes, windshield wipers, seat belts, fuel tanks, and rearview mirrors (Mashaw and Harfst 1990b).

Haddon's successor, Douglas Toms, served as administrator from 1971 to 1973 and was the first administrator to head the agency after it was removed from the Federal Highway Administration. Toms was succeeded by James Gregory in 1973. Gregory had no background in auto safety and was a cautious leader. When John Snow took over from Gregory in 1976, he reorganized the agency, introducing a seventeen-step rule-making process known as the flowchart procedure. This procedure institutionalized the inclusion of the agency's different professions but did so in a way that was both adversarial and cumbersome (Mashaw and Harfst 1990b).

During the Carter years, NHTSA's administrator was Joan Claybrook. Claybrook, who had close ties to Ralph Nader, took an activist stance toward regulation and held a rather negative view of the auto industry (Mashaw and Harfst 1990b; Weinraub 1992; Wood and Waterman 1994). According to Mashaw and Harfst (1990:194), "The contrast between Claybrook and Snow was stark." The contrast between Claybrook and the administrators appointed to NHTSA by Reagan was equally stark. Claybrook reorganized the agency, issued a passive restraint rule in July 1977 that required automatic occupant restraints in all new cars by the early 1980s (often referred to as the air-bag rule), and issued a number of "midnight" regulations shortly before Carter left office in 1980.

During the Reagan years, NHTSA's employees were divided into five divisions, each headed by a career associate administrator: Rule Making, Traffic Safety Programs, Enforcement, Research and Development, and Plans and Policy. The Traffic Safety Program Office focused on driver behavior and state grants-in-aid. The Office of Enforcement was responsible for investigating defects and deciding on recalls, and the Office of Planning and Policy Evaluation conducted cost-benefit analyses and was home to most of the agency's economists and political appointees. The agency also had an appointed deputy administrator and a chief counsel's office. Before Reagan, the position of chief counsel had been held by a career civil servant, but during the Reagan administration, it was filled by a Schedule C appointee.

REAGAN'S POLICY OBJECTIVES AT NHTSA

NHTSA was one of several agencies targeted for deregulation by the Reagan transition team. Relief for the ailing auto industry and deregulation in general were high priorities for the Reagan administration (Leone 1984; Public Papers, Reagan 1982:113; Weekly Compilation, Reagan 1981:403; Wines 1983). In April 1981, a Reagan-commissioned vice-presidential task force issued a report entitled "Actions to Help the U.S. Auto Industry." The report singled out the Environmental Protection Agency (EPA) and NHTSA for regulatory review. It directed NHTSA to undertake twenty-two specific actions, including terminating pending agency rulemakings and rescinding previously issued regulations (U.S. Task Force of the Vice President 1981).[3] Among the regulations targeted in the task force report were the passive-restraint rule, bumper standards, tire-grade requirements, and field-of-view rules (Leone 1984:90). Reagan signaled his personal support for the report by announcing its release. In his announcement, he blamed the auto industry's plight in part on "strangling regulations" and vowed to "reduce unnecessary regulation by the EPA and NHTSA" (Public Papers, Reagan 1982:332–333; Weekly Compilation, Reagan 1981:113).

Many of the careerists I interviewed felt that this report set the tone for the president's NHTSA policy for the duration of Reagan's two terms. Its call for regulatory relief stood in stark contrast to Joan Claybrook's agenda at the agency, which had been to increase the speed with which regulations were issued and the quantity of those regulations. One analyst observed that "the Reagan proposals for regulatory relief were quick in coming and much more generous in proffered relief than a less conservative administration would likely have recommended" (Leone 1984:91).

The Reagan administration's efforts at NHTSA concentrated primarily on deregulation, but recalls were also affected. Recalls declined dramatically under Reagan, and the agency's approach to recalls was much more accommodating toward the auto industry (Center for Auto Safety 1989; Thornton and Work 1983).

In addition, NHTSA experienced significant budget cuts. Its overall operating budget fell from $259 million in 1979 to $211 million by the end of Reagan's tenure in office.[4] Over the same time period, the budget for highway safety was reduced from $17 million to $4.5 million, and the budget for research and analysis was cut by one-third. The highway safety cuts particularly affected funding for grant-in-aid programs to the states, and the cuts in research and analysis primarily affected NHTSA's research and development division.

The Administrative Presidency at NHTSA

NHTSA was the target of a number of administrative actions aimed at controlling the agency and altering the direction of its policy. Besides suffering budget and personnel cuts, it was headed by antiregulation administrators and was initially overseen by an antiregulation Secretary of Transportation (Drew Lewis), although he was later replaced by the more moderate Elizabeth Dole. Although Dole was less adversarial than Lewis in her approach to the agency, she too sought to redirect the agency by shifting its focus away from regulation and toward a behavior modification approach to auto safety (Thornton and Work 1983). Her efforts to find alternatives to regulation by promoting voluntary industry initiatives and driver education were consistent with Reagan's policy orientation. Her efforts to centralize decision making in the secretary's office were also in keeping with the management strategy of the administrative presidency and reflected a distrust of the career bureaucracy.

The Office of Management and Budget (OMB) also played a role in the president's attempts to bring about policy change at NHTSA. Due to the regulatory nature of its work, NHTSA was subject to review by OMB's Office of Information and Regulatory Affairs (OIRA). Although OIRA's role at NHTSA was largely indirect, it was nonetheless significant. The people I interviewed contended that although OIRA rarely vetoed the regulations that it reviewed, agency appointees used OIRA's regulatory review process as a threat, thus deterring regulatory activity. In addition, OMB was in the lead in securing the budget cuts desired by the president.

NHTSA's Political Appointees

During the Reagan years, NHTSA had two administrators. The first was Raymond Peck, an attorney and coal industry lobbyist known for his combative style (Lynn 1984). His credentials as a strategic political appointee were revealed in a Heritage Foundation report that emphasized his conservative ideological beliefs and his commitment to the administration's goal of reducing the regulatory burden on the auto industry (Wines 1982b). This preference for regulatory relief over regulation went hand in hand with Peck's sympathy for the auto industry and contrasted sharply with that of his predecessor, Joan Claybrook (Wood and Waterman 1994). Peck's support for the administration's regulatory relief program was evident in his testimony at his confirmation hearing:

> It is now time, I believe, for a period of review and consolidation of all regulatory efforts of the Federal government. This is especially true with respect to agencies charged with regulation of those industries most directly affected by current and adverse economic conditions. The automobile industry and its supporting industries are of course in this category. . . . I understand my regulatory philosophy to be in keeping with that of the President. . . . I share the view that the Federal government should regulate only where regulation can be shown to be cost effective and there is no practicable alternative to regulation. . . . Some of the regulations issued by the agency in the past may be found not to be effective under application of these criteria. These should and will be considered for revocation.
>
> (U.S. Senate 1981b:12)

By the time of his departure in 1983, Peck had revoked, rescinded, or delayed seventeen existing safety regulations or rule-making procedures in addition to his unsuccessful attempt to rescind the Carter-era air-bag regulation (Hines 1983).

Peck was succeeded by Diane Steed, a graduate of the University of Kansas and a former intern for Senator Robert Dole, who had served as NHTSA's deputy administrator during Peck's tenure. Steed's entire career had been spent in government, mainly at the OMB where she headed the regulatory policy branch from 1978 to 1981. According to careerists, Steed continued the administration's policy of minimizing new regulations and reviewing existing ones, but her personal style was much less strident than Peck's had been. Careerists felt that her appointed chief counsel, Erika Jones, was also very influential in the agency's operation; for example, it was Jones who read drafts of rules and ran staff meetings.

Two aspects of the Reagan appointees' approach to running the agency warrant attention here. The first is illustrated by Peck's decision-making process for the passive-restraint (air-bag) rule. Peck made a unilateral decision to rescind the passive-restraint regulation that was in place when the Reagan administration took office. The decision was "sent down" by Peck rather than percolating up through the agency, as was customary for agency policy. More-over, when the U.S. Supreme Court overturned and remanded Peck's rescission of the air-bag rule, Secretary of Transportation Dole took the issue out of NHTSA's hands and moved it "upstairs" (the careerists' term for the secretary's office). This pattern of removing both the decision-making process and deci-sion-making authority from NHTSA and placing them in the secretary's office occurred in a number of prominent issues in addition to the highly visible air-bag rule.

The second telling aspect of the appointees' management style was the man-ner in which the Reagan appointees handled rule-making activity. Both Peck and Steed ran the agency in a way that agency careerists felt slowed productiv-ity without directly challenging the agency's mission. For example, career rec-ommendations were rarely rejected outright. Instead, Peck and Steed would send proposals back to the lower levels of the agency and request more research without ever directly commenting on the merits of the proposals or vetoing them. The interviewees' comments in this regard are revealing:

- "No one ever straight-out said deregulation."
- "In most cases, the decision was long delay but not rejection."
- "Everything was researched to death."
- "They just called for more research."
- "Under Reagan, decisions just were not made but were sent back to gener-ate more information. Things were left hanging."

An example is illustrative. In the mid 1980s, the agency was considering a proposal for a rule requiring child-restraint hooks in the rear seat of automo-biles. Although the estimated cost was one dollar per car, Peck kept sending the proposal back and requesting a hook that could be installed for ninety-seven cents per car. The engineer who related this story to me added, "Ray never said, 'I just don't want to do it.'" Yet it was clear to this engineer that Peck did not want to issue this regulation; he just did not want to go on record as op-posing it.

BUREAUCRATIC BEHAVIOR AT NHTSA DURING THE REAGAN YEARS

The mettle of career personnel at NHTSA was often tested during the Reagan years, particularly when the administration tried to review, rescind, and repeal previously issued agency rules as well as to stall those currently being considered by the agency. Yet, their response can best be characterized as passive and acquiescent. Overall, at NHTSA the voices of career professionals were generally muted, and agency careerists chose to follow a cooperative path during the Reagan years. There was no rebellion at NHTSA; in fact, there were rarely even arguments between career staff and presidential appointees. Careerists felt both that it was their job to cooperate and that there was no compelling reason to defy that principle by resigning in protest, arguing, or sabotaging their appointed bosses' policy plans.

VOICE

VOICE BY ARGUMENTATION

Although career civil servants at NHTSA employed voice by argumentation under some circumstances, overall it was relatively rare. Voice by argumentation was used by some NHTSA career officials when they expressed their criticism of Reagan administration policies regarding air bags, bumper standards, and fuel-economy requirements to Peck and Steed. In these instances, the few agency careerists who spoke up supported air bags, a five-mile-per-hour bumper standard, and higher fuel-economy requirements. Most of their colleagues, however, were silent on these issues.

Where voice was used, it was only at specific times, such as when decisions were still under consideration. In Peck's rescission of the passive-restraint rule, an estimated twelve careerists "lobbied" him before he announced his decision. They did not do so collectively, and their concerns were not identical, but they all expressed their concerns to Peck. When he called top-level careerists into his office on the Sunday that he decided to rescind the passive restraint rule, a few not only disagreed with him but also "angrily disputed" his decision. One of those present told Peck that he thought Peck was "completely wrong." But that was the extent of the dissent. Once it was clear that Peck's decision was final, the careerists did not try to deter him from proceeding, as they felt that they had no other avenues of recourse beyond this type of voice. In addition, the views expressed by NHTSA's careerists fell on deaf ears; they had no apparent impact on Peck's decision.

There was also some voice in the form of back-and-forth discussion in the case of the automobile-bumper standard. Here, by law, NHTSA had to issue a standard; the debate was between a two-mile-per-hour or a five-mile-per-hour standard. Careerists lacked consensus among themselves on this issue, in part owing to controversies over data, a point to which we will return later. Nonetheless, individual careerists, armed with their own data and their own opinions, forthrightly presented their cases to Peck.

However, over the course of the eight Reagan years, there were a host of other issues regarding the redirection of agency policy or procedure where almost nothing was heard from the careerists. Careerists at NHTSA tended to avoid engaging in disputes that required them to take what they viewed as political stands. They did not view this as their proper role and hence consciously avoided arguing with appointees on many matters.

COLLECTIVE ACTION

None of the people I interviewed at NHTSA provided any examples of collective voice or collective resistance during the Reagan years. An incident that occurred during the Bush administration, however, sheds light on both what *does* provoke civil servants to act collectively and how NHTSA careerists viewed agency policy during the Reagan years.

In 1989, career personnel from the office in NHTSA responsible for recalling defective automobiles wrote a letter to the Center for Auto Safety, a consumer advocacy organization, chastising it for what the careerists argued was unjustified criticism of the agency's recall record during the Reagan years (Brown 1989). The letter, signed by fifty members of the NHTSA career staff, also accused the consumer organization of selling information about defective automobiles, information that the agency asserted was available from the agency for free. The letter was also leaked to the *Washington Post*.

This incident is noteworthy for several reasons. It was not an objection to the policy direction in which the president was attempting to lead the agency. Nor did it have to do with a conflict between Bush appointees and agency careerists. Instead, the collective action of NHTSA's career staff was directed at an interest group, allegedly their ally in their battles with the president. But far from seeing them as an ally, NHTSA careerists regard the Center for Auto Safety, and its director Clarence Ditlow, with disdain. Although the Center is the leading consumer group concerned with auto safety, NHTSA careerists view its policy agenda as frequently at odds with their agency's mission. In my interviews, NHTSA careerists frequently criticized the Center for basing its decisions on faulty, shaky, inadequate, and insufficient scientific information. This criticism is relevant to our discussion of leaks because the Center would have been a logical place to leak information during the Reagan administration, but careerists did not want to have anything to do with Ditlow's organization. It also is relevant to our discussion of what causes careerists—NHTSA's careerists in particular—to protest. Careerists objected to the center's sloppy science as much as its policy agenda. Equally important, they were not willing to accept sloppy scientific evidence even for a cause in which they believed. Nor did they necessarily wholeheartedly endorse the Center's agenda. The NHTSA careerists I interviewed who mentioned the Center for Auto Safety viewed its agenda as ideologically driven and did not view themselves as ideologues. Finally, we should note that NHTSA careerists defended their agency when it was criticized. They were loyal to their agency and defended the job they had been doing on recalls. They could have been pleased that policies enacted during the Reagan administration were receiving negative attention, but instead, they viewed those policies and that recall record as their own, rather than attributing them solely to the Reagan appointees.

LEAKS AND SABOTAGE

Although the preceding incident occurred in 1989, after Reagan had left office, some information was also leaked to Congress and interest groups during Reagan's tenure. In my interviews, both the careerists and the recipients of the leaked information were vague about the content of these leaks and the motivation for the leaking. When Tim Wirth moved from the House to the Senate and his top aide moved back to Colorado, NHTSA lost its principal advocate in the House of Representatives. According to my interviewees—both those in the agency and those on the Hill—without a sympathetic recipient for the leaks, fewer occurred, though agency careerists continued to provide information to Senator William Danforth's office (Danforth chaired the committee responsible for oversight of NHTSA in the Senate). The disdain toward the Center for Auto Safety expressed by many of those I interviewed further limited the outlets for leaks. For leaks to be an effective tool of resistance, there must be an interested and reliable external recipient in a position to use the supplied information. For the most part, NHTSA lacked such a recipient. In short, leaking was minimal at NHTSA, not only due to its careerists' ethical principles and the absence of serious rifts between careerists and appointees, but also as a result of NHTSA's external environment, which failed to provide a suitable outlet for "insider information." As noted in chapter 1, an agency's clientele is a primary source of its power. An agency with strained relations with its clientele and without a strong patron in Congress is not as well positioned to challenge the president.

Sabotage was not viewed by careerists at NHTSA as appropriate conduct for members of the civil service. Engineers and attorneys alike expressed their belief that the administrator was the legitimate decision maker and that once his or her decisions were made, they were binding. Ray Peck's decision to rescind the air-bag rule illustrates this principle. Most interviewees were convinced that Peck had acted unilaterally on this decision, disregarding staff advice (though Peck claimed to have read the entire docket on the subject). Although they disliked the decision, careerists felt that decision-making responsibility fell appropriately within Peck's purview. The telling aspect of this episode is the comment that consistently followed the recounting of the episode, the gist of which was that if Peck had let the careerists write the order rescinding the regulation, it would not have been dismissed by the Supreme Court as "arbitrary and capricious." If the goal had been sabotage, careerists would have viewed this as an opportunity to weaken the notice of rescission. Instead, their comments indicate a desire to follow the decision made by their appointed superior and to use their expertise to strengthen that decision. Careerists told me that if they had had the opportunity, that is, if they had not been excluded from the process, they would have used their expertise to write an effective rescission order, one complete with the type of evidence and arguments that could have withstood the Courts' scrutiny.

Exit

Exit was seldom used as a form of resistance at NHTSA. Although a few individuals left the agency because they opposed a particular policy or decision, most of those who left did so between election day and inauguration day in reaction to anticipated rather than real changes. This type of exit was most common among the legal staff.

Most of the staff who left NHTSA between 1981 and 1988 had no protest motivation. The turnover was mostly the result of RIFs (reductions in force) or, more frequently, because of the anticipation of RIFs. Interviewees often mentioned the fear of RIFs as a factor that led careerists—mainly junior engineers who believed that their jobs were vulnerable—to begin looking for other employment. Interviewees believed that actual RIFs were less relevant to agency turnover because even though positions were constantly being reshuffled and redefined, few people were actually fired. Nonetheless, by the end of the Reagan administration, the agency had almost two hundred fewer full-time employees than it had had at its start (U.S. Office of Management and Budget 1979–1990). Moreover, those who remained at the agency speculated that the atmosphere created by RIFs had an additional effect on exit: Those whose jobs were secure but who might otherwise have considered leaving NHTSA ruled out such a move because they had a greater appreciation of their job security.

Another factor reducing the use of exit at NHTSA was the limited availability of alternative jobs—in an era of deregulation, Detroit was hiring fewer auto safety engineers. In addition, one interviewee pointed out that auto safety engineering does not have a large research community in universities and research institutes. The job market for attorneys was substantially better, however, and several did leave the agency. But even the lawyers did not leave because of policy conflicts but because of the boredom caused by the slowdown of agency activity.

Some interviewees, in fact, were surprised that more of the high-ranking career officials in their agency did *not* leave, particularly those who had been closely identified with the Carter/Claybrook administration and proregulatory activity. While the factors just discussed partially explain this group's lack of exit, their less ideological orientation and more centrist views of regulation also help explain their behavior. Even those careerists who had worked most closely with the Carter administration appointees did not feel the same degree of ideological incompatibility with the Reagan administration that led their peers at the Civil Rights Division to exit.

LOYALTY

Almost everyone at NHTSA can be characterized to some extent as a loyalist. Careerists at NHTSA worked hard to comply with the directives and initiatives of the agency's appointees. This loyal behavior had two sources. First, loyalty resulted from the beliefs—widely shared at NHTSA—regarding the role of the career staff vis-à-vis the president's appointees. As one career engineer observed, "Career staff are here to do the job we're told to do. We try to do our best whether it's regulation or deregulation. We carry it out in the best manner. . . . It's up to the elected officials to decide what they want to do." This belief cannot be emphasized enough. Throughout the agency's history, the administrator (who has always been a political appointee) has been the ultimate decision maker concerning both rules and recalls. As a result, careerists view these decisions as political ones, which, although they draw on the research of the experts, are appropriately made by individuals in political positions. One NHTSA attorney regarded decisions about regulatory proposals to be "matters of judgment," with the administrator or secretary as the appropriate judge.

Cooperation also stemmed from the lack of disagreement over policy, which in turn stemmed from the fact that the majority of NHTSA careerists did not hold strong policy convictions. Careerists at NHTSA are essentially proregulation. They believe that their enabling statutes mandate the development of auto safety regulations. "NHTSA careerists have a regulatory orientation," explained one former careerist. In addition, a former NHTSA attorney contends that "careerists wanted more regulation than the Reagan people. They believe, in general, in the necessity of regulation." But many civil servants at NHTSA felt that Joan Claybrook had gone too far on the regulatory side, sacrificing thorough research for speed, and they were critical of her hostility toward the auto industry. According to the people I interviewed, under Claybrook, NHTSA careerists had tried to temper her agenda. Thus, at least initially during the Reagan administration, they were not averse to a slightly slower pace of regulation than what they perceived as Claybrook's excessively quick one.

Most careerists at NHTSA were committed to regulation as a necessary part of improving auto safety and interpreted the agency's mission as including regulatory authority. But from their perspective, there was less to be frustrated about under Peck and Steed than there had been under Claybrook. Moreover, overall, NHTSA's career personnel did not view their frustration as sufficient to necessitate action; it was something they could live with. The absence of policy differences between careerists and appointees thus partially explains the cooperation that I found among high-ranking NHTSA careerists as well as the compliance that interviewees reported predominated in the lower ranks of their agency.

Neglect

There was a great deal of acquiescence, apathy, and neglect at NHTSA. As one congressional staffer characterized the reaction to the Reagan administration at NHTSA, "There was a bunker-down mentality at NHTSA—a ride-out-the-storm mentality, if you know what I mean. Some careerists were fairly docile and cooperative, but there were others who were clearly not pleased by the situation but felt powerless to do anything."

Several factors contributed to the prevalence of neglect. One was the looming threat of RIFs. One mid-level careerist claimed that "because of RIFs, you kept your mouth shut and your head low to keep your job." Attention was focused on job security rather than "the public interest." At NHTSA, this factor should not have affected those on the higher rungs of the career ladder who were not threatened by RIFs, but it did nonetheless, and it particularly affected those in middle management who were constantly being shuffled around and reassigned.

Another factor that explains neglect among one group of NHTSA careerists—the engineers in R&D (research and development)—is that they actually gained autonomy during Peck's and Steed's tenures. Since both appointees shared the goal of no new regulation, they did not have a specific research agenda and therefore did not communicate any research priorities to the R&D staff. As a result, researchers were "left to their own devices" and "could study whatever they wanted to—anything that interested them." In essence, the behavior of R&D careerists was compliant and cooperative for two reasons. First, since they were not given any direct orders, they had little to disobey. They were cooperative by default. But second, they were content because they preferred autonomy in their work environment, even at the expense of an activist regulatory agenda. Their professional norms led them to care more about research qua research than about translating their research into new regulations.

An additional factor contributing to neglect was the lack of consensus among careerists. There were, and always had been, disagreements among the different professions in NHTSA, as well as disputes within the professions over data and the appropriate conclusions to be drawn from them. Careerists had traditionally debated among themselves and then turned to the administrator for the final decision. This pattern was institutionalized in the procedure by which draft regulations were circulated throughout the agency, and in the lengthy process involved in reviewing them. This internal decision-making process, which was maintained by Reagan's appointees at NHTSA, further limited voice and increased neglect because it highlighted those issues for which careerists lacked the consensus to present a united front to the Reagan appointees.

Finally, and the factor that best accounts for neglect at NHTSA, the political appointees quickly adopted and maintained an approach to running the agency that involved slowing down the rule-developing machine through increased research and data requirements. As one interviewee characterized it, "Under Reagan, decisions just were not made but were sent back to generate more information. Things were left hanging." Careerists found this atmosphere demoralizing. As one career supervisor commented, "Morale went down because our work wasn't going anywhere." Many careerists contrasted their attitudes and behavior during the Reagan years with the long hours and hard work they put in during the Carter years, and some also contrasted it with their work patterns and morale during the early Bush years. They attributed their less apathetic behavior during this later time period to Bush appointee Jerry Curry, who, though not pursuing an activist agenda, nonetheless gave careerists specific goals and timetables. And they attributed their enthusiasm during the Carter years to the atmosphere of energy and excitement that Joan Claybrook generated.

Conventional wisdom makes a great deal of the fact that bureaucrats can derail the president's plans by dragging their feet and stalling until the president forgets about his directive or leaves office (Heclo 1977; Neustadt 1990). At NHTSA during the Reagan years, however, it was the appointees who used this strategy of stalling agency activity to thwart careerist initiatives.

Analysis

In the following section, I shall expand on my discussion of the factors that prevented NHTSA careerists from feeling tempted, or compelled, to resist the Reagan administration—its appointees or its policy agenda. These factors, which resulted in careerist passivity, include the management style of the Reagan appointees, the lack of consensus among agency professionals, and the more tempered ideological culture of the agency. I shall also discuss the impact of the agency's historical legacy.

The Role of Appointees

Two components of the approach to management used by Reagan appointees Dole, Peck, Steed, and, to a lesser extent, Lewis, reduced the number of opportunities available for voice. These were (1) moving decision-making authority from the agency to the secretary's office and (2) delaying the release of the agency's work product without actually rejecting it. One excluded NHTSA careerists from the decision-making loop, and the other kept them spinning their wheels.

Both components limited the opportunities for rebellion or sabotage, the first by removing agency careerists from the loop and the second by keeping career experts engaged, by appealing to their professional desire to act only after all scientific doubts had been fully addressed, and by not giving them a concrete decision to rally around. The experience at NHTSA highlights the difficulty of rallying around "nondecisions" and the efficacy of this administrative micromanagement technique as a way to limit career resistance to presidential policy goals.

Agency Context

DOMINANT AGENCY PROFESSION
The multiplicity of professions at NHTSA inhibited the agency's response to the Reagan administration. Each profession brought with it its own perspec-

tive regarding the formulation and issuance of regulations and decisions regarding the recall of vehicles. There was no internal unity or consensus among the different agency professions or even within the engineering staff. In fact, the agency had a history of infighting between engineers and lawyers and squabbles within the engineering group (Mashaw and Harfst 1990a). Unity may well be a prerequisite to mounting an effective attack on presidents and their appointees, for without it, there is no consensus on the preferred policy direction or agency goals. Moreover, the engineers and other scientists were more concerned with achieving scientific certainty than with recommending specific actions. Such scientific certainty is rare at NHTSA, where data are often incomplete or inconclusive. Careerists in these professions, therefore, were hesitant to exercise voice when they lacked the scientific certainty to back up their recommendations.

I have argued elsewhere that attorneys may be more inclined to use voice than scientists or technicians because of their professional training and because their day-to-day work requires proficiency in the art of argument (Golden 1992). This hypothesis is borne out here. Professional background and the extent to which work routines are technical in nature account for the different types of behavior found among different groups of NHTSA careerists. Most of those who did exercise voice at NHTSA were attorneys, and another, though not an attorney, had a generalist liberal arts rather than a scientific background. Voice was rare among NHTSA's engineers, physical scientists, and highway safety professionals. These professionals seemed more comfortable providing research evidence and data, presenting both sides of an issue, and leaving the decision making to others. Government engineers rely heavily on research and data, and at NHTSA, they viewed their jobs as presenting those data for others to use as the basis for decisions. NHTSA engineers frequently commented that the only thing they did not like about their jobs was "the politics."

The profession of agency careerists also affected exit as a form of resistance. Attorneys were more optimistic about alternative job prospects outside their agency than were other NHTSA professionals. Other than attorneys, NHTSA careerists' expertise was too narrowly focused to facilitate transfer to other government agencies, and these same professions offered few job opportunities in the private sector, especially at a time when the automobile industry was downsizing. There is no doubt that the availability of alternative job prospects affected the likelihood of exit. It is equally clear that careerist profession played a major role in determining the availability of alternative employment opportunities.

IDEOLOGY

The partisan and ideological composition of NHTSA was mixed. The thirteen survey respondents were split ideologically, with seven careerists identifying themselves as conservative and six as liberal. And while there was only one Republican, seven considered themselves independent of party affiliation, with the remaining five identifying themselves as Democrats. A career attorney described NHTSA as an agency that did not attract "crusaders," and my findings about the agency and the people in it support that characterization. Agency careerists constantly distanced themselves from Joan Claybrook, whom all considered to be a crusader. Their policy views reflected their attempt to balance the interests of the auto industry and those of consumers. Their reasons for joining the agency had nothing to do with crusading or ideological commitment. Instead, they were "car nuts" who joined the agency out of an interest in cars, not politics. In essence, NHTSA was not an agency distinguished by a "liberal" culture or a "crusading" spirit.

AGENCY HISTORY

An examination of NHTSA's history best explains why careerists did not put up a resistant front during the Reagan years. The history of NHTSA before Reagan included a few accomplishments in which agency careerists took great pride, such as the recall of the Ford Pinto and a number of the regulations that careerists believed improved auto safety. However, NHTSA's history was also one of frequent repudiation of its regulatory efforts by Congress, the courts, the regulated community, and even public-interest groups. For example, the agency was still reeling from its embarrassment over a regulation it issued in 1973 on automatic ignition interlock systems. This regulation had been so controversial and produced such a public outcry that Congress repealed it through a legislative veto.[5] Mashaw and Harfst (1990b:220) argue that the lesson learned from "the agency's interlock fiasco" was that "not all improvements in safety are acceptable" and that the agency needed to gauge the public mood as well as technological feasibility.

The agency also carried in its historical baggage the rejection by a federal court of one of its earlier attempts to issue a passive-restraint rule (Standard 208), in which the court held [*Chrysler Corp. v Department of Transportation,* 472 F2d 659 (6th Cir 1972)] that the evidence on which the agency relied was not conclusive because the test dummies used in the studies of the air bag's effectiveness were not properly specified (Graham 1989). The court's decision directly questioned the agency's scientific capabilities. This court decision was only one of many setbacks in the decades-long debate over air bags, a debate that has lasted for most of the agency's history. And it was only one in a series of court cases in which the agency's rule-making decisions were remanded or rejected by the courts. Other cases included the H&H Tire case in 1972 [*H&H Tire Co. v DOT,* 471 F2d 350 (7th Cir 1972)], the Paccar case in 1978 [*Paccar v NHTSA,* 573 F2d 632 (9th Cir 1978)], and countless others, leading Mashaw and Harfst (1990b:100) to conclude that after all these court battles, NHTSA was "haunted by the specter of judicial invalidation" and "could hardly be faulted for taking a very cautious approach."

These experiences taught NHTSA careerists to be very cautious and to move slowly and carefully on any agency initiatives. The lesson learned by NHTSA careerists from these setbacks was that they were operating in an environment of great uncertainty. Because the agency's history was marked by unpredictable interventions into its actions by the courts and Congress, NHTSA careerists sought to avoid such embarrassment in the future and thought the best way to do so was to be cautious and prudent. This attitude is best captured by a careerist's response to congressional questioning in 1974 that was echoed by the careerists I interviewed almost a decade later:

SENATOR: Isn't it a lot better to get knocked down by the court than to concede before you start?
MR. SCHNEIDER [NHTSA]: No.   (Mashaw and Harfst 1990b:122).

The agency's history has also been marked by repeated attempts to satisfy the competing demands of the auto industry and of consumer-advocacy groups. We have seen that NHTSA's personnel do not fall into an ideological camp. Neither have they historically identified exclusively with either the auto industry or consumer groups. Rather, they have always had ties to both sets of "clients." This has influenced the kinds of decisions the agency has made in the past and the type of policy direction preferred by agency careerists. As Mashaw and Harfst (1990b:121) have observed, "Life with Ralph Nader and General Motors as constant companions was not easy."

Equally important, careerists found themselves caught between the zealotry of Joan Claybrook, a proponent of passive restraints and of increased regulation in general, whose views they had tried to temper, and the slowdown of agency activity promoted by the Reagan appointees. The civil servants I interviewed commented just as often about the Carter years as about the Reagan years. Had they bought into Claybrook's agenda to a greater extent, there might have been more voice and exit at NHTSA. But most high-ranking career officials expressed some reservations about Claybrook's approach and hence did not react to Peck and Steed in the same way that Claybrook herself would have. The legacy of the Carter years thus led not to resistance but to a desire by the career staff to slow down what they viewed as Claybrook's rash issuance of regulations.

In short, based on the agency's historical legacy, especially the prior reactions of external actors to their actions, NHTSA's career civil servants lacked the confidence to resist the Reagan administration and its agenda for regulatory reform and instead opted for a more cautious path. In this case, the cautious path was one of neglectful cooperation.[6]

AGENCY ESPRIT DE CORPS

Of the seventeen people I interviewed at NHTSA, only one described the agency as having a strong sense of esprit de corps. This absence of esprit is surprising, since everyone I talked to seemed quite congenial and spoke of their colleagues in friendly and respectful terms. But their responses to the question about agency esprit were clear—it was not an operating force at NHTSA. Part of the explanation seems to stem from the historical divisions among careerists over policy. These divisions were exacerbated (or possibly created) by the agency's structure and by an internal review process that entailed circulating drafts of proposed regulations and other agency documents to each office within NHTSA for comments, thus pitting groups of careerists (those in research, policy evaluation, rule making, crashworthiness, etc.) against one another. The professions in the agency also were divided according to these same structural and policy cleavages. Although this process could have fostered cooperation by forcing different groups to interact with one another in developing regulations, the interviewees reported that the process had traditionally exacerbated internal cleavages and highlighted the differing perspectives of agency personnel from different units and professions rather than promoting unity.

In addition, as a number of interviewees noted, the agency is filled with "car nuts," not "crusaders." And although Joan Claybrook tried to create a more crusading spirit in the agency during her tenure, she was not particularly successful. If NHTSA had had a more crusading spirit, it might also have had a stronger sense of esprit de corps, and this might have produced less cooperative behavior than what I found at the agency during the Reagan years.

SELF-INTEREST AND ROLE PERCEPTION

What about self-interest and role perception? At NHTSA, self-interest and role perception, while important, are less central to the story than the roles played by either the administrative presidency or the agency's culture. To the extent that they did play a role, however, they complemented those factors by further fostering an already compliant atmosphere.

First, almost to a man,[7] top-level careerists at NHTSA shared similar conceptions of their role. In their view, politics could (and should) be separated from administration, and therefore, the appropriate locus of "political" decision making was the *political* appointees. They felt quite strongly that their role was to present the scientific evidence and then to defer the decision to their appointed superiors; it was not to engage in politics. Second, self-interest, although not a dominant factor at NHTSA during the Reagan years, did have some impact on bureaucratic behavior. It was manifested primarily by a preoccupation with job security. This led NHTSA careerists to be even more cautious than they already were; as noted earlier, it led them to keep their heads low and their mouths shut. In other words, at NHTSA, self-interest complimented careerists' preexisting hesitance to use voice and led them to cooperate with Reagan's appointees.

In sum, the cooperation I found at NHTSA can be explained in part by how NHTSA's careerists viewed their proper role and in part by the fact that civil servants were somewhat concerned about job security. But the primary determinants of bureaucratic behavior at NHTSA were the management style adopted by Reagan's strategic appointees, which limited the careerists' role in the decision-making process, and the culture of the agency, which led the careerists there to take a cautious approach to policymaking. Irrespective of the occupant of the White House, his policy goals, or his administrative strategy, NHTSA was not an agency destined by its culture, history, or personnel to rock the boat.

This chapter has demonstrated that at least in one agency, the anticipated careerist revolt in response to Ronald Reagan's policy agenda and approach to policy change did not materialize. There was minimal voice or non-RIF-induced exit and considerable quiescence. I have explained these findings by relying heavily on the culture of the agency, though the actions and behavior of Reagan's appointees also colored the careerists' response.

Examining agency context in this way illustrates five points. First, career civil servants at NHTSA did not hitch their wagon to an expanded role for their agency by issuing large numbers of hastily conceived regulations. If they had, they would have embraced Joan Claybrook and fought the Reagan appointees. And they would have done more to ensure their agency's continued regulatory activity during the Reagan years. Second, careerists viewed the avoidance of future embarrassments like the ones experienced in the past as a high-priority goal. This goal was more important than expanding the agency's budget or engaging in high-volume regulatory activity. Third, different types of agency careerists, in different professions and with different functional positions, had different priorities. This lack of unity in the career ranks led to more compliance than orchestrated resistance. Fourth, NHTSA careerists were simply not an ideological bunch—before, during, or after the Reagan years. It was not just that half of them held no party affiliation or that they were evenly split along ideological lines. Rather, the clear impression that emerges from the interviews I conducted—both inside the agency and with outside observers—is of an agency peopled by relatively apolitical technocrats not inclined toward partisanship of any stripe. Cars, not politics, led them to careers at NHTSA, and career and professional concerns, not political ones, motivated their behavior. Finally, none of these factors alone accounts for the careerists' compliance at NHTSA. Rather, appointee management techniques interacted with the agency's modus operandi and individuals' attitudes and professional norms to create a behavioral pattern characterized by caution and cooperation rather than either subtle sabotage or vocal objections to the administration's policy.

CHAPTER 4

THE FOOD AND NUTRITION SERVICE: LIMITED OPPORTUNITY, LIMITED RESISTANCE

Shortly after Ronald Reagan took office in 1981, the Department of Agriculture proposed regulations that included allowing ketchup to be used to fill the vegetable requirement in the school lunch program. This proposal received considerable publicity, evoked a significant amount of controversy, and was even ridiculed in a Doonesbury cartoon, but it is just one example of the Reagan administration's efforts to reorient social welfare programs and establish greater executive control over the agencies administering them.

This chapter focuses on Reagan's administrative presidency at one such agency—the Department of Agriculture's Food and Nutrition Service (FNS)—and on how the career civil servants in that agency responded to Reagan's intervention into their agency's activities. It presents the findings generated by this case study, the second of the four cases examined in this book. Using the framework of exit, voice, loyalty, and neglect to characterize bureaucratic behavior, I found that, like their counterparts at the National Highway Traffic Safety Administration (NHTSA), most careerists at FNS were passive and acquiescent. They exhibited little voice or exit. Careerists did not resign in protest from the agency, nor did they try to sabotage presidential policies. In fact, only rarely did they so much as verbally confront presidential appointees. Their behavior and my explanation for why they did not resist form the nucleus of this chapter.

Agency Background

The food stamp program has always been controversial, the school lunch program popular, and the women, infants, and children program (WIC) held up as a model program. During the Reagan years, all were housed in the Food and Nutrition Service of the Department of Agriculture (USDA), an agency targeted by the administration for budget cuts and the reduction of waste, fraud, and abuse.

The Food and Nutrition Service was not established until 1969, but many of the programs that it administers predate that year: the National School Lunch Act was passed in 1946, the School Milk program in 1954, and the Food Stamp Act in 1964. Earlier versions of these programs were enacted during the Depression but were terminated following World War II. The catalyst for the creation of the FNS was a study, book, and television exposé, "Hunger in America," in the late 1960s.[1] The agency was housed in USDA because many of its programs involved distributing surplus farm produce. But the FNS has fit uneasily into this home. Its mission, unlike that of the parent department, has a distinctly social service orientation and is more redistributive than distributive. Its clientele base of poor people, women, and children is also different from USDA's traditional farming constituency. In addition, career civil servants at FNS tend to be generalists and managers rather than agricultural or forestry professionals, as is true elsewhere in USDA.

The FNS is a small agency in terms of staff—during the Reagan years it had only 1,800 full-time employees (2,400 at the start) and four career members of the Senior Executive Service (SES). It has seven regional offices and is headquartered in Alexandria, Virginia, eight miles from the main USDA headquarters building in southwest Washington, D.C. Its operating budget, however, is proportionally quite large, making it one of the biggest (in dollars) agencies in the USDA. During the Reagan years, the FNS had an operating budget of $24.5 billion; its school lunch program served 23 million students a day; WIC had an average monthly participation of 3 million women, infants, and children; and the food stamp program served more than 20 million participants a month (Hoagland 1984; U.S. Department of Agriculture 1995a,c; U.S. Office of Management and Budget 1985).[2]

Characteristics of FNS Careerists

High-ranking career civil servants at FNS share a "do-gooder" attitude and joined the agency out of "social altruism." I interviewed twelve careerists at

FNS, four of whom came to the agency from the Peace Corps or the Public Health Service; two more came from other social service agencies like Health and Human Services.[3] They were, even after the White House had been occupied by a Republican for ten years, solidly Democratic and liberal.[4] Eight of ten survey respondents affiliated themselves with the Democratic Party, and the other two described themselves as Independents—there were no Republicans. Six considered themselves to be liberal; three "middle of the road," and only one conservative.

The careerists at FNS identified their expertise more by their function in the agency than by their professional training. For example, one interviewee described himself as an expert in budgeting, two in finance, and several in management. Others described their expertise in terms of policy analysis or program evaluation. Their educational background ranged from liberal arts to psychology, from economics to MPAs (master of public administration), with no one kind of training predominant.

Careerists at FNS did not describe the kind of esprit de corps and camaraderie that we will see later among careerists at the Civil Rights Division. There was, however, consensus that the agency had a distinctly "social service–oriented" culture. Careerists also boasted of a high level of collegiality, which they attributed to the agency's relative youth and the fact that most high-ranking careerists had worked their way up the ranks and "grown up" together in the agency.

The FNS has witnessed a number of changes during its history. Its organizational home has always been somewhat controversial, with plans for reorganization that would move FNS out of the Department of Agriculture and into the Department of Health, Education and Welfare (now Health and Human Services), where it would be merged with other needs-based programs.

More important, the agency has undergone significant shifts in its political environment. To some extent, the agency's history has been rocky owing to the controversial nature of its programs. At first, Food and Nutrition programs were criticized for serving too few Americans and, later, for serving too many. In the early 1960s, before the FNS had been formally established but after most of its programs were operational, careerists enjoyed considerable autonomy. They ran the programs, wrote the rules and regulations, and did so without much intervention from political appointees in the USDA or from Congress (Berry 1984). But this began to change around the time the FNS was formed in 1969. Between 1968 and 1972, George McGovern chaired the Senate Nutrition Committee and viewed "hunger" as one of his principal issues. Congressional intervention increased correspondingly. At the same time, interest groups that became known as the "hunger lobby" were forming (Melnick 1994). These groups were critical of the new agency because its programs—the food stamp program in particular—did not serve enough people (Berry 1984). Key careerists retired at the same time that the agency lost much of its autonomy over rulemaking to an assertive Congress and was being criticized by liberals on the Hill and in the emerging hunger lobby (Berry 1984).

In the later years of the Nixon administration, under the helm of Secretary of Agriculture Earl Butz, and through the Ford years, both public opinion and presidential leadership turned against FNS programs, charging that they served too many unqualified participants and were plagued by program abuse (Melnick 1994). The pendulum swung again during the Carter administration, when FNS's appointees came almost exclusively from the lobbying groups who monitored the agency, and the agency's emphasis shifted back to outreach (publicizing agency programs and actively encouraging eligible individuals to participate in those programs) and nutrition.

The school lunch program, however, has been consistently popular with members of Congress and parents across the United States, even if not with all school-age children, and every year at congressional hearings, parents, educators, and nutritionists attest to its importance. WIC is even more popular, although it serves a politically inactive clientele. One observer of WIC (Rauch 1984:2198) explained the program's popularity by asking, "What Congressman wants to go home and say he voted against pregnant women and children?" Physicians' support for the program is also widespread. Its scale, though, is fairly small; during the Reagan years it served 3 million to 4 million participants at a cost of less than $1 billion a year (Hoagland 1984; Rauch 1984; U.S. Department of Agriculture 1995).[5] Thus, the program is held up as a model of success, although some people in the food and nutrition community criticize its diet as being too heavy in butter and cholesterol.

In short, FNS's programs have experienced differing historical paths and exist in different political environments. Careerist confidence has been affected by the varied histories and circumstances of the agency's different programs.[6] Moreover, careerists are aware that the interest groups who monitor the agency—FRAC (Food Research Action Center), CNI (Community Nutrition Institute), and the Center on Budget and Policy Priorities—do not have much political clout. These interest groups, known collectively as "the hunger lobby," are all public-interest groups with few actual program participants as members. The agency has some friends in Congress, but especially between 1981 and 1986 when Republicans controlled the Senate and Jesse Helms chaired the Senate Agriculture Committee, it had many critics on the Hill as well.

Food and Nutrition Service careerists all believed that their agency's mission was clear: to provide food assistance to those with "low incomes." However, historically, there has been some tension between those who viewed the agency as serving a primarily nutritional function and those who viewed its mission as "income maintenance" or "income transfer" (Melnick 1994; Nathan 1976). This has created some uncertainty within the agency regarding the implementation of its mission. As was the case at NHTSA, the Carter administration had attempted to make significant changes at FNS, specifically to shift the emphasis more toward nutrition and away from mere income transfer. The Carter agenda stood in stark contrast to the agency's early orientation under Nixon, Ford, and Earl Butz, and to the later Reagan agenda. During the Reagan years, careerists perceived a decided shift by the administration and its appointees away from the nutritional role for the agency that Carter appointees Carol Tucker Foreman and Robert Greenstein had emphasized.

These changes in the agency's direction had an effect on careerist confidence. Most of the people I interviewed for this study were more sympathetic to the Carter view of the agency and were committed to the agency's mission of providing food assistance—whether it was food stamps, hot school lunches, milk, or surplus foods—to those in need. But at least one interviewee reported that at the lower levels of the agency, employees felt they were being buffeted from side to side. In short, the agency was influenced not only by Reagan's agenda but also by what one former Carter appointee described as the "roller coaster ride" that agency civil servants had been on as they experienced transitions and the concomitant changes from Johnson to Nixon/Ford and from Carter to Reagan.

REAGAN'S GOALS AT FNS

At the heart of the Reagan administration's interest in FNS was a desire to spend less money on "social" programs and to cut program costs as a way of reducing the budget deficit. The administration did not so much have specific policy goals regarding food stamps or school lunches as it had a general desire to curb the growth of the general class of social programs to which FNS's programs belonged. Its food assistance policies "were designed to reduce or slow budget outlays" (Hoagland 1984:49). Reagan complained unceasingly in his State of the Union addresses, at press conferences, and in public appearances about the bloated food stamp budget, which he claimed had grown 16,000 percent ("like Topsy") to the detriment of military spending (Public Papers, Reagan 1983:74, 389, 436, 555, 1260, 1398).

Reagan's second goal was to cut program costs by reducing waste, fraud, and abuse.[7] Nine of the ten careerists whom I interviewed mentioned program "accountability" as the Reagan administration's primary administrative goal. They stated that "accountability and cost control" or "accountability and productivity" became the agency's top priority and noted that this was a marked change in direction from the agency's earlier emphasis on outreach. As one interviewee commented, "Accountability became the big issue," which contrasted with the Carter administration's concern with "making sure that everyone who qualified received the program."

An important subset of this policy goal was Reagan's oft-remarked desire to limit programs to the "truly needy" and to get the "nonneedy" working poor and lower middle class off the "payroll." He had a number of anecdotes about food stamp abuse, including one about a college student who was allegedly collecting food stamps even though his parents' income was in the "six figures" and another about an investigation that revealed that 57 percent of retailers sold banned items in exchange for food stamps (Public Papers, Reagan 1983:120, 404). Reagan also expressed support for "cutting back on [school lunch program] meals for children of families who can afford to pay" (Public Papers, Reagan 1982:111). His goals here were both philosophical and pragmatic. Philosophically, Reagan wanted to limit participation in FNS programs to those for whom benefits were "morally or materially justified" (Public Papers, Reagan 1983:1340). Pragmatically, he viewed attacks on waste, fraud, and abuse as a means to save money. For example, he estimated that more than $1 billion could be saved by dropping ineligible participants from the food stamp rolls (Public Papers, Reagan 1982:111; see also Hoagland 1984 for further estimates of cost savings). Philosophical or otherwise, the administration's emphasis on eliminating food assistance to those above a "safety net income standard" or otherwise ineligible represented a marked departure in orientation from the agency's approach during the Carter administration.

Finally, the FNS was a target for Reagan's new federalism. Reagan proposed a "swap" with the states. Under his plan, the federal government would turn over the administration of both AFDC (Aid to Families with Dependent Children) and food stamps entirely to the states. In return, the federal government would assume responsibility for Medicaid. Reagan campaigned very hard to promote his plan. The proposed AFDC–food stamp–Medicaid swap featured prominently in at least eleven different speeches, including his 1982 State of the Union message, that Reagan gave to a variety of audiences between February 1981 and July 1982 (Public Papers, Reagan 1982, 1983). Although his policy initiative was eventually abandoned in the face of congressional opposition, its prominence in Reagan's early speeches indicates that it was a high administrative priority (see Sanders 1988 for a discussion of Reagan's proposal and its eventual withdrawal). It was also a priority that posed a threat to the career staff at the FNS.

To achieve these goals, the Reagan administration used both an administrative and a congressional strategy. Although the administration consistently sought budget cuts from Congress and required congressional approval for its federal-state program swap, it attempted to achieve its policy goals mainly by employing the bureaucracy to work for its reforms.

The Administrative Presidency at FNS

The Reagan administration relied primarily on two tools of the administrative presidency strategy in its attempt to achieve its policy aims at FNS: the Office of Management and Budget (OMB) and strategic appointments.[8]

The Office of Management and Budget was a key factor in Reagan's administrative strategy at FNS. Six of ten survey respondents attributed "a great deal" of influence to OMB. In response to a question about who had the most influence over agency policy during the Reagan years, the same six respondents ranked OMB first or second. OMB's influence was felt at the agency primarily through its role in promoting budget cuts. FNS suffered from massive budget cuts, especially in the food stamp program (Melnick 1994). The biggest of these cuts came in the Omnibus Reconciliation Bill of 1981 (OBRA) and therefore were made with the consent of Congress. These cuts affected all of FNS's programs: food stamps, school lunch, WIC, milk distribution, and so forth. As has been well documented elsewhere, the 1981 budget was the product of David Stockman's OMB and Congress, with little input from the agencies themselves (see, e.g., Benda and Levine 1988; Berry 1984; Sanders 1988). Many of the budgetary decisions were made by OMB early in 1981 before confirmed appointees were even in place. In addition, the use of the reconciliation process prevented the logrolling that had always taken place between the vote on the budget for FNS programs and the farm bill (Berry 1984).

The most striking of these early OBRA cuts was a drop from $156 million in 1980 to $20 million in 1982 for the special milk program, a program that provides milk to school districts that do not have a school lunch program (U.S. Office of Management and Budget 1984). Child Nutrition, the bureau administering the school lunch program, saw its budget allocation fall from $3.2 billion in 1980 to $2.9 billion in 1982 (Wholey 1984). And as Melnick has observed, "few programs sustained as many cuts as food stamps did in the first two years of the Reagan presidency" (Melnick 1994:230). Food stamp cuts enacted during the early Reagan years totaled $6 billion (Melnick 1994). As a result of these budget cuts, the agency also experienced a 14 percent decline in personnel between 1980 and 1983 (Wholey 1984).

After 1981, however, Congress did not grant Reagan's requested cuts for FNS programs, and the budget levels crept back up (Melnick 1994). But except for WIC, they never returned to pre-1981 levels. In addition, the administration, through OMB, continued to seek budget cuts every year after 1981.

During the Reagan years, FNS had two subcabinet-level appointed positions: Assistant Secretary for Food and Consumer Services and Administrator of FNS.[9] During that time, FNS experienced considerable turnover in both positions, with two different assistant secretaries and four different administrators in the eight years. These appointees received widely varied marks from careerists regarding their impact on the agency's policy and direction. Six of ten survey respondents believed that John Bode, Assistant Secretary for Food and Consumer Services from 1985 to 1988, was one of the two most influential political actors during the Reagan years. Seven of ten felt that he had "a great deal of influence." By contrast, all ten respondents gave Administrator Sam Cornelius (1982 to 1983) ratings of slight or no influence.[10] Cornelius is the best example of a failure of the administrative presidency's use of strategic appointments because he was overwhelmingly regarded by careerists as incompetent and ineffectual. Comments about Cornelius showed little variation, ranging only from "incompetent" to "just not competent." Moreover, according to the careerists, he spent most of the day in his office either sleeping or watching soap operas and was known to fall asleep in meetings.

William Hoagland, the agency's first administrator (1981–1982), is another interesting example. Careerists liked Hoagland because they considered him an "expert" based on his experience working on food and nutrition issues "on the Hill" before his appointment to FNS. Careerists believe that he was forced out of his appointed position by the White House because he was too moderate and not ideological enough, and they also feel that his short tenure limited his effectiveness.

Two women were appointed to FNS at various times during the Reagan administration. The first was Mary Jarrat (assistant secretary from 1981 to 1985) who, although she came from the Hill, started out as a secretary and had a business degree from the Katherine Gibbs secretarial school. Careerists considered her to be a "lightweight" who lacked the necessary background and experience to effect change in the agency. The second female appointee was Anna Kondratas (1987–1989), who served in the waning years of the Reagan administration. Almost all the careerists I interviewed felt that she was the most ideologically committed of the Reagan appointees to serve at FNS, having come from the Heritage Foundation where she had written extensively on welfare policy. Interviewees commented that "Kondratas was really the only ideologue" and that "she was a pure, driven-snow ideologue." Nonetheless, they respected her expertise and management skills and felt that her ability to carry out her agenda was hampered not by careerist resistance but by her short tenure and its timing in the lame duck years of Reagan's presidency.

Administrator Robert Leard (1984–1987) was not plagued by a short tenure and elicited mixed reactions from careerists. No one objected to his ideology, which they did not feel was a significant motivating factor. In fact, most felt him to be "Secretary Block's man" rather than a "Reagan man." Instead, what evoked controversy about Leard was not his policy goals but his military background, which heavily influenced his management style. According to some careerists, this enabled him to run the organization effectively, but according to others, it "strained" relations with careerists. Overall, he was considered to be an effective manager but lacking the agenda and clear policy goals associated with a strategic appointee. One careerist described him as "competent but no policy sense."

Despite these wide-ranging differences in influence, certain shared characteristics describe the appointees' strategy at FNS. Foremost among these were secrecy and limited access for careerists. According to careerists, Reagan's appointees "held policy decisions more closely to their chest" than Carter and Nixon appointees had, and they "didn't want a lot of careerists at meetings." In fact, the appointees distrusted FNS careerists to such an extent that they took away the SES status of three of the four agency careerists who had been promoted to the SES during the Carter administration.

Reagan's appointees at FNS adopted a management style that circumvented careerists. They did so by removing careerists from the tasks for which they had traditionally been responsible, or by reviewing and changing their work product. Two examples in which this strategy of superceding careerists was employed illustrate this management style.

One instance involved a decision to rewrite the food stamp regulations. According to the careerist who related this incident to me, the appointees felt that the existing food stamp regulations were too "liberal" and that new regulations could eliminate loopholes, tighten the requirements, reduce fraud, and limit access to food stamps to the "truly needy." Moreover, the appointees believed that careerists could not be trusted to write the new regulations, since they were the people who had written the old "liberal" regulations in the first place and who were perceived by the appointees as the repository of liberalism in the agency. Accordingly, the administration hired an outside consultant to rewrite the regulations. Thus, the appointees removed the opportunity for careerist sabotage by bypassing civil servants and assigning the work to someone whom they viewed as more ideologically "trustworthy." One consequence of this approach was that it also removed the opportunity to utilize careerist expertise. Bureaucrats had neither an opportunity to defend the existing regulations nor a voice in formulating the new ones.[11]

The second example pertains to a study evaluating the effectiveness of the WIC program. The FNS's Office of Analysis and Evaluation had been commissioned to conduct a study of WIC toward the end of the Carter administration, but the report was not completed until well into Reagan's term of office. When the completed report was submitted to the Reagan appointees, however, they were displeased because it painted the WIC program in a very favorable light. Because the Reagan administration was anxious to persuade Congress to drastically reduce WIC's funding, it did not want to provide program advocates with empirical evidence supporting the program's value. Reagan appointees in the agency thus tried to suppress the report's findings. First, they rewrote the introduction to the report and added false statistics to the summary section to cast the findings in a different light (U.S. General Accounting Office 1989). Second, appointees took advantage of a loophole in the rules for printing government reports so that only a handful of reports were actually printed for distribution (U.S. General Accounting Office 1989; interview).

Careerists were not included in any of the decision making regarding the report's revisions, nor were they involved in the rewriting. Instead, when appointees were presented with a report that reached conclusions contrary to those they desired, they reacted by taking over the traditionally careerist function of preparing reports, by rewriting parts of the report themselves, and by shielding their activities from the career civil servants in the agency. They reacted by taking matters into their own hands and attempting to achieve their policy goals without careerist input. One significant consequence of this appointee behavior was to lessen the role traditionally played by careerist expertise, to limit bureaucratic decision-making discretion, and to reduce the amount of line responsibility traditionally exercised by career staff.

FNS experienced clear and significant instances in which career civil servants—their expertise, line responsibility, and institutional memory—were bypassed by political appointees to facilitate achievement of the administration's goals at FNS. This management technique was not used universally by appointees but, rather, was used strategically. This technique reduced the discretion of career civil servants and limited potential efforts to disrupt the administration's attempts to revamp FNS programs.

Lower-level appointees such as Schedule C special assistants and noncareer members of the Senior Executive Service also played a role in reducing bureaucratic discretion by assuming tasks traditionally performed by career staff. For example, when the incident involving the rewriting of the WIC report was made public in 1990, congressional testimony revealed that the person who actually rewrote the introduction to the revised report was a Schedule C appointee (U.S. Congress 1990). In fact, I argue that large numbers of lower-level appointees are a prerequisite to a presidential administration's ability to leave career civil servants out of the loop. Such a strategy requires sufficient numbers of "loyal" personnel serving in high- and low-level appointed positions to carry out the tasks traditionally performed by careerists. By increasing the number of appointees at FNS and using outside contractors when it lacked sufficient appointed personnel, the Reagan administration was able to capitalize on this approach to carrying out agency tasks.

Moreover, increasing the number of Schedule C and noncareer SES appointees at FNS and giving positions that had traditionally been held by careerists to political appointees reduced the high-ranking careerists' opportunities for advancement. During the Reagan years, appointees held positions, such as office director, traditionally held by top careerists. Finally, appointees complemented the president's strategic use of OMB by continuing to support OMB's budget cuts before Congress. Year after year, they testified in support of cutting the agency's budget (U.S. House 1982c, 1985c; U.S. Senate 1981a).[12]

THE BUREAUCRATIC RESPONSE

The situation just described provided FNS careerists with plenty of reasons to resist—exactly the reasons depicted in the literature as causes of bureaucratic resistance: change from the status quo (from outreach to accountability); desire for agency and budgetary expansion, or at least maintenance of current levels of spending (as contrasted with budget cuts); desire to serve their clientele (not reduce it); and loss of careerist autonomy and discretion. Yet the career civil servants I interviewed at FNS reported that they and their colleagues seldom resisted and generally tried to comply with their political superiors.

EXIT

During the Reagan years, the agency turnover rate at FNS remained consistently at 10 to 12 percent per year—the same as during the pre-Reagan years.[13] Exit was minimal at this agency despite the demoralization of career personnel. In this section, I look at the two clearest incidents in which exit was used in response to the Reagan administration's behavior at FNS and then I turn to the factors that limited exit.

Reagan appointees at FNS suspected the four careerists who had been appointed to the Senior Executive Service during the Carter years of being Carter lackeys. As a result, they demoted three of the four out of the SES. One careerist left FNS after being demoted in this manner, because she felt that her "Carter" label was impossible to dispel. However, her reason for exit was not dissatisfaction with administration policy but a feeling of being forced out against her will. When she was invited to return to a different agency in the USDA later in the Reagan administration, she jumped at the chance and returned. Despite their demotions, the other two FNS careerists who were removed from the SES did not resign.

The incident involving the WIC study and report precipitated a cluster of exit from FNS's Office of Policy Analysis and Evaluation. A group of industrial psychologists who had had line responsibility for the study left FNS after the report evaluating the WIC program was tampered with by appointees. They resigned because they felt that they had been excluded from the decision to alter the report. Moreover, they felt that the politically motivated revisions disregarded and belittled the integrity of the scientific process.

In general, the individuals I interviewed reported that researchers, such as those in the policy office, were "harder hit" and suffered more under the Reagan administration than did the people in the program offices. They were also more likely to leave. But because of their professional background and training, these researchers were also in a better position to get jobs outside the government. Most were Ph.D.s who were able to secure academic positions after they left FNS. In addition, their unit was a relatively new one, so their tenure was shorter. They had invested less time in FNS. They also were more marketable because they had not spent their entire careers at the agency.[14]

The more common behavior at FNS was remaining with the agency rather than exiting, a response best explained by one interviewee who asked, "Where can you get a job?" Most careerists at FNS had devoted their entire careers to government service, often starting with the Peace Corps or Public Health Service and then joining the FNS. To them, the logical place to look for a new job was with the government, but this option was not possible for two reasons. First, the problems that beset the FNS were also present in other social welfare agencies such as the Department of Health and Human Services (HHS) and the Department of Education. More significantly, other federal agencies with responsibility for social welfare programs were not hiring any new personnel, as they were operating under the same hiring freezes and RIFs (reductions in force) that were being experienced throughout the federal government during the Reagan years (Goldenberg 1984; Rubin 1985). Furthermore, with the exception of those in the Office of Policy Analysis and Evaluation just discussed, most of the careerists at FNS were generalists and so lacked the marketable expertise of an attorney or a nuclear physicist.

A bleak job market was only one factor that kept careerists from leaving the FNS. Some chose to stay because they remained committed to FNS's programs and client population. Finally, several careerists reported that they had considered resigning, but not because of objections to policy change or other "political reasons." Rather, their unhappiness was rooted in the demoralization resulting from the "bureaucrat bashing" of the Carter and Reagan years. This group did not seek to resign in protest but did consider fleeing an occupation that had lost its luster. At the same time, however, they felt confined to the agency because they had no other job prospects, and this constraint proved to be the overriding factor in their decisions. As we shall see shortly, this dependence on the FNS for job security and job satisfaction also affected the way career personnel behaved within the agency.

VOICE

The Reagan years at the Food and Nutrition Service demonstrate that appointees can squelch voice by creating an atmosphere in which careerists become preoccupied with self-preservation. According to the careerists, the appointees came in suspecting innocent people of engaging in voice tactics such as leaking and sabotage. As described earlier in the chapter, this suspicion led to the demotion of three of the four SES members. One of these former SESers was banished to a regional office "in the hinterland." Appointees assumed that careerist resistance would be widespread, and they acted accordingly. This created an atmosphere that made careerists quite hesitant to exercise their voice.

Fear is too strong a word to describe the feeling that the political appointees created, but the atmosphere was one that led careerists to focus more on survival and self-preservation than they had during the Carter years. Careerists viewed the fate of their colleagues in the SES with alarm and became increasingly concerned with avoiding demotion or job transfer. They decided that the best survival strategy was toeing the line, avoiding any action that might draw the appointees' attention, and keeping their opinions to themselves. As one careerist explained, "[There was] no gag rule, but for survival you didn't say, 'You're killing these programs—don't.'"

Appointees also limited the opportunities available to agency careerists to use their voice by their approach to agency management. In some areas, they simply did not let the careerists participate in policy decisions. The example of the food stamp regulations is the clearest illustration of this practice. In that instance, careerists had no opportunity to use their voice, either to defend the existing regulations or to formulate revised ones, because they had been removed from the process altogether.

This is not to say that all FNS careerists were silent throughout Reagan's tenure. One high-ranking careerist described his colleagues as follows: "[There are] six people in [the] agency who will say, 'My job is to protect the programs.' These six are so vocal that they create a perception that everyone is like that." Yet all the careerists I interviewed described themselves and the majority of their colleagues as being reluctant to use their voices too loudly.

VOICE BY ARGUMENTATION

At the FNS, voice by argumentation took a particularly mild cast, especially when compared with the use of voice by argumentation at the Civil Rights Division (CRD). At the CRD, career attorneys argued with appointees, whereas at FNS, careerists gingerly presented existing agency policy—its advantages and disadvantages—to appointees. Careerists at FNS strove to avoid confronting the Reagan appointees in their agency. Overall, the limited policy discussion that did take place at FNS did so without the combativeness and confrontation traditionally associated with argumentation and debate between career civil servants and political appointees.

FOOT-DRAGGING AND SABOTAGE

There were no reports of sabotage at the FNS, in part because the opportunities to engage in this type of behavior were limited by the appointees' exclusionary management style. But there was some foot-dragging that stemmed from a lack of enthusiasm for some of the policy changes that careerists were charged with implementing. This behavior did not include outright resistance but was closer to the stereotypical bureaucratic response of waiting out an administration. One careerist told me, "I did what I was told to do but wouldn't fight for their policies. I did what was technically required. . . . I would just explain but not be an advocate." Another commented, "In [my division], we fought a holding action. . . . All we were able to do was stem the tide."[15]

LEAKS AND WHISTLE-BLOWING

Careerists characterized the majority of civil servants in their agency as "straight shooters" and were critical of colleagues who leaked. They reported that while some leaking did occur at FNS, whistle-blowing did not. One explained, "Appointees suspected leaks a lot. The more suspicion, the more likely it is to happen. It became a self-fulfilling prophecy. Some things did leak, maybe one or two people doing it. One leaker left. Leaks did happen, but not as much as appointees thought." Others agreed that there was some leaking in their agency during the Reagan years, but again argued that it was all done by a few people.

Key events such as the school lunch regulations and the controversy over the release of the WIC study, however, were not leaked by careerists in the FNS. President Reagan accused bureaucrats of leaking the new school lunch regulation to concerned interest groups, who used the incident to generate considerable publicity in support of the program (Community Nutrition Institute 1981). In fact, as Reagan himself later acknowledged, the decision to classify ketchup (as well as pickles) as a vegetable was not made by FNS bureaucrats, nor was the leak that revealed the decision made by career civil servants in the agency (Community Nutrition Institute 1981). Rather, both the decision and the leak came from the USDA's Office of General Counsel and involved political appointees from that office.[16] However, the leak was blamed on an FNS careerist who was then "banished." This banishment highlighted the potential costs of using this type of voice and thus discouraged its use.

In the second case, it was an outside consultant (the university scientist who had been hired by FNS to direct the WIC study), not an agency careerist, who drew attention to the altered WIC report. No careerist participated in leaking that information; the consultant was the only person who contacted Congress, the "hunger lobby," or the press.[17] In both this episode and the school lunch controversy, career civil servants were passive, and attention was drawn to internal agency events by other political actors.

COLLECTIVE ACTION

Although the careerists at FNS shared a sense of camaraderie, a common sense of purpose, and Peace Corps–type roots, this did not lead to any coordinated group action during the Reagan years. No such activity was reported by any of the interviewees at FNS or by any of the outside observers I interviewed.

LOYALTY

Cooperation at the FNS had two sources. First and foremost, the careerists believed that the appointees had a legitimate role at the helm of federal agencies and departments. Overall, they felt that the proper role of careerists was to point out the different options and implications to political appointees, but that then it was their duty to follow the directives of those political superiors.[18] Careerists articulated this belief with comments such as these:

- [You] need to give them the information and point out background of issues. But then it's your job to fall into line.

- A good bureaucrat has to point out the pros and cons. Once they make a decision, you support it or you leave.

- I always followed the direction of my political superiors. In doing so, you have to explain the implications as you see [them], [but] once you explain, you have got to carry policy out to the best of your ability.

The careerists, however, also believed that this norm went only so far, and that if a matter of illegality were to arise, they might act differently. But all claimed that no such questions of legality arose during the Reagan years.

The fact that most of the careerists, at least initially, supported some policy change also encouraged cooperation. An eighteen-year FNS veteran stated, "It may have been time to cut back on outreach." Another observed that "there were aspects of the program that needed this [cost and paperwork reduction], and it hadn't been high on the agenda under Carter." He felt that "there was fertile ground for cost cutting, at least initially." But this type of policy congruence–based loyalty waned somewhat over time as the effects of Reagan's policy goals were felt.

NEGLECT

As at the other agencies described in this study, neglect was pervasive and resulted from both the loss of careerist autonomy and discretion, and the exclusion of agency careerists from agency decision making. The lack of activity and reduced responsibility over a number of years fostered apathy, inertia, and passivity on the part of the FNS careerists.

The Role of External Political Actors

This chapter has established that most of the careerists at the FNS were liberal and supported a generally liberal orientation for their agency and its programs. It has also established that despite their personal views regarding policy, civil servants were usually cooperative and compliant with the Reagan administration and its appointees. Nonetheless, the Reagan administration was prevented from achieving some of its policy goals regarding food and nutrition programs. I believe that the source of obstruction did not lie internally within the agency but externally with Congress and interest groups.[19] In fact, many of the Reagan administration's attempts to reorient policy at FNS were challenged by groups outside the bureaucracy.

Constituency support is commonly acknowledged as a critical source of bureaucratic power (Meier 1993; Rourke 1984). But the experience at FNS leads me to argue that this resource is not expressed in the manner suggested by textbook accounts of iron triangles. Instead, I argue that the role of bureaucrats and external political actors at the FNS highlights the passive role of agency bureaucrats in soliciting the involvement of external political actors. Although careerists may benefit from the involvement of outsiders, they do not directly initiate that involvement. Constituency support can indeed be a potent resource for bureaucrats, but the FNS experience during the Reagan years demonstrates the precariousness of this bureaucratic resource. Bureaucrats do not command this resource at will but, rather, depend on the sympathies, policy goals, and political agendas of Congress and relevant interest groups.

Three incidents demonstrate the critical role played by external political actors and the passive role played by career bureaucrats. In one episode, the Reagan administration attempted to rewrite the regulations governing the nutritional content of children's school lunches. Their effort was never completed. Following the publicity generated by an interest group–led petition, interest group–initiated media attention, and extensive congressional hearings, the administration withdrew its proposed regulation and did not introduce any further changes to school lunch regulations for the rest of its time in office (Community Nutrition Institute 1981; U.S. House 1981b). Moreover, after the publicity generated by interest groups and Congress, the administration made no further attempts to reform other aspects of the school lunch program, nor did it seek additional budget cuts. As one FNS career official said about the episode, "Ketchup as a vegetable saved the school lunch program. After that they left it alone."

Agency careerists did not initiate this external voice. As described earlier in this chapter, a political appointee leaked the controversial material. The ball was picked up by the Center for Science in the Public Interest and the Community Nutrition Institute (among others), who used it to attract public and congressional attention. Congress also picked up the ball and, through its House Subcommittee on Elementary, Secondary and Vocational Education, held a hearing on the matter (U.S. House 1981b). This combination of activities persuaded the administration to drop the matter. Although the career civil servants benefited from the activity of these external institutions, they had no direct contact with them.

A second incident involved the administration's decision to hire an outside consultant to write new food stamp regulations, a decision that also attracted congressional attention. The mere threat of a congressional investigation was enough to cause the administration to abandon this strategy. Congress never held formal hearings on the matter, but as soon as outsiders became aware of the agency's action and informally expressed their disapproval to the FNS and White House appointees, the agency dropped both the consultant and the planned regulations. No further attempts were made to write regulations "out-of-house."

Finally, with respect to the WIC study, the Reagan administration was thwarted by the behavior of one maverick epidemiologist. The WIC study was a commissioned study because the agency lacked the technical expertise and manpower to conduct such a large study in-house. Dr. David Rush, an epidemiologist then at Albert Einstein College of Medicine and the director of the study, became suspicious about the status of his report, not because careerists leaked information to him about it, but because careerists began to avoid him. That is, career personnel in the Office of Policy Analysis and Evaluation with whom he had been in frequent contact during the study stopped returning his phone calls. Then, when Rush was invited to testify before Congress, an FNS appointee called him and told him he should not testify. When the few copies of the report that were printed were finally released in 1986 and he saw the changes that had been made to his work, he contacted concerned interest groups and members of Congress and held his own press conference. In addition, at considerable personal expense, he published his original results in a scientific journal.[20] Following the media attention generated by Dr. Rush's press conference, Congress assigned the General Accounting Office (GAO) to investigate the WIC evaluation study (Anderson and Van Atta 1990; Cowen 1990). The GAO concluded that the agency had indeed altered the report's scientific evidence (U.S. Congress 1990; U.S. General Accounting Office 1989). The result, after a considerable time lag, was an affirmation by Congress of the scientifically proven benefits of the WIC program. In all of these episodes, Reagan's policy initiatives were thwarted, but the chorus of resistance was sung by external political actors, not career civil servants.[21]

ANALYSIS

The following analysis focuses on my findings regarding the relative absence of bureaucratic resistance and the presence of bureaucratic cooperation at the Food and Nutrition Service. The explanation I offer has three elements: careerists' inability to resist; the way in which their desire to resist can be altered by the behavior of their appointed principals; and the finding that even where resources for resistance were available, most careerists at FNS chose not to capitalize on them as a matter of principle.

First, the presidential control strategies used at FNS diminished the ability of bureaucrats to resist the Reagan administration. These control strategies included micromanagement techniques that bypassed career civil servants and that employed political appointees to perform agency tasks. When such strategies were used, career civil servants were unable to use their expertise, autonomy, line responsibility, institutional memory, and program knowledge to resist presidential attempts to change policy. By cutting them out of the decision-making loop, political appointees denied careerists the chance to translate their resources into resistance. In the incident involving the proposed nutritional guidelines for the school lunch program, for example, responsibility for regulation writing was removed from FNS careerists and placed in the hands of cabinet-level appointees, thereby removing possible opportunities for foot-dragging or sabotage.

Second, political appointees also altered agency careerists' self-interest calculations in ways that dampened their propensity to challenge the appointees. This approach led careerists to believe that their self-interest—their path to job security and career advancement—lay in cooperating with appointees. The experience at FNS during the Reagan years shows that incentives can be structured so that bureaucrats view their self-interest as better served by promoting the president's policy goals, even when those goals are at odds with their agency's mission and their own personal policy preferences, than by defending their own preferences.

Finally, bureaucratic behavior at the Food and Nutrition Service is partly a function of the conviction—expressed by almost all the careerists I interviewed—that the proper role of the career civil servant is cooperation with duly elected presidential administrations. Even when the FNS careerists could have used their resources—for example, by leaking information about appointees' activities in their agency—they consciously chose not to do so, based on principles that they believed should govern their relationship with their political superiors.

The experience at the Food and Nutrition Service during the Reagan years shares a number of elements with the experience at the National Highway Traffic Safety Administration. The most striking is the predominance of cooperation in both agencies. The management style of the Reagan appointees was similar in both cases, as were some key features of the agencies' contexts and histories. These similarities, in turn, influenced the behavior exhibited in both agencies during Reagan's presidency.

Thus, we can begin to see a number of potentially generalizable propositions from these two case studies. First, the management strategies of political appointees can limit the opportunities for resistance available to career bureaucrats. Second, the actions of these political principals affect the way bureaucrats calculate their self-interest. Third, bureaucrats are motivated by principles as well as self-interest. And finally, as the FNS case underscores, the presidency and the bureaucracy cannot be discussed or evaluated in isolation. In our system of separate institutions sharing power, bureaucratic responsiveness is not a guarantee that the president will prevail. Congress and interest groups both play a role in shaping the president's ability to achieve his policy goals, even when he seeks to achieve those goals administratively.

CHAPTER 5

THE CIVIL RIGHTS DIVISION: LAWYERS WHO LOVE TO ARGUE

The Civil Rights Division of the Department of Justice has long been a symbol of the nation's commitment to enforcing civil rights laws and to eradicating discrimination on the basis of race, gender, age, handicap, national origin, and religion, in the areas of voting, education, employment, and housing. Its policies safeguard the rights of African Americans, Native Americans, women, institutionalized persons, and other groups that Congress, presidents, and/or the courts have determined need to have their civil rights protected by the federal government. This chapter examines how the Reagan administration tried to use the administrative presidency to alter agency policy at the Civil Rights Division, and how the career civil servants who staff the agency reacted to these changes.

The Civil Rights Division (CRD) during the Reagan years is a case in which (a) the administration had a clear policy agenda, (b) that agenda entailed significant policy change, (c) the administration sought to implement its agenda administratively rather than legislatively, and (d) the administrative presidency was the approach adopted by the administration to achieve these policy goals. The CRD differs from the other cases examined in this book, however, in the way the agency's careerists reacted to these circumstances. That is, the Civil Rights Division is the only agency in this study in which careerists mounted any significant opposition to Reagan's policy initiatives and in which civil servants exercised both exit and voice to any significant degree.

But even here, as this chapter demonstrates, bureaucratic opposition was limited to a few, narrowly delineated response options, and by what the agency's careerists considered to be ethical constraints on their behavior. Moreover, the same factors that enabled us to explain bureaucratic behavior at the National Highway Traffic Safety Administration (NHTSA) and the Food and Nutrition Service (FNS) prove to be equally applicable to the very different behavior exhibited at the Civil Rights Division. The agency's organizational features (particularly its professional composition) provided the impetus for resistance, but the civil servants' ethics, role perception, and professional norms restricted the nature and extent of their resistance, and the management style of the agency's appointees limited its effectiveness.

THE AGENCY SETTING

The Civil Rights Division is a subcabinet division of the Department of Justice. The Justice Department, which was established in 1870, is headed by the attorney general, a cabinet post. The Civil Rights Division was elevated to the status of a division in 1957 and is headed by the assistant attorney general for civil rights, a politically appointed position requiring Senate confirmation. In terms of its location in the Justice Department, it is comparable to the Tax Division, Antitrust Division, and Criminal Division, each of which is also headed by an appointed assistant attorney general.

At the time Ronald Reagan took office, the Civil Rights Division was responsible for enforcing the Civil Rights Acts of 1957, 1960, 1964, and 1968, the Voting Rights Act of 1965 (renewed and amended in 1982), the Fair Housing Acts of 1968 and 1978, the Equal Credit Opportunity Act of 1974, the Equal Education Opportunity Act of 1974, the Rehabilitation Act of 1972, and the Civil Rights of Institutionalized Person's Act of 1980 (CRIPA). The Civil Rights Division shares responsibility for enforcing many of these statutes with other federal agencies, including the Equal Employment Opportunity Commission (EEOC), the Office of Civil Rights (OCR) in the Department of Education, and the U.S. Commission on Civil Rights, but the division shoulders the primary responsibility for a number of the enforcement activities mandated by these laws.[1] In addition, it differs from other civil rights agencies in the scope of its responsibilities. The OCR is limited to educational rights, and the EEOC to matters of employment discrimination, whereas the CRD has responsibility in both these areas.

During the Reagan administration, the division's approximately 150 attorneys were divided into seven functional units or "sections," each section specializing in a policy area: Voting, Educational Opportunity, Employment, Housing, Criminal Activity, and Special Litigation. The Appellate Section handled all cases at the appeals stage. Before 1969, the division's sections were organized geographically rather than functionally, with different sections responsible for enforcing all civil rights laws in different regions of the country. The overall effect of creating functional sections was to increase the specialization of career attorneys. As a result, CRD attorneys develop expertise not just in civil rights law broadly defined but in educational rights, voting rights, the rights of institutionalized persons, and so on. Each section is headed by a section chief, who is typically a career civil servant. Section chiefs are usually the highest-ranking civil servants in the agency. Enforcement at the Civil Rights Division is carried out through litigation (including the filing of suits and amicus curiae briefs), investigation, and negotiation.

Between the time that President Dwight Eisenhower elevated the civil rights wing of the Justice Department to the status of a division and Ronald Reagan was elected to the White House, civil rights policy in the United States proceeded on a fairly straight path toward increased presidential commitment to its enforcement (Amaker 1988; Shull 1989a). Eisenhower was at the helm for the first pieces of major civil rights legislation to be enacted in this century—the Civil Rights Acts of 1957 and 1960—legislation that created the Civil Rights Commission and strengthened the CRD. Kennedy advanced the national civil rights agenda through his use of federal marshals and National Guard troops, the issuance of executive orders, the introduction of civil rights legislation in Congress, and his outspoken and oft-repeated sense of moral outrage at racial injustice (Amaker 1988). With respect to Lyndon Johnson's civil rights achievements,

> There can be no question that the presidency of Lyndon Johnson exhibited the greatest amount of sustained executive leadership in this field in the nation's history. . . . During the period from his succession in November 1963 to his departure in January 1969, enforcement of civil rights by the executive branch of government became a firmly established reality.
>
> (Amaker 1988:19)

A number of important pieces of civil rights legislation were enacted under Johnson, including the Civil Rights Act of 1964, the Voting Rights Act of 1965, and the Fair Housing Act of 1968, and from his speeches, scholars have discovered a "clear, unequivocal statement repeated time after time to the nation about how imperative it was to enforce civil rights throughout the country." (Amaker 1988:21).

The Nixon administration approached civil rights with less vigor than did its predecessors and was opposed to the use of busing to achieve school desegregation (Amaker 1988). But civil servants who served at CRD under Nixon stated that their agency did not alter its mission or overall agenda in any fundamental way during Nixon's tenure. And Gerald Ford, although he continued to oppose busing, "did not seek to dismantle the machinery for executive enforcement of civil rights protections" (Amaker 1988:25). Jimmy Carter increased the attorney general's authority in the area of civil rights enforcement and appointed the first black assistant attorney general for civil rights, Drew Days.

In reviewing the three decades of civil rights enforcement before the Reagan administration, legal scholar Norman Amaker (1988:28) contends that although the "vigor" with which civil rights enforcement was pursued varied under Democratic and Republican administrations, "the record of none of them (including that of Richard Nixon) manifested a tendency to subvert in any fundamental way the protective goals of civil rights laws that had evolved over nearly three decades."

REAGAN'S POLICY OBJECTIVES AT CRD

Ronald Reagan arrived in Washington with a clear agenda for policy change. His policy goals in the area of civil rights were clearly and forcefully expressed not only in his speeches and press briefings but also in the special analyses prepared by the Office of Management and Budget (OMB) that accompanied the president's budget to Capitol Hill (U.S. Commission on Civil Rights 1981; U.S. Office of Management and Budget 1981, 1982; Public Papers, Reagan 1982, 1984). Shull (1989a:64–65) has observed that "more than any president since Johnson, Reagan revealed the ability of presidential policy statements to initiate government's agenda." He also (1989a:xii) notes that "Ronald Reagan consciously returned civil rights to the forefront of the public policy agenda." According to Shull (1989a:3), "Ronald Reagan reversed the direction that civil rights policy had taken during the past generation. Such a drastic change revealed the president as a major catalyst for policy innovation." Amaker (1988:157) concurs, writing, "The record clearly manifests an effort to turn back the clock in the enforcement of civil rights laws—not merely in comparison with prior administrations . . . but in a more fundamental sense."

At the forefront of this agenda, the Reagan administration sought to eliminate the remedies of affirmative action, quotas and timetables, and school busing used by the government and the courts in discrimination cases (Amaker 1988; Bawden and Palmer 1984; Govan 1989; *National Journal* 1985; Wines 1982a; Yarbrough 1985). The administration not only rejected the concept of affirmative action but also sought to limit the long-standing policy of redressing discriminatory practices to cases of proven intent and to limit compensation for the effects of discrimination to those cases in which individual victims could be identified (Amaker 1988; Bawden and Palmer 1984). All the components of Reagan's civil rights agenda were directed toward reversing long-standing policies and often involved reversing pending court cases in midstream.

Although Reagan's pronouncements were not detailed, there is little doubt in the minds of scholars, CRD careerists, or Reagan's appointees that the subsequent administrative implementation of his agenda was consistent with his policy goals (Amaker 1988; Shull 1989a; Smith 1991). Career attorneys at the Civil Rights Division, while attributing little day-to-day influence over agency policy to the president, credited Reagan, the Heritage Foundation, and the Federalist Society with developing the agenda and setting the tone on which the changes in division policy were based.

The Civil Rights Division was not the only target for these policy goals. They are also reflected in Reagan's appointments to the federal courts, his appointments and actions at the EEOC, OCR, and Civil Rights Commission, and in his legislative battles with Congress (Amaker 1988; Shull 1993; Weekly Compilation, Reagan 1983:1080–1081). However, the Civil Rights Division was among those singled out as a place to implement the administration's civil rights agenda and achieve its civil rights goals (Ball and Greene 1985). And the fact that all these agencies were targeted reflects the importance that the administration attributed to this policy area.

THE ADMINISTRATIVE PRESIDENCY AT CRD

Reagan's use of the administrative presidency at the Civil Rights Division was quite simple. At its core was the use of strategic appointments, especially the appointment of an ideologically committed attorney, William Bradford Reynolds, to the position of assistant attorney general for civil rights. All the survey respondents at CRD credited Reynolds with having had "the most influence" over agency policy during the Reagan years, more than that of the president, Congress, or the attorney general.[2]

The Civil Rights Division did not experience budget cuts or reductions in force (RIFs), and because it is not mainly a regulatory agency, it escaped the intervention of OMB's Office of Information and Regulatory Affairs (OIRA). In fact, in every year but one, the budgets requested by the assistant attorney general, approved by the OMB and granted by Congress, featured spending increases (U.S. Office of Management and Budget 1979–1990). Moreover, none of the CRD careerists who completed my questionnaires attributed "a great deal of influence" to either the OMB or the OIRA, and only one respondent indicated that the OMB had even "moderate influence" over agency decisions.[3] With respect to the OIRA specifically, a number of the civil servants I interviewed at CRD had never even heard of the office—a rather telling indication that it had not played a prominent role.[4]

Nowhere was the strategy of appointing ideologically committed individuals to cabinet and subcabinet posts more evident than at the Civil Rights Division of the Justice Department. Although it was the subcabinet appointee who was key to implementing Reagan's change agenda at the Civil Rights Division, his superiors also played an important role as spokesmen for the administration's policy views, expressing those views, setting a tone for the department, and conveying their support and consensus for the work of their subordinate.

The Justice Department had two attorneys general over the course of Reagan's eight years in office. The first was William French Smith. Smith's role in bringing about policy change was not pivotal. In fact, only one respondent felt that Smith had "a great deal of influence" in agency decision making. He did his part, however, by articulating the administration's views concerning civil rights in public appearances and in a series of special reports that he issued to department employees (U.S. Department of Justice 1983, 1985). Foremost among these views were Smith's opposition to both mandatory busing in school desegregation cases and racial quotas in cases of employment discrimination, and his desire to uphold and implement "conservative principles of both law and social policy" (Smith 1991:89–90). His policy views on civil rights were remarkably congruent with those of the administration (Ball and Greene 1985; Lees and Turner 1988), and his memoir reveals his continuing commitment to Reagan's civil rights agenda, philosophy, and beliefs (Smith 1991). Despite his lack of direct involvement in the division's day-to-day operations, it is clear from my interviews that the career bureaucrats at CRD viewed Smith as a messenger for the civil rights agenda, lending another voice in support of the president, the Heritage Foundation, and the Federalist Society (see also Ball and Greene 1985).

Edwin Meese took over the post of attorney general in Reagan's second term. Meese had been actively involved in the activities of the Civil Rights Division even before he became attorney general. During Reagan's first term, he had played the lead role in the White House's monitoring of civil rights policy, and some career attorneys indicated that he had more influence while he was at the White House than after he joined the Justice Department. One-third of my survey respondents felt that Meese had the second most influence over agency decisions (behind Assistant Attorney General Reynolds), and more than half of those surveyed attributed a great deal of influence to him. Meese's relationship with Reynolds was close and personal, and after he became attorney general, careerists believed that Reynolds essentially became his right-hand man (in spite of Reynolds's failure to win Senate confirmation as associate attorney general). Meese's policy views were also consistent with those of the other three members of the civil rights tetrarchy, Reagan, Smith, and Reynolds (Ball and Greene 1985). When Meese took over the helm at Justice, the *National Journal* (1985:1143) observed that while criminal issues "may be closer to Meese's heart," it was "on civil rights that the department is pressing its most ambitious agenda." This agenda, the *National Journal* reported (1985:1143), was the same one initiated by Smith and Reynolds at "the outset of the first term," an agenda that "made clear that the Administration would oppose employment quotas, mandatory busing, and other remedies traditionally used in civil rights cases." Neither Meese's title change nor his change of address (from 1600 Pennsylvania Avenue to 1000 Constitution Avenue) caused any disruption in the president's management of the Civil Rights Division, nor did it portend any change in policy goals.

Neither of Reagan's two attorneys general appear to have been overly active in the division's day-to-day affairs, certainly not any more so than Carter's attorney general, Griffin Bell. Instead, their influence came from the impression they conveyed that all members of the team were consistent in their policy goals and, even more important, that Assistant Attorney General Reynolds had their backing and support.

William Bradford Reynolds was only forty years old when he took over the Civil Rights Division. A 1964 graduate of Yale with a law degree from Vanderbilt University, he had spent most of his career in private practice except for three years in the Solicitor General's Office under the tutelage of Nixon's solicitor general, Erwin Griswold. Like most of Reagan's civil rights appointees, Reynolds was white, male, and conservative and had no significant civil rights experience (though he had helped prepare one civil rights brief during his stint in the Solicitor General's Office).[5]

There was no doubt as to Reynolds's views on civil rights. They were clearly and frequently articulated and were consistent with Reagan's policy pronouncements (Ball and Greene 1985; Brownstein and Easton 1982). In his 1985 confirmation hearing to be associate attorney general, Reynolds testified:

> Senator, the policy of this administration in the civil rights area is one that was set, I think very firmly, by the President at the beginning of his first term, and by Attorney General Smith when he came into office, and probably was outlined in the first instance in a speech given by Attorney General Smith back in May of 1981. . . . I subscribe to the policies of the administration and I have certainly followed those policies.
>
> (U.S. Senate 1985c:61)

Even a cursory examination of Reynolds's testimony before Congress, his legal writings, and his public speeches reveals his policy views, including his opposition to school busing and racial quotas (see, e.g., Ball and Greene 1985; Brownstein and Easton 1982; Reynolds 1986). At his first confirmation hearing in 1981, Reynolds testified that "compulsory busing of students in order to achieve racial balance in the public schools is not an acceptable remedy" (U.S. Senate 1981e:97). And in a speech given a few years into his tenure, he stated that "remedial goals, quotas or set-asides based on race perpetuate the very evil that the 14th Amendment seeks to remove" (U.S. Commission on Civil Rights 1983:22). Career staff had no doubt about Reynolds's policy intentions. In fact, careerists stated that it was through his speeches, as well as personal discussions, that they learned of his civil rights aims, rather than through explicit memos or directives. It is also clear that Reynolds's statements regarding civil rights were remarkably consistent with those expressed by Reagan, Smith, and Meese.

MANAGEMENT AT CRD

Reynolds ruled the Civil Rights Division with an iron hand, centralizing control of the agency in the assistant attorney general's office, instituting a system under which almost all the work of the career attorneys was reviewed by politically appointed special assistants or by Reynolds himself, and generally reducing the autonomy and discretion of the career attorneys. Reynolds also increased the number of political appointees in the agency by hiring a large number of Schedule C special assistants to serve in the office of the assistant attorney general.

The first things to note about Reynolds as a manager are some of his personal attributes. As we have already seen, he had firm and clearly articulated views concerning civil rights that he was able to translate into specific decisions. He was also unusually intelligent. Even his critics acknowledged his intelligence and talent as an attorney (U.S. Senate 1981e, 1985c). On top of that, he was a notoriously hard worker. In fact, according to one interviewee, he was such a workaholic that one evening his wife stormed into the office and berated him for never being home. They were divorced before the administration left office, and interviewees attest that his dedication to his job continued unabated. Finally, although Reynolds had almost no civil rights experience to speak of, he was an attorney with a fair amount of litigation experience in an agency filled with attorneys whose principal activity was litigation. He also learned very quickly. Most of the career attorneys I interviewed credited Reynolds with having mastered civil rights law within six to twelve months of taking office (though many claimed that he mastered it without understanding it). Since Reynolds served as assistant attorney general for seven years, he spent a considerable amount of time at the top of his learning curve, a clear managerial asset, and a rare one for subcabinet appointees who typically spend only twenty-two months at their posts.

Reynolds personally reviewed a significant portion of the pleadings that career attorneys intended to file in court. This contrasted sharply with the management style during the Carter administration, in which, according to interviewees, once things got past the desk of the section chief (a career position), they were usually rubber-stamped by the political appointees and were rarely scrutinized very carefully. Reynolds's work habits, however, gave him the time for such scrutiny. Reynolds rejected the recommendations of the Voting Section attorneys (and the Voting Section chief) when they recommended that the agency file objections to the redistricting plans submitted by the states under section 5 of the Voting Rights Act. He rejected the recommendations of attorneys in the Special Litigation Section when they recommended that the agency investigate prison conditions. In earlier administrations, line attorneys (careerists) could personally request FBI investigations into prison conditions, but Reynolds required that these requests be cleared with him first. He required a detailed memo justifying the need for such an investigation. He also edited the agency's court submissions and amicus curiae briefs.

Even with all his personal skills—his expertise in the law, his intelligence, and his diligence—Reynolds could not have controlled an agency of 150 attorneys alone. So he reorganized the division and developed an internal system of central clearance. He increased the number of politically appointed (but not confirmed by the Senate) deputy associate attorneys general. Although there had been only two such positions under Carter's assistant attorney general Drew Days, Reynolds's Civil Rights Division had three. The main effect of this reorganization was that it allowed the appointees to more closely monitor the sections' activities.

Reynolds also increased the number of Schedule C special assistants, all of whom were appointees (and none of whom were confirmed by the Senate). This group was led by Charles (Chuck) Cooper, an active member of the Federalist Society, and J. Harvie Wilkinson, among others. These appointees were the ones who had the most impact on the careerists' environment. And they were viewed by the careerists as ideological zealots.

The strategy of increasing the number of appointees had two effects on the agency's workings. The first was that appointees began handling cases themselves, something that had traditionally been the exclusive domain of the careerists. In more than a few cases, this cadre of appointees actually wrote the legal briefs or tried the cases themselves. This had the effect of taking the agency's work product out of the careerists' hands altogether.

The second effect of this control strategy was a closer review of the careerists' work by the appointees. When appointees were not actually doing the agency's work themselves, they were carefully monitoring the careerists' work product. This routinely involved vetoing staff recommendations and extensively editing legal pleadings. One career attorney complained that "they looked at every single piece of paper you filed."

The careerists believed that the rationale behind the appointees' management strategy was their open and outright distrust of career attorneys in the agency. According to careerists, the appointees believed that agency bureaucrats could not be trusted to reliably enact the president's agenda.

THE BUREAUCRATIC REJOINDER

Career attorneys at the Civil Rights Division were clearly provoked by the Reagan administration. The agency's career personnel were being told to reverse themselves in court, to work to have earlier court decisions obtained by their agency overturned—decisions that they had previously worked to achieve—and their recommendations to initiate investigations and proceedings were being carefully reviewed, challenged, denied, and overruled. In addition, they had new political superiors who openly distrusted them. We turn now to their response to these circumstances.

Voice

Voice was by far the most common response by career attorneys of all ranks in the Civil Rights Division. Even the most loyal careerists used voice in response to some incidents, and almost all those who left the agency during the Reagan years expressed their disagreement before resorting to exit.

The CRD's career attorneys used voice because they held strong convictions that many of the Reagan administration's civil rights policies were seriously misguided, detrimental to the effective enforcement of civil rights, and in conflict with existing statute and case law. As one CRD attorney put it, "[Our] ultimate boss is not Reagan or Reynolds, but the courts. They set the law. That's why attorneys disagree. They take an oath to carry out the law."

VOICE BY ARGUMENTATION

Career attorneys argued vociferously, both orally and in written memoranda, with Reynolds and the other appointees. As one attorney commented, "One thing attorneys like to do is argue." Another said, "We're a noisy lot." These were clear expressions of voice by argumentation, and division attorneys did not hesitate to use this avenue of resistance. People were frank and open about their disagreements with Reynolds. They did not hesitate to express their point of view when it differed from Reynolds's, and most were not worried about reprisals or other repercussions.

One thing for which all the careerists I interviewed gave Reynolds credit was being accessible and willing to listen to their arguments, whether or not he was persuaded by them. These attorneys felt comfortable presenting their cases to him, whether it was in person or in the form of memos. "Brad would hear you out," a number of interviewees commented. "He might not do [what you wanted], but his door was open," added one. A section chief described the standard operating procedure in his section: "We had lots of meetings . . . and lots of arguments with Brad on [it]."

Some of the issues about which careerists felt compelled to use voice by argumentation are surprising. In a case in which careerists wanted to use CRIPA to prosecute a prison with substandard conditions, one attorney was required to defend his belief that prisoners were entitled to have soap. Ultimately the career attorney prevailed, but he came to feel that Reynolds consciously and deliberately employed a strategy of forcing careerists to go to a lot of trouble to prevail. This careerist believed that Reynolds's strategy was designed to wear down the line attorneys in the hope that over time they would become more neglectful and decide that it was not worth the time and effort required.

On the big issues that lay at the heart of the Reagan agenda, such as busing and affirmative action, agency careerists acknowledge that they did not even try to persuade Reynolds to use traditional remedies. Instead, line attorneys directed their efforts toward devising the "best acceptable" remedies, such as the "best" magnet school plan, rather than trying to persuade Reynolds to recommend busing as the appropriate remedy in a particular school desegregation case.

Although careerists were not hesitant to argue, they did not often win. The practice of line attorneys (with the section chief's approval) recommending and Reynolds vetoing was a constant theme throughout Reynolds's seven years. Line attorneys continued to argue vociferously in support of their recommendations, whether it was recommending an appeal in a school desegregation case or recommending a section 5 objection under the Voting Rights Act. One attorney explained, "I felt that the key was to keep trying, to keep arguing with Brad [Reynolds], and sometimes you'll win and some cases will be filed."

The lawyers at the Civil Rights Division admitted that they became quite adept at formulating those arguments most likely to win over Reynolds. They came to know the types of arguments that he found persuasive. For example, the 1982 Voting Rights Act specifically stated that it was not necessary to establish discriminatory "intent" in redistricting plans and that an "effects test" was sufficient under the law. Nonetheless, CRD careerists worked hard to meet the more difficult "intent" standard in order to win Reynolds's approval to file objections. They believed that this approach increased the chance that their arguments would succeed, since Reynolds personally favored the "intent" standard, the will of Congress notwithstanding. It was in this way that they developed their voice—incrementally, one pleading, brief, or case at a time, using the same voices they were accustomed to using in court, to attempt to point civil rights policy in the direction that they believed was more consistent with the law.

Voice by argumentation—that is, careerists trying, verbally and in writing, to persuade appointees to pursue certain courses of action—was the predominant response of CRD career attorneys to the Reagan administration. It was exercised throughout the Reagan years (albeit to varying degrees) by significant numbers of CRD careerists. Indeed, career attorneys felt that they spent more time "writing memos back and forth" and "arguing about what should be done" during the Reagan administration than they spent on what had been their main pre-Reagan activity, litigating.

COLLECTIVE ACTION

A number of incidents of what I call collective action took place at the Civil Rights Division during the Reagan years. In one incident, career attorneys in the Civil Rights Division joined together to write a protest memo following the decision of the Justice Department to side with the administration against the Internal Revenue Service in the Bob Jones University case. The case involved the tax-exempt status of religious schools with racially discriminatory policies, in this case a racially discriminatory admissions policy and a rule prohibiting interracial dating. Careerists in Civil Rights collectively expressed their objection to the department's decision in a memo to Reynolds. They urged Reynolds to side with the IRS, which was arguing that schools with discriminatory policies should lose their tax-exempt status.[6]

A second example of collective action involved a petition containing the signatures of one hundred careerists. It was drafted in response to a controversial memo written by political appointee Robert D'Agostino, one of Reynolds's Schedule C special assistants. The memo pertained to a much-publicized case involving the city of Yonkers, New York, and concerned both housing and educational discrimination. In the memo, D'Agostino stated that "blacks, because of their family, cultural and economic background are more disruptive in the classroom" and therefore "would benefit from programs for the emotionally disturbed" (Brownstein and Easton 1982:39). Careerists at CRD objected to what they perceived to be D'Agostino's insensitive, if not racist, attitudes, and in the petition they submitted to Reynolds, they called for D'Agostino's resignation.

Collective action also occurred early in the administration when career attorneys who were themselves members of racial or ethnic minorities met with Reynolds to discuss their policy disagreements. According to one attorney who attended the meeting, Reynolds was receptive to meeting with them but not to their policy views.

A final instance of collective action pertained to the annual office Christmas party, traditionally an eagerly anticipated event. It was spontaneous and had little bearing on policy, but it does provide insight into the prevailing sentiments among CRD careerists at that time. Reynolds decided to change the format of the party and raised the cost (paid for by employee contributions) significantly. Since no one wanted to socialize with Reynolds and his deputies anyway, almost everyone decided that the party was too expensive and, in effect, boycotted it. While this symbolic act of rebellion hardly impeded the administration's civil rights policy, it does demonstrate how all facets of behavior were colored by the schism between careerists and the Reagan appointees.

The extent of collective action at the Civil Rights Division can be viewed in either of two ways. Initially, I was struck by its rarity. But when the behavior of career bureaucrats in the Civil Rights Division is compared with the behavior I found in the other agencies, its extent is striking. Nonetheless, on a daily basis, solitary voice by argumentation—rather than collective voice—was the norm. This pattern seems to be due to a combination of professional and bureaucratic norms as well as the nature of the careerists' work. While there is often more than one lawyer assigned to a case, the nature of the work precludes more than two or three attorneys from working together on a given case. The grievances that emerged were on a case-by-case basis, stemming from disagreements about how to handle those individual cases. Reynolds contributed to this by rarely issuing memos with specific guidelines or blanket statements of policy direction. One former Civil Rights attorney felt that Reynolds did this to avoid providing ammunition for leaks or, as another put it, "to avoid seeing his memos turn up in the *Washington Post*." But it also had the effect of not giving groups of bureaucrats anything to rally around. Even the highest-ranking career people, the section chiefs, usually learned of policy on this case-by-case basis. As a result, disputes, for the most part, focused on individual cases.

By contrast, three things about D'Agostino's remarks made him a target for collective action. First, his remarks provided a concrete statement behind which careerists could rally. Second, the careerists' action did not directly concern a policy issue over which appointees could claim to have decision-making authority but instead involved what careerists viewed as inappropriate behavior that reflected poorly on the agency. And third, the subject did not involve a pending court case to which professional norms such as rules of confidentiality and attorney-client privilege would apply.

LEAKS

The attorneys I interviewed at the Civil Rights Division felt that leaking was not appropriate behavior for civil servants in general and lawyers in particular and consequently did not engage in this mode of resistance. In fact, many of the lawyers I talked to were offended merely by being asked about whether they had participated in or knew of leaks. In an agency like theirs, leaks usually pertain to specific cases, and lawyers are prohibited by professional norms and the bar association's ethical guidelines from discussing pending cases. Moreover, CRD careerists view internal agency deliberations on pending cases as "predecisional material," and predecisional material is exempt from disclosure by the Freedom of Information Act. These professional norms (of the legal and civil service professions) thus prevented CRD attorneys from leaking material regarding the agency's position in pending civil rights cases. Furthermore, these norms outweighed the outrage that careerists felt about many of these cases.

The Civil Rights Division, however, was not immune to leaks. But the leaks that did occur rarely involved specific cases. Rather, when careerists leaked, it was generally to disclose what they viewed as egregiously racially insensitive comments made by Reagan appointees. For example, a remark made by Reynolds in which he referred to the black parents in a South Carolina desegregation case as "those bastards" was leaked (U.S. Senate 1985c).

There appears to have been more leaking in the Special Litigation Section than elsewhere in the agency.[7] This section also experienced more exit, and in fact the leakers subsequently exited. These lawyers were younger, more zealous, and less imbued with the agency's culture. Moreover, the subject area of Special Litigation was new and evolving. This had two consequences. One was that it attracted these younger, more zealous bureaucrats. And the second was that because policy was being defined and shaped for the first time, there was more to leak.[8]

SABOTAGE

Sabotage could conceivably take place at the Civil Rights Division in a number of guises: deliberately losing cases, deliberately missing court deadlines, providing false information to political superiors, or failing to follow the specific orders or instructions of those political superiors. According to current and former agency careerists, the political appointees openly expressed their distrust of the career staff and continually anticipated sabotage.

Sabotage, however, was anathema to the CRD attorneys. Deliberately presenting weak arguments in a case, or deliberately losing a case, was simply not considered. Comments on this behavior showed little variation: "You try to win a case, or you don't go on the case"; "It is unprofessional and unethical to act as a double agent"; "The only example I know of is Griswold. He threw it" (a decade before Reagan). Rather than sabotage a case, if an attorney felt that he or she could not in good conscience make the arguments that the appointees wanted made, that attorney would ask to be removed from the case. Attorneys did in fact ask to be taken off cases during the Reagan years, though it was not a common occurrence. However, as a number of them commented, "If you need to be taken off enough cases, then it's time to leave."

Nor did attorneys provide their political bosses with false information. The interviews I conducted at CRD did not reveal any instances in which careerists misled, or even considered misleading, or withholding information from, the appointees.[9]

These findings regarding the absence of sabotage are all the more striking given the fact that even with centralized review, the opportunities for sabotage seem to have been endless. It would have been very easy to insert a weak argument or flawed logic into a legal brief. In fact, the opposite occurred. Career attorneys felt that they were more effective and more successful at presenting the administration's policies and arguments in court than their appointed counterparts were and that the agency would have been *more*, not *less*, successful at achieving the president's civil rights agenda if Reynolds had relied more heavily on careerist-prepared court documents.

FOOT-DRAGGING

Foot-dragging, a type of behavior commonly attributed to recalcitrant bureaucrats, would not have been an effective strategy for bureaucrats whose agenda was the active prosecution of civil rights violations. Slowdown would have resulted in less aggressive enforcement of civil rights laws—the goal of the Reagan administration but not of the career civil servants. Therefore it is not surprising that respondents did not give any indication of a deliberate slowdown of work in the agency. CRD attorneys reported that they continued to vigorously prosecute the cases assigned to them; in fact, by some measures, such as the number of criminal prosecutions filed, the agency's productivity actually increased.

EXIT

Attorneys at the Civil Rights Division did engage in exit, although precise numbers of those who left the agency because they disagreed with Reagan's policies are difficult to find, for several reasons. First, turnover is always relatively high in the Justice Department. Many young attorneys view service at Justice as a career stepping-stone. For example, thirty-one lawyers left the division in 1974, and twenty-four each in 1978 and 1982 (U.S. Senate 1985a,c; see also Landsberg 1997). Because of the prestige of the Justice Department, CRD attorneys feel more confident than do civil servants elsewhere in the federal government that their job prospects outside government are fairly promising. Few of the respondents interviewed for this study joined the agency expecting to make a career of government service (although many have ended up staying for more than twenty years). Thus, it is not possible to attribute all turnover during the Reagan years to dissatisfaction with the presidential administration or its policy goals. Second, in congressional testimony, Reynolds denied that there was any turnover due to protest (U.S. Senate 1985a,c). As a result, no data are publicly available on what proportion of those who left the agency did so in protest.[10]

Nonetheless, I have acquired evidence from a variety of sources that seem to indicate that some of the attorneys who left the agency during the Reagan years did so out of frustration with the redirection of policy in their agency. This evidence leads me to estimate that twenty-five or more attorneys left the agency in protest during this time period. This number is derived from (1) interviews with former members of the agency, (2) the signatures on a letter sent to Congress during Reynolds's 1985 confirmation hearing (U.S. Senate 1985c), and (3) information provided to me by those interviewed in the study, about other careerists who left the agency.

In the context of the CRD, this figure is strikingly large. No one is alleged to have left the agency in protest during the Carter administration. Moreover, turnover at CRD is normally attributed to career advancement or retirement not to policy disagreement.

Turnover in some sections was greater than in others. In the Special Litigation Section, it almost amounted to a mass exodus (Holt 1998). By 1984, only one line attorney and the section chief remained out of the eighteen attorneys who had worked in the section in 1979. In general, however, exit was more of a trickle, occurring over the eight years of the Reagan administration, than the flood that occurred in Special Litigation. In the agency at large, exit was precipitated, for the most part, by specific cases or incidents that served as catalysts for specific individuals, or as one person put it, "Reynolds's veto of my recommendation in the . . . case was the straw that broke the camel's back."

Most of those I interviewed told me that a variety of factors influenced their decision to leave the Civil Rights Division. I interviewed eight attorneys who left the division in the 1980s, and all attributed their decision to a mix of factors. For all but one, however, dissatisfaction with the agency's policy direction was one of those factors.[11] To an unprecedented extent, according to those interviewed, both junior and senior career attorneys felt that they had no choice but to leave the division because they could not, in good conscience, comply with the policy changes they were being asked to make. One respondent explained his reason for leaving as follows: "It became impossible to prosecute cases when ideologues were running the division, so I felt that I had no choice but to leave." Ten of the attorneys who left the Special Litigation Section submitted a letter to the Senate during Reynolds's 1985 confirmation hearing, in which they stated, "All of us vigorously opposed Mr. Reynolds's narrow views of the rights of institutionalized persons and resigned in part due to that opposition" (U.S. Senate 1985c:937). Others wrote exit letters to Reynolds or held exit interviews with him outlining their disagreements. Some attorneys did not draw attention to their resignation because they were seeking employment elsewhere in the government and were afraid of jeopardizing their job prospects, but they told me or their colleagues that the direction of agency policy was a significant factor in their decisions to leave CRD.

Exit was not taken lightly and was often a last resort. Exit was more common in the Special Litigation Section, in part because careerists there were younger and more optimistic about their job prospects outside government, and in part because they felt thwarted from actively enforcing the law to a greater extent than did those in other sections. Older, more senior attorneys were more concerned about their job prospects in the private sector. In addition, the lawyers in Special Litigation felt thwarted to a greater extent because agency restrictions left them with less work to do. In the Education Section, for example, attorneys could bring suit, though the remedies they could seek were limited; in Special Litigation, career attorneys found they were restricted from conducting investigations or bringing suits at all.[12]

Exit was viewed by career bureaucrats as an extreme action. Nonetheless, quite a few career attorneys at the Civil Rights Division found the situation there so extreme that they felt they had no choice but to leave. They believed that they could not, in good conscience, help execute policies that they viewed as antithetical to the vigorous enforcement of civil rights laws.

Exit was limited not only by the availability of other employment but also by the condition observed by Hirschman (1970:37) that "once you have exited, you have lost the opportunity to use voice but not vice versa; in some situations, exit will therefore be a reaction of last resort after voice has failed." Those who resigned from the agency were no longer in a position to influence policy from the inside and gave up the opportunity to influence the agency's direction in the future. This is why some lawyers chose voice over exit. Many felt that they could play a more positive role in shaping the Reagan administration's policy by remaining in the agency. One career supervisor hoped to "help keep the Division on the moderate course it had steered [in the past] through both Republican and Democratic administrations" (Selig 1985:785–786). Another said that she was committed to seeing civil rights laws enforced and felt that the resources of the Justice Department, even under Reagan, enabled her to do so more effectively than she could in a public-interest law organization.

Loyalty

As described in chapter 2, loyal behavior can be either the result of policy agreement with political appointees or the belief that loyalty to the president is proper bureaucratic behavior. The former view was inconceivable at the Civil

Rights Division. The Civil Rights Division during the Reagan years was without question an agency in which conservative appointees confronted liberal bureaucrats. As was established earlier in this chapter, Reagan's appointees at the Civil Rights Division were Federalist Society conservatives, committed to a conservative agenda (see also Smith 1991). There were no conservatives among the seventeen CRD survey respondents and only one Republican.[13] Nor were there many indications of policy agreement except in those areas, such as the prosecution of criminal civil rights violations, in which the Reagan administration did not seek major policy changes. As one attorney described it, the overall relationship between careerists and appointees was one in which "there was more disagreement than agreement." Nor did any of my interviews provide evidence of this type of loyalty.[14]

I did find, however, considerable evidence of loyalty based on bureaucratic norms. Most interviewees felt that the attorney general was their legitimate boss. The attorneys at the Civil Rights Division understood and respected the authority and legitimacy of their political superiors. On the surface, this may seem to conflict with the extensive use of voice discussed earlier. But when the relevant conditional variable, the time of behavior, is introduced, it explains when and where voice rather than loyalty was present. Agency lawyers exercised voice at all the predecisional points in the process. They argued for the conduct of an investigation or against a section 5 voting rights preclearance. But once Reynolds made a decision, that decision was accepted. The same norms that deterred sabotage led to loyalty at the later stages of decision making or after Reynolds had edited a pleading to be submitted in court.

The presence of both voice and loyalty at the Civil Rights Division is an important finding. The further finding that these behaviors occurred at different points in the decision process (for a particular case or policy) sheds considerable light on our stereotypes concerning bureaucratic resistance. The point I want to emphasize here, however, is that careerists were quite explicit that they viewed their job as winning the case and serving their client, and that in this case their client was the Reagan administration. They were quite explicit that they made the arguments they were told to make, even though they believed that many of the arguments were misguided.

An additional bureaucratic quality that led to loyal behavior at CRD was political expedience. Although there was much less of this type of loyalty at CRD than at the other agencies I examined in this study, it still was present. The best illustration of politically expedient cooperation involved two attorneys assigned to the same employment discrimination case. An already existing consent decree governing the hiring practices of a municipality's police force

had been challenged by white employees, and a decision had to be made regarding the agency's response. The two line attorneys disagreed over the appropriate response. Most of the attorneys in the section felt that one attorney's response was "shaped by what Brad [Reynolds] wanted" rather than the
attorney's own understanding of the law. It was this attorney's approach that
was adopted as the agency's position in the case, and he was later promoted to
section chief. According to colleagues, the second attorney acted based on his
professional judgment in the case. The appointees discounted his recommendation, he was subsequently passed over for promotion a number of times, and
he ultimately left the Civil Rights Division.

Overall, this type of loyal behavior based on personal career advancement
seems to have been rare in the Civil Rights Division, especially in comparison
with the behavior at the other agencies in this study. But a few CRD careerists
did cooperate with the appointees in this manner. They were not "converted"
to the administration's point of view. As I have already reported, CRD attorneys remained overwhelmingly liberal and Democratic, even at the end of the
Reagan years. However, a few careerists were motivated by political expedience
to cooperate with their political superiors. They were more concerned with career advancement than their peers, and they may have been somewhat less
zealous in their commitment to traditional civil rights policies as well. Their
behavior reveals the possibility that "capture" is a two-way street and that committed appointees can capture career people as well as be captured by them.
Appointees, in their positions of authority, have managerial carrots and sticks
that can be used to aid in this capture.

NEGLECT

In the Civil Rights Division, neglect was more common during the later years
of the Reagan administration than during the earlier ones. According to the interviewees, they and almost all their colleagues initially voiced their objections
to Reynolds and his assistants about the redirection of civil rights policy. As
time went on, however, the response of some career attorneys shifted from
voice by argumentation to neglect. Respondents, who described their own behavior during the later Reagan years as complacent, pointed with respect to
those who continued to voice their opposition and "fight the good fight"
throughout the eight years of the Reagan administration. But they also described a leveling off of voice and its replacement by neglect. Again, time turns
out to be an important explanatory variable. In the case of understanding neglect, however, the relevant units for measuring time are not the point in the decision process but the point in the term of the president.

Neglect took the form of not recommending investigations or suits that would have been recommended before 1981 but that under Reynolds were unlikely to be approved. In the early years of the Reagan administration, careerists made such recommendations in spite of the fact that Reynolds was likely to reject them. But by the later years, careerists, recognizing the futility of such recommendations, did not pursue them. Overall, neglect took the form of less arguing, less activism, and fewer initiatives by agency careerists.

The interviewees' comments make it clear that neglect resulted from their becoming worn down and tired and adopting a more defeatist attitude. "The problem," according to one section chief, "was that the lawyers stopped proposing things because they got discouraged after a while." A deputy section chief noted that "the career people were beaten down and stopped trying as hard." An attorney who ultimately left the division observed that after a while, it was "not worth breaking your neck to prepare lawsuits that they won't file anyway." Another exiter commented, "Once you realized it was futile, you stopped trying." This is not to suggest that the civil servants at CRD abandoned their commitment to what they viewed as the proper approach to civil rights enforcement. However, as attrition (through exit) took its toll, it was more difficult for those who remained to retain their zeal and diligence, especially when they saw little payoff for their efforts. Traditional political science wisdom makes a great deal of the fact that bureaucrats can simply outlast politicians because politicians come and go (Heclo 1977; Light 1987). In this case, Reagan and Reynolds outlasted many careerists and beat those who remained at their own waiting game.

Analysis

Three aspects of the bureaucratic response at the Civil Rights Division require further examination and explanation. The first is the extensive use of voice by argumentation, a behavior not prominent in any of the other case studies. The second is the significant exodus from the agency over the course of the Reagan years. And the third is the absence of other tactics of resistance, the presence of loyalty, and the increased presence of neglect over time.

All these findings can be explained in large part by the profession of CRD career civil servants. Their legal training and perspective are significant factors in understanding their actions. Three other factors also played a role. One is that career attorneys at CRD were ideologically liberal. Another is the role played by the agency's history and culture. Finally, the president's appointees had a considerable effect on bureaucratic behavior, albeit quite a different effect from that found at the other agencies. Thus the same set of variables used to analyze cases of bureaucratic passivity also helps explain the different pattern of behavior detected in the Civil Rights Division.

DOMINANT AGENCY PROFESSION

The profession of the civil servants in the Civil Rights Division affected their use of exit and voice, and it also affected their willingness to cooperate loyally with the president and his emissaries in their agency.

First, attorneys were not hesitant to use voice by argumentation, because their professional training and their day-to-day work entails arguing, rebutting, and counterarguing. They are well trained in the arts of arguing and debate. Indeed, the attorneys at the Civil Rights Division seemed comfortable arguing, constantly and forcefully.

Moreover, professional norms influenced the behavior of attorneys at CRD in that a number of these lawyers spoke of their obligation "to the law." When this professional obligation to enforce and uphold the law (which to CRD attorneys encompasses both congressional statute and judicial precedent) conflicted with appointees' decisions, it often led to voice or exit. Careerists at CRD defended their disagreements with appointees on the grounds of "the law" rather than on ideological grounds or on the grounds that the agency had always done it that way. They felt that the sources of conflict between careerists and appointees were issues of "legal principle," "not just political or policy issues." They objected to the fact that Reagan's appointees "distorted the law" and "wanted to do things that were inconsistent with the law." Careerists felt that to the appointees, "the law and the Supreme Court didn't matter." To the CRD careerists, because they all were lawyers, the law, legal precedent, and the rulings of the Supreme Court mattered very much, and this led them to challenge the appointees and/or to leave the agency. According to one CRD veteran, "Careerists dislike White House intervention because they make decisions on a political basis. Attorneys make it based on the law."

The profession of agency careerists also had an effect on exit as a form of resistance. Attorneys were relatively optimistic about alternative job prospects outside their agency. In fact, a few CRD careerists who chose to leave were able to transfer to other bureaus within the Justice Department. There is no doubt that the availability of alternative job prospects affected the likelihood of exit. It is equally clear that profession played a major role in determining the availability of alternative employment opportunities.

Finally, the fact that CRD was peopled with attorneys increased the presence of loyalty and cooperation. While it is true that agency careerists argued predecisionally, they were quite explicit that once they were preparing a case, their goal was to win the case. This is part of the lawyer's ethic: Whomever you are representing, whoever your client is, it is your task to present the best case for your client. The attorneys at the Civil Rights Division were loyal because they felt a professional obligation to represent their client as best they could.

CAREERIST IDEOLOGY

Careerists at the Civil Rights Division were, for the most part, liberal and Democratic. Twelve out of seventeen respondents identified themselves as liberal and none were self-identified conservatives.[15] Only one of the seventeen was a Republican.[16] This ideological portrait must be contrasted with the ideological composition of Reagan appointees in the agency. Reynolds, Edwin Meese, and Charles Cooper (one of the most visible and influential of the Schedule C appointees) all were active members of the Federalist Society, an organization of lawyers committed to a conservative agenda. Career respondents overwhelmingly viewed Reynolds as an "ideologue" and a "zealot." When asked about the degree of partisanship among the Reagan appointees, careerists often noted that it was not partisanship that set these appointees apart from those who had served in previous administrations; it was their ideological fervor. Overall, this clash between ideologically committed conservatives and more liberal careerists contributed to the presence of voice and exit at the Civil Rights Division.[17]

AGENCY ESPRIT DE CORPS

All but one interviewee at the Civil Rights Division characterized the agency as having a strong esprit de corps. The reason for the strong sense of esprit at CRD is readily apparent: Agency personnel share a strong commitment to the active pursuit of civil rights. Interviews revealed that CRD careerists joined the agency out of either a commitment to civil rights or a desire to practice public-interest law. Before the Reagan administration, that commitment was further cultivated inside the agency. For example, many interviewees referred to the intense bonding experience that resulted from spending months "on the road" with two or three other attorneys during the trial portion of cases. Other intangible features of agency culture fostered this sense of esprit, including the fact that until the Reagan years, CRD personnel often socialized as well as worked together. I detected this sense of camaraderie and the intensity of their pride in their agency and their colleagues in every interview I conducted.[18]

It is interesting that even with this strong sense of camaraderie, voice was rarely collective. But it also is likely that without these strong feelings of esprit de corps, there would have been no collectively produced petitions or memos at all. It is also relevant to note that the strong feelings of esprit de corps at CRD served to limit the use of exit even while it facilitated voice. Careerists indicated that their sense of camaraderie increased as they shared the experience of what was, from their perspective, an attempt to "endure" the Reagan years.

AGENCY HISTORY

The Civil Rights Division entered the 1980s with an almost impeccable record in court. It had won major victories in the areas of voting rights and school desegregation, and it had recently succeeded in obtaining the legislation it desired from Congress regarding the rights of institutionalized persons. These experiences led careerists to view their agency as the one responsible for setting the precedents that over the two decades preceding 1981 had established the existing body of civil rights case law, the very precedents and case law that the Reagan administration sought to challenge. Careerists were very proud of their record and quite confident of their prowess in the courtroom.

Moreover, resistance to presidential directives was not new to the agency. In 1969, sixty-five Justice Department attorneys signed a petition critical of President Nixon's and Attorney General Mitchell's stance on the issue of delaying the implementation of desegregation consent decrees in the South. According to Dennis Thompson (1978:40), CRD attorneys defended their actions because they "believed the policy [of delay] violated the law and would require them to act contrary to the ethical canons of the legal profession." Thus, the Civil Rights Division had a history of career attorneys willing to speak out for what they believed were legal principles and professional norms. Their actions and behavior under Reagan were not novel but, like their policy beliefs, were based on precedent. Nor is it coincidental that many of those in the upper career ranks under Reagan were junior attorneys in the agency in 1969.

This combination of historical experiences and agency esprit resulted in "careerist confidence": Careerists at CRD shared a past and a spirit of camaraderie that gave them the confidence to challenge the executive branch's political leadership.

THE ROLE OF APPOINTEES

The careerists' behavior was also partly a function of the appointees' behavior. First, appointees presented a united front ideologically and with respect to policy goals. Careerists knew where the appointees stood and where the appointees' agenda conflicted with their own policy preferences. There was little obfuscation, few mixed signals from different appointees, and minimal infighting among appointees. Careerists had something specific to object to and to rally around. This contrasts with the approach to management at NHTSA, where appointees never directly stated their policy agenda and gave careerists the runaround rather than rejecting their policies outright. At CRD, careerists had something concrete with which to agree or disagree.

In addition, the appointees, and Assistant Attorney General William Bradford Reynolds in particular, allowed attorneys to argue. Careerists felt that they could risk arguing because, although the appointees were ideological, they did not engage in reprisals, demotions, or scare tactics. As we will see in chapter 6, this contrasts sharply with the management style of Anne Gorsuch at the Environmental Protection Agency, who expressed annoyance when challenged by careerists, did not enjoy the give-and-take of a good argument with careerists, was bored by long presentations, and maintained lists of potential troublemakers in the career ranks. It is readily apparent that these contrasting management styles led to different behavior by career bureaucrats.

However, Reynolds's management style also limited opportunities for resistance. The strategy of removing career attorneys from cases and assigning cases to political appointees reduced the number of cases over which careerists had any influence. They could not argue about cases that "never even got assigned to sections" or that "we never saw or heard about until the court rendered its decision." Thus, although Reynolds did not suppress careerists' voices, his steering of controversial cases away from career staff to his large cadre of appointees limited opportunities for voice at the CRD. This pattern is strikingly similar to the management approach adopted at the FNS and the EPA.

SELF-INTEREST AND ROLE PERCEPTION

As was the case at NHTSA, self-interest was not the most important determinant of behavior at the Civil Rights Division. However, including self-interest in our analysis reveals that the extent to which self-interest can be used to explain behavior depends on what assumptions are made about what it is that civil servants are trying to maximize. If one assumes that defending agency policy is a sign of self-interested behavior, then the attorneys at CRD behaved self-interestedly. But if one assumes that civil servants' self-interest lies in job protection and career advancement, then the civil servants at CRD did not act self-interestedly. This is because their career enhancement lay in abandoning agency policy and hitching their wagons to the policies of Reynolds, Cooper, and the rest of the appointed crew. Yet few CRD careerists jumped on that wagon. Therefore, unless it can be demonstrated that civil servants stood to gain from defending agency policy, the reason that careerists so vigorously defended agency policy had to have been based on something other than self-interest. This is not to say that no one at CRD was motivated by self-interest or abandoned agency policy to protect their jobs. But it does mean that those were not the predominant motives or behaviors at the Civil Rights Division during the Reagan years.

It is more difficult to assess the extent to which role perception was a motivating factor at CRD because, in this case, it is difficult to distinguish between the professional norms of lawyers and the way that CRD careerists perceived their role as civil servants. But it is possible to state that some facet of the way that they perceived their role—either as lawyers or as civil servants—led them to limit their resistance to two activities: voice by argumentation and exit. Whether due to the professional norms of lawyers or a civil service ethic, the career attorneys at CRD were quite explicit in expressing their belief that other activities—such as leaking and sabotage—were improper. The civil servants at CRD had been trained and socialized to work hard, take pride in their craft, and fight to win, but they also perceived their role as serving their client loyally and following the etiquette of the courtroom.[19] Thus, the way they viewed their role both explains and constrained their behavior to a considerable degree.

Conclusion

The behavior of the career civil servants in the Civil Rights Division of the Justice Department during the Reagan years was strikingly different from that found in the other three agencies examined in this study. There was considerably more voice by argumentation and exit at CRD than elsewhere. Yet even here, there was no sabotage, and although bureaucrats argued, they also cooperated. They cooperated with Reynolds by doing their best to win the cases that they were given. Resistance was limited to attempting to influence the appointees' decisions, not to affecting the execution of those decisions.

Careerists at the Civil Rights Division accepted the authority of politically appointed officials to have the final say once they had exercised their voice.

While this behavior may not be the strict neutral competence envisioned by adherents of the politics/administration dichotomy, it is also not the intransigent, insubordinate behavior feared by politicians. Instead, it suggests a model that is adversarial in that divergent views were expressed when the Reagan administration sought policy change, and in that careerists were active in voicing their opinions; but that is also cooperative, in that disagreements were limited to a predecisional time frame, and sabotage was anathema.

The previous section offered a variety of explanations for this pattern of behavior—the agency's culture, the profession of CRD career bureaucrats, their ideology, and the attitudes and behavior of the agency's political appointees. In some ways, the factors that best explain bureaucratic behavior in this agency fit the existing stereotypes of bureaucrats. Most of the bureaucrats at the CRD were liberal and, it can be argued, acted according to their personal ideologies. Even more significant, although couched in the language of legal precedent and respect for the court system, CRD attorneys fought to maintain the status quo in civil rights policy. Yet at the same time, by arguing and exiting, CRD careerists took risks and undertook tasks that increased their workload, decreased their on-the-job leisure time, and could have damaged their careers. This chapter has reported at least one instance in which one careerist was passed over for promotion for preparing a case according to his beliefs and another was promoted for toeing the party line, and a number of instances in which careerists sacrificed job security for what they believed in. Thus, examining how bureaucrats reacted to the Reagan administration at this agency both highlights the limits of relying solely on self-interest to explain bureaucratic behavior and provides evidence of an agency very much characterized by "clashing beliefs" between career and appointed personnel.

However, this chapter also suggests an alternative normative interpretation of some of the factors that led civil servants to defy their appointed superiors and some of the response options that they employed in that defiance. This interpretation emphasizes the potential value of voice by argumentation and the possible virtue of civil servants who both differ from their appointed principals with respect to their ideological persuasion and policy preferences, and are not afraid to articulate those differences.

The case of the CRD during the Reagan years suggests that it is possible to have discussion between civil servants and political appointees without that discussion leading to more perverse behavior or undermining the appointees' authority. It also suggests that such discussion may lead to better deliberation and possibly even better decisions as a result.[20] At a minimum, federal prisoners are now entitled to soap as a result of a predecisional discussion between a career attorney and his appointed supervisor. At a maximum, voice by argument takes better advantage of the talents of both agency careerists and their appointed principals in making public policy than do the arrangements prevalent at the other agencies examined in this study.

CHAPTER 6

THE ENVIRONMENTAL PROTECTION AGENCY: A TALE OF TWO REAGAN ADMINISTRATIONS

The case of the Environmental Protection Agency (EPA) can be told as a tale of two Reagan administrations, because, by their own accounts, career civil servants there found themselves reacting to two radically different sets of circumstances during the first three years of the Reagan administration and during the final five.[1] During the first three years, when Anne Gorsuch served as its administrator, the EPA is best characterized as an agency under siege, in which strategic appointees acted like an invading army who did not trust their new subjects, even though those subjects were actually quite accepting of the invading force and, in most cases, did not even view it as an invasion at all. By contrast, during the following five years, under the tutelage of William Ruckelshaus and Lee Thomas, the EPA is better characterized as a love fest between the career civil servants and Reagan's appointees.[2]

Examining the agency in this light not only reveals how bureaucrats reacted to these two Reagan administrations but also highlights the pivotal role played by an agency's appointed leadership. In the first case, the management style of Reagan's strategic appointees achieved compliance through micromanagement and intimidation. In the second case, Reagan's less strategic appointees obtained compliance through dialogue and respect. In both cases the behavior reported by the careerists was similar. But its causes were very different. Thus, examining each Reagan administration separately offers two distinct paths to compliance. One relies heavily on the administrative presidency to remove civil servants' opportunities for resistance and to alter their self-interest calculations. The other relies heavily on leadership in tune with the agency's culture and ethos to build trust between agency careerists and their appointed principals.

The EPA case is also a tale of two agencies, because the civil servants at different levels of the agency reacted quite differently to Reagan's application of the administrative presidency at their agency.[3] At the upper levels, the subject of this study, EPA careerists were quite responsive to the appointed leadership. But at the lower levels, there appears to have been some strong resistance, even guerilla warfare (Johnson and Kraft 1990; O'Leary 1995). Although this resistance appears to have been limited to a few individuals, it demonstrates the dangers of overgeneralizing about bureaucratic responsiveness or resistance. As was the case at the other agencies examined in this study, the civil servants at the EPA for the most part responded to the direction and directives of their appointed bosses, but this does not mean that all bureaucrats were responsive all the time. In critiquing one stereotype about bureaucrats, I do not wish to create another.

In addition, viewing the EPA as a tale of two agencies also draws attention to the role of agency context in explaining bureaucratic behavior. Here, the agency's historical development—particularly its patterns of promotion and advancement—produced an agency whose upper levels were peopled by moderate, consensus-building pragmatists who, for the most part, accepted the redirection of their agency but whose lower ranks housed some very vocal zealots who resisted the changes sought by the Reagan administration.

Because these two features distinguish the EPA from the other agencies discussed in this book, this chapter's organization deviates somewhat from that of the preceding chapters. First, after a brief background discussion of the EPA, the chapter is divided into two sections, one for each Reagan administration. Second, the chapter is further subdivided to include a separate discussion of the agency's lower-level whistle-blowers and a case-within-a-case of the agency's Office of Enforcement. The latter is included to compensate for the fact that the EPA is larger than any of the other agencies examined in this study. Examining one subunit of the agency in depth enables me to identify any behavior I might have missed in my broad overview of the agency at large.

The Agency Setting

The Environmental Protection Agency is an independent agency headed by an administrator, a presidentially appointed position requiring Senate confirmation. Independent agencies in general, and the EPA in particular, do not have cabinet rank and status, although there has been talk over the years of elevating the EPA to cabinet rank. Independent agencies also differ from independent regulatory commissions (IRCs), which are governed by multimember boards of commissioners, because they have a single administrator who serves at the pleasure of the president who appoints them. The EPA was organized as an independent agency to avoid its being susceptible to "capture" by industry, a problem that had plagued earlier regulatory agencies organized following the more traditional IRC design (Waterman 1989).

During the Reagan years, the EPA had about 10,000 employees working at the two EPA headquarters, in Washington, D.C., and Arlington, Virginia, eleven regional offices, and research and laboratory facilities located throughout the country. These employees represented a variety of professions, including lawyers, scientists, economists, and engineers.[4] The agency administered a budget of billions of dollars and was responsible for implementing more than a dozen major statutes.[5]

The EPA was ten years old when Ronald Reagan took office. A quick glance at those ten years sheds light on the agency that Reagan and his appointees inherited in January 1981.

The Early Years at EPA

President Richard Nixon established the EPA via a reorganization plan in 1970 (operations began officially in December of that year). Congress gave it its tasks through the passage of a wide range of legislation in the decade that followed, and William Ruckelshaus, the EPA's first administrator, made a lasting imprint on the agency's structure and decision-making processes.

By creating the EPA, Nixon brought together under one roof a host of previously disparate agencies, offices, and bureaus from the Departments of Health, Education and Welfare, Agriculture, and Interior, and the Atomic Energy Commission—ten different programs in all (Marcus 1980b; O'Leary 1993).[6] At first, the new EPA employed six thousand people, most of them transferees from the aforementioned agencies, but the young and vibrant agency quickly attracted new people as well.

Nixon's reasons for establishing a single environmental agency are not entirely clear, as environmental issues were not at the top of his policy agenda (Dobel 1992). But he was concerned with the organization of the executive branch and had established the Ash Council to make recommendations for reorganization with the goal of streamlining the federal government's many departments and agencies into a smaller number of more centralized departments or "superdepartments." Although Nixon never enacted some of the Ash Council's more ambitious proposals, he did create the EPA. He may also have been trying to jump on the bandwagon of rising ecological awareness that was spreading through the country at this time. Rachel Carson's *Silent Spring* and Ralph Nader's *Vanishing Air* had drawn public attention to issues of pollution and ecology. This new public awareness reached a peak on April 22, 1970, when millions of Americans participated in Earth Day. Nixon submitted his reorganization plan for the EPA to Congress the following July.

In Congress, Senators Edmund Muskie of Maine and Henry (Scoop) Jackson of Washington wholeheartedly embraced the environmental movement and kept the bandwagon rolling with the introduction of legislation aimed at addressing ecological concerns (Harris and Milkis 1989; Landy et al. 1994). They were aided (and in some cases prodded) by newly formed or revitalized environmental groups, with whom they worked to produce the legislation that the EPA was charged with implementing. In the decade between that first Earth Day and Reagan's election in 1980, Congress passed laws to tackle the problems associated with air, water, and noise pollution, and the hazards posed by toxic substances, pesticides, and the handling, transport, storage, and disposal of hazardous waste.[7]

At the time Reagan entered office, the EPA was responsible for enforcing at least a dozen statutes, which gave the organization a wide variety of responsibilities.[8] With respect to air pollution, the agency was charged with setting standards for national ambient air quality and stationary and mobile source emissions.[9] It was also required to review the states' plans to achieve emissions goals and to review environmental impact statements. With respect to water, the EPA was required to set standards for pollutants in drinking water systems as well as for industrial and municipal discharge into water, including oceans and underground sources of drinking water; and to dispense grants to states for water treatment projects. In the area of noise pollution, the 1972 Noise Control Act charged the EPA with establishing noise emissions standards for air traffic and commercial products. Statutes regarding pesticide usage required that all pesticides be registered with the EPA, and they empowered the agency not only to regulate the testing of pesticides but also to regulate or ban the usage of pesticides determined to be hazardous. The fact that the agency currently reviews between 35,000 and 40,000 products each year provides some sense of the scope of this undertaking (Bryner 1987:94).

The "second wave" of legislation dealt with toxins and hazardous waste and set standards for testing toxic materials. It also gave the EPA the power to ban or regulate toxins that posed an "unreasonable" risk to health or the environment. The hazardous waste legislation was designed to establish a comprehensive system for controlling hazardous waste from "cradle to grave"—that is, from creation through disposal—accounting for all the stages in between, including handling, transport, and storage. Superfund legislation authorized the EPA to spend money to clean up hazardous waste emergencies and toxic dump sites and to assess the liability for those sites.

In short, EPA's responsibilities included promulgating regulations in the areas of air, water, and noise pollution, toxic substances, and hazardous waste; licensing and monitoring polluters and users of pesticides; reviewing and approving environmental impact statements; and conducting its own research and development (Bryner 1987:93–94). The earlier legislation focused on imposing standards and timetables on industry, while the more recent legislation both "attempts to bring efficiency criteria into environmental regulation" and grapples with the "more technical and complex ecological problems" of toxic waste management and acid rain (Harris and Milkis 1989:246–247). Three Senate committees, six House committees, and countless subcommittees are needed to oversee the agency's implementation of these statutes.[10]

Because Nixon's commitment to the EPA was unclear, William Ruckelshaus, the EPA's first administrator, set out to create a constituency for the agency and to quickly produce visible accomplishments (Marcus 1980; Waterman 1989). However, his first step was to create an organizational structure for the new agency.

A combination of the recommendations produced by the Ash Council and the politics of pragmatism produced the EPA's internal structure (Marcus 1980b; Landy et al. 1994). The Ash Council wanted to organize the new agency along functional lines (e.g., monitoring, enforcement, research, abatement). But the agencies that had recently been transferred into the EPA operated along media lines (i.e., by program or "medium"—air, water, radiation). In an effort to facilitate a smooth transition, avoid protracted turf battles, and get the new agency up and running quickly, Ruckelshaus adopted a compromise arrangement that included both media and functional offices operating in tandem (Marcus 1980b). Eight offices initially formed the core of this arrangement, five media offices (Air, Water, Pesticides, Solid Waste, and Noise and Radiation) with functional offices for Enforcement, Research, and Planning and Management. This structure was intended to be temporary, with the gradual phasing out of the media offices in favor of organizing fully along functional lines. However, with the exception of incorporating new media and functions into the existing organizational structure (such as the addition of the Office for Toxic Substances in the late 1970s when toxins were added to the EPA's agenda), the dual structure remained intact well beyond Ruckelshaus's tenure and in fact remained in place as the agency's modus operandi when Reagan took over administration of the agency. Each office, whether media or functional, is headed by an appointed assistant administrator; these positions require Senate confirmation.

One result of this structure was the need for an internal agency decision-making process that took into account the needs of the different offices and utilized their respective expertise. Ruckelshaus developed a process that involved working groups composed of members of all the functional offices and the lead media office (and often other "interested" media offices) hammering out drafts of proposed regulations (Dobel 1992; Marcus 1980b). These drafts were then reviewed by a steering committee made up of representatives from the offices of all of EPA's assistant administrators. This decision-making process was not always a smooth one, and it was not geared toward producing quick results. But what emerged was a tradition of openness and of consensus building (interview). The EPA has continued to use working groups and steering committees in the formulation of regulations, and EPA careerists have also tried to maintain the tradition of seeking consensus on agency decisions.

The other important thing to note about Ruckelshaus's first tenure at EPA was his emphasis on enforcement (Marcus 1980b; Landy et al. 1994; Waterman 1989a). He sought quick results and wanted to establish a reputation for the new agency as a vigorous enforcer of pollution control laws (Marcus 1980b). In the agency's early years, lawsuits were brought against ARMCO Steel, Jones and Laughlin Steel, U.S. Plywood, and the cities of Atlanta, Detroit, and Cleveland, for discharging industrial waste and sewage into the waterways. Ruckelshaus's approach set the EPA apart from its independent regulatory commission cousins, who were accused of being captive to the industries they regulated.

The Ford years at the EPA were a continuation of the Nixon era (Harris and Milkis 1989; Landy et al. 1994). Russell Train, who had replaced Ruckelshaus as EPA administrator in 1973, remained in the position throughout Ford's administration. Ford did not attempt any major policy initiatives, and Train provided continuity for Ruckelshaus's personnel and policy goals.

During the Carter administration, under the direction of Administrator

Doug Costle, the agency experienced two types of changes. First was a change in the nature of the problems confronting the agency, as new issues like acid rain, groundwater contamination, and hazardous waste site emergencies appeared on the environmental agenda. Second was the introduction of regulatory reform at the EPA. This manifested itself in the adoption of methods to take into account cost considerations in the promulgation of new regulations and the adoption of alternatives to command-and-control regulation, such as bubble policies and emissions trading (for explanations of these policies, see Cook 1988; Harris and Milkis 1989; Landy et al. 1994; Levin 1982; Meidinger 1989).

Entering the 1980s, the EPA was a large, geographically dispersed, and professionally diverse agency with responsibility for a large number of ambitious and controversial environmental laws. Its mission required it to wrestle with issues at the cutting edge of existing scientific and technical knowledge and to regulate a wide range of industries under the watchful eye of environmental and public-interest groups.[11]

THE "FIRST" REAGAN ADMINISTRATION: THE GORSUCH ERA

As discussed at the beginning of this chapter, EPA careerists viewed their agency as having experienced "two" Reagan administrations. Accordingly, these two eras are treated separately here. We turn our attention first to Anne Gorsuch's short-lived tenure at the EPA.[12]

REAGAN'S POLICY OBJECTIVES AT THE EPA

The environmental policy that guided the first Reagan administration was multifaceted. One goal fell under Reagan's general plan to reduce the size of government. Here, reducing the EPA's budget and personnel was seen as a way to reduce the deficit as well as to achieve more specific objectives vis-à-vis the environment and environmentalists. A second goal fell under Reagan's broader plan for the "New Federalism." The administration sought to redefine state and local roles and responsibilities in the area of enforcing environmental regulations, with a greater role for the states and a smaller federal presence in both funding for the states and enforcement activities. A third goal was directed at the EPA itself. The Heritage Foundation report "focused the attention of regulators on the bureaucracy as a problem" (Harris and Milkis 1989:253). This goal, like that for smaller government, resulted in policies aimed at cutting EPA personnel and reducing the size of the EPA workforce. In short, the administration saw the career bureaucracy as an obstacle to achieving its other policy goals at the EPA. This focus on the career bureaucracy took on a life of its own apart from the rest of the policy agenda and resulted in the EPA's appointees' devoting considerable time to a variety of micromanagement techniques that targeted the EPA's career bureaucrats; these will be discussed later.

Finally, and at the heart of Reagan's policy agenda at the EPA, was the goal of regulatory relief (Goodman and Wrightson 1987; Harris and Milkis 1989). The rationale behind this policy was that environmental and other social regulations hindered economic growth and industry profitability (Harris and Milkis 1989). The Reagan administration actively sought to build a stronger economy and viewed social regulation—and environmental regulation in particular—as adding costs to industry—the costs of complying with regulations—and thereby reducing profits. As a result, the core of the administration's agenda at the EPA was to lighten the regulatory burden on industry.

This view is clearly expressed in Reagan's first State of the Union address in 1981.

> American society experienced a virtual explosion in governmental regulation during the past decade. . . . The result has been higher prices, higher unemployment, and lower productivity growth. Overregulation causes small and independent business men and women, as well as large businesses, to defer or terminate plans for expansion. And since they're responsible for most of the new jobs, these new jobs are not created . . . we must come to grips with inefficient and burdensome regulations, eliminate those we can and reform others.
>
> (Public Papers, Reagan 1981:113)

Reagan's assault on regulations took two forms: instituting a process of regulatory review "designed to slow the growth in new federal regulations" and using this same process to review existing regulations with the goal of eliminating those onerous to industry (Goodman and Wrightson 1987:127).

Carter, too, had tried to reform the EPA's approach to regulation, but Reagan's approach was quite different. Reagan was primarily concerned with relieving industries of the burden of regulation. Carter's reforms (such as emissions trading and bubble policies), however, were grounded in the view that command-and-control regulation was inefficient and unnecessarily costly because the real-world complexities of companies emitting different types of pollutants from different sources made them difficult to monitor and made it difficult to determine the best available technology to reduce the pollution. The solution Carter offered was to create a marketplace for pollution so that pollution could be reduced more efficiently. The main goal remained the reduction of pollution in the air and water, based on the belief that creating a marketplace for polluters offered a more efficient means to achieve that goal.

The Reagan administration gave lip service to this plan and certainly used the academic wisdom to debunk command-and-control regulation. However, it was suspicious of the initiative because of its origin in the Carter administration (Goodman and Wrightson 1987:141; Landy et al. 1994; Mosher 1981b). Moreover, Reagan's principal objective was not to reform the way we regulated but, rather, to try to relieve industry of what industry viewed as the burdens imposed by regulation. Thus, whereas the Carter administration worked to develop a comprehensive plan for emissions trading (i.e., to create a market in which to trade emissions), the Reagan administration was satisfied with trying to provide relief to industry on a case-by-case basis. In short, as the *National Journal* (Mosher 1981a:743) noted in 1981, Reagan's policy agenda for the EPA amounted to "a 180-degree turn away from the Carter administration's beginning [in 1976]."

THE ADMINISTRATIVE PRESIDENCY AT EPA DURING THE GORSUCH YEARS

Reagan's approach to achieving his policy objectives at the EPA set him apart from his predecessors as much as the objectives themselves did. The Reagan administration adopted an administrative rather than a legislative strategy toward environmental policy (Goodman and Wrightson 1987; Kraft and Vig 1984; Lees and Turner 1988), making use of all the components of the administrative presidency in its execution.

The president appears to have followed the advice of the Heritage Foundation that the administration's goals could best be achieved through "proper administrative direction and not legislative remedy" (Heatherly 1981:970). Thus, the administration passed up opportunities to change environmental statutes, such as the Clean Air Act, which was up for renewal in 1982, in favor of bringing about change administratively. As a result, it was able to focus its legislative strategy on the budget (Lees 1988), avoid squandering Reagan's personal political capital (Kirschten 1981), avoid appearing at odds with public opinion (Kirschten 1981), defuse a potential rallying point for interest groups (Kirschten 1981), and minimize the adverse publicity that would have resulted from efforts to alter environmental statutes (Kraft and Vig 1984). Moreover, by using an administrative approach, the Reagan administration positioned itself to reap the benefits available from the administrative tools at the president's disposal.

THE OMB, BUDGET CUTS, OIRA, AND REGULATORY REVIEW

Even before David Stockman began his tenure as the director of the Office of Management and Budget (OMB), he was on record as a staunch opponent of the EPA, regarding it as an obstacle to economic growth. He also held a negative opinion of its career bureaucrats. In a "Dear Colleague" letter to members of Congress before he left Congress to head OMB, Stockman wrote,

> For ten years we've been in an environmental time warp. EPA and its minions in the press and the professional environmental lobbies have assumed an absolute monopoly right to flood the American economy with regulations, litigation, and compliance costs that are out of proportion to any environmental problem—real and imagined—that has reached the congressional calendar.
>
> It's time to get off this super bureaucracy kick unless you really believe that the present drastic deterioration of our economy, productivity, international competitiveness, and living standards will soon miraculously fade away.
>
> It won't happen so long as we keep writing blank checks that authorize hotshot junior lawyers and zealots ensconced in the EPA to bleed American industry of scarce funds needed for investment, modernization, and job creation.
>
> (Burford and Greenya 1986:29; Goodman and Wrightson 1987:119)

Stockman got to work right away. Every budget that the OMB submitted to Congress during the time that Gorsuch headed the EPA contained massive cuts. Carter's final budget (FY1981) was $1.35 billion. Two years later, in 1983, the agency's overall operating budget was down to $1.04 billion (Davis 1983f). OMB's request for 1984 sought to cut another 9 percent from EPA's budget, reducing the budget total to $948.6 million (Davis 1983f). Cuts were sharpest in research and development, in which OMB proposed to reduce funding by 38 percent by 1983 (using 1981 as the base year), but other agency activities, such as enforcement and abatement and control, were also impacted by budget cuts (Goodman and Wrightson 1987; Kirschten 1983; Rubin 1985; Waterman 1989b).

Career personnel were largely helpless in the face of this onslaught, as they relied on agency appointees to take on OMB and its Office of Information and Regulatory Affairs (OIRA) subdivision. The careerists were not in a position to challenge these organizations themselves. As one veteran careerist explained,

"We'd shake our heads," but that was "about all we could do." The careerists' impotence was exacerbated by the fact that OIRA in particular "did nothing in writing," which made it difficult to challenge it (interview). Instead, proposed regulations were stalled, "held up for a year," "just not approved," this careerist added. Other interviewees also noted that OMB and OIRA "slowed everything down," "held everything up," and "vetoed by dragging their feet."

These OMB and OIRA techniques have been observed elsewhere (see, e.g., Benda and Levine 1988; Percival 1991; Tolchin and Tolchin 1983; Waterman 1989b). What is interesting is the feeling the careerists shared that there was nothing they could do about it. It is also interesting that this type of foot-dragging and stalling behavior is frequently attributed to bureaucrats, yet in this case it was not federal agencies but parts of the Executive Office of the President that were engaging in this behavior. Moreover, the OMB and OIRA were employing these strategies without having to comply with any of the checks, such as the Administrative Procedure Act, that govern bureaucratic behavior (Benda and Levine 1988; Bowers 1993; Percival 1991). Hence, they were able to avoid keeping written records of their decisions and telephone conversations, and they faced no penalties for taking longer than the time period suggested in Reagan's executive orders (Bowers 1993; Harris and Milkis 1989; Percival 1991).

With two notable exceptions (see Burford and Greenya 1986), Reagan's EPA appointees did not challenge the OMB or OIRA. The appointed team at the EPA under the leadership of Anne Gorsuch both shared OMB's goals and viewed their own role as team players, with OMB as the team's captain. As one high-ranking careerist explained, "Anne viewed OMB as the leader in regulatory reform. She was just there to implement, not to lead." Another put it more bluntly: "Initially she loved OMB."[13] In fact, Gorsuch testified before Congress in support of OMB's proposed budget cuts for her agency (Davis 1981). Richard Waterman (1989b:124) provides a useful description of this teamwork between OMB and agency appointees and its consequences:

> In the budgetary process, Administrator Anne Burford was a strong advocate for the Reagan administration's proposed budget cuts. She defended the reductions before congressional committees. . . . Burford's support for the administration's position enhanced the credibility of the budget reduction proposals. Perhaps more importantly, it removed a potential source of resistance to the reductions, a source that congressional critics of the president's program could have rallied around. Had Burford and other political appointees at EPA argued that the proposals would seriously undercut their agency's ability to perform its legally mandated functions, Congress could then have more easily justified smaller reductions in EPA's budget. . . . In-

stead Congress heard a united chorus of support for the president's economic recovery program.

In general, with the exception of the two incidents discussed in Gorsuch's
memoir, agency appointees rarely went to bat for the agency against the OMB
but remained committed to the policy goals of budget cuts and regulatory review. Moreover, and particularly germane to our present concerns regarding
bureaucratic behavior, careerists were not able to challenge OMB or OIRA on
their own because they had to get past the appointees before they could take on
other tools of the administrative presidency, such as the OMB, that lie outside
their agency's walls. And as we shall see, the appointees' internal management
techniques seriously restricted all but a few agency careerists from getting past
the political appointees and, for the most part, from even attempting to do so.

STRATEGIC APPOINTEES AT EPA: POLICY GOALS AND MANAGEMENT STRATEGIES

More than any other aspect of the administrative presidency, the president's
appointees had the most direct impact on the EPA's career civil servants, as they
were the people with whom the careerists dealt on a daily basis and the ones
who carried out Reagan's policy agenda.

Anne Gorsuch, administrator of EPA from 1981 to 1983, quickly became a
household name. Three-quarters of the careerists I interviewed credited her
with having "a great deal" of influence over the EPA, and more than half identified her as one of the two most influential figures at the EPA during the entire
eight years of the Reagan administration. As one careerist put it, "Anne really
ran the show." Gorsuch came to the EPA with firm convictions about the negative impact that environmental regulations had on economic growth. She ful-
filled all the criteria Reagan sought in a strategic appointee: She was an ideological conservative; she shared the president's environmental policy agenda;
and she was personally loyal to Ronald Reagan (Harris and Milkis 1989).

Gorsuch's testimony at her confirmation hearing makes it clear that she
shared the president's policy goals and that these were at odds with the agency's
status quo. At the top of this list was regulatory reform and relief for industry:

> The president is committed to regulatory reform and here I believe it is im-
> portant to emphasize that the reform is not limited to withdrawal of unnec-
> essary or overly burdensome singular regulations but envisions a much

broader scope involving the process by which new regulations are formulated and current regulations are evaluated.

(U.S. Senate 1981c:28)

Behind that goal was a desire to reduce the agency's size in terms of both budget and personnel and to turn over its tasks to the states. Gorsuch testified that

the President is committed to achieving a new federalism in which the decisions and the power to implement those decisions will be shifted from the banks of the Potomac back to the level of government which is closest and most accountable to the people it serves. I share that commitment.

(U.S. Senate 1981c:28)

With two exceptions, Gorsuch's team of subcabinet appointees were chosen for her by the White House personnel team (Landy et al. 1994:247). As a group, they were as committed to Reagan and his agenda as Gorsuch was. As recounted in an interview with a former career subordinate of Rita Lavelle, this was true to the extent that while in prison, Lavelle punched a fellow inmate who had criticized Ronald Reagan.

The goal these appointees seem to have taken most to heart when they arrived at the Waterside Mall (the EPA's headquarters) was the one contained in the Heritage Foundation report and in Reagan's and Stockman's speeches about the bureaucracy's being the problem. They focused as much on controlling the career bureaucrats in their agency as they did on effecting changes in environmental regulation and enforcement. In fact, a certain amount of goal displacement took place among Reagan's first set of appointees, as they became so preoccupied with taming the bureaucrats in their agency that they lost sight of their broader goals for policy change.

The appointees at EPA, including those in the administrator's office, the subcabinet appointees, and the special assistants all employed a variety of micromanagement techniques in their attempts to "tame" the career civil servants in their agency. Foremost among these techniques were the following:

1. The use of hit lists to target career employees for firing, transfer, or demotion
2. Three reorganizations of the Enforcement Division
3. Secrecy and the exclusion of careerists from the decision-making process
4. The replacement of careerists with appointees to produce the agency's work product

5. Centralization of the rule-making process so that all work was extensively reviewed by appointees

6. Disparagement of the role of career civil servants

Hit lists were, in essence, lists compiled by one or more special assistants in Gorsuch's office containing the names of EPA bureaucrats whose alleged political or ideological leanings were suspect (Kennedy School 1984a,b; Lash et al. 1984; *National Journal* 1984; Waterman 1989b). Individuals on the lists were not only targeted to be transferred, demoted, or fired, but in many cases the transfer or demotion was carried out. The ability of appointees to use this strategy was facilitated by the 1978 Civil Service Reform Act, which removed traditional civil service protections from members of the Senior Executive Service. Moreover, one common consequence of transferring employees outside the Washington area was that they were forced to resign from the agency if they were unable or unwilling to relocate. It is likely that this was intended.[14] One careerist from my sample, who himself had left the agency, personally knew three colleagues who were reassigned by this method—two from Washington to regional offices and one from a regional office to Washington.

Hit lists were important at the EPA because they impacted a much wider spectrum of career staff than those directly affected by the transfer strategy. However many individuals were directly impacted, the existence of the hit lists and the application of the transfer strategy were known throughout the agency.

The overall management style engaged in by Gorsuch-era appointees was one of secrecy and the exclusion of careerists. Careerists felt that decisions were made "on the twelfth floor," a reference to the top floor of EPA headquarters and home to the offices of the administrator and her closest aides. One seventeen-year veteran claimed that he did not have a single meeting with Gorsuch during her entire tenure—a record that contrasted sharply with his experience during previous and subsequent administrations. Another veteran reported that he was also excluded from meetings until he received "clearance from upstairs." He contrasted this experience with that during the Bush administration, when anyone could attend meetings that concerned them. And another felt that "a large number of decisions were made behind closed doors."

Appointees also rewrote the work product of career staff. For example, careerists prepared a document (required by law) to provide guidance in implementing Superfund's Emergency Contingency Plan. The document was substantially rewritten by appointed staff. As one careerist related, Gorsuch "took the responsibility for writing it away from us." This was not an isolated incident but a common practice. However, it was not practiced uniformly or with an eye to achieving specific policy goals. For example, in the rewriting incident just described, Gorsuch's objection was not to the policy content of the document but to its length. She felt that it was too long and so directed her special assistants to produce a shorter document. In other cases, appointees simply did not believe that the careerists' work product could be objective, so they assigned the projects to noncareer special assistants (interview).

These are but a few of the micromanagement techniques employed by Gorsuch and her team at EPA. In essence, they attempted to remove discretion from, and keep close tabs on, career bureaucrats, and to centralize decision making and work products so that they were consistently reviewed by appointees. Gorsuch herself tried to read every rule and regulation and would often edit them on a page-by-page basis (interview). This management style contrasted sharply with that of previous administrations in which, for example, under Carter's administrator Doug Costle, a dozen people were authorized to sign off on documents such as regulations and interagency memoranda that required the administrator's signature. But under Gorsuch, only Gorsuch herself and her close aide John Daniels (a special assistant who never went through the Senate confirmation process) were authorized to sign off on such documents. This management policy clearly diminished bureaucratic discretion and changed the environment in which bureaucrats worked.

Anne Gorsuch reorganized EPA's Office of Enforcement three times in a twelve-month period. One of the reorganizations abolished the office entirely and dispersed its staff to other divisions of the EPA. As a result, Enforcement attorneys were separated from the office's technical staff. Some attorneys were sent to EPA's Office of General Counsel, which was retitled the Office of Enforcement and Legal Counsel, and others were sent to the media offices for air, water, and hazardous waste.[15] Scientific and engineering staff were relocated to media offices and hence separated from one another. Another reorganization resulted in two political appointees competing for authority over the Enforcement staff, with the careerists unclear about whom they should report to.

The true intent of these reorganizations remains unknown. Neither scholars, nor subsequent appointees, nor those I interviewed are sure about the true intent of reorganization at the EPA (Kennedy School 1984a; Kurtz 1983; Lash et al. 1984; Mosher 1983; Waterman 1989b). Some claim that it was to slow down enforcement in an administration that did not believe in enforcement. Others claim that it was to centralize decision making in the hands of the appointed head of the Office of General Counsel. Still others view it as a management improvement strategy designed to enhance the agency's efficiency and performance. And finally, some view it as a failed attempt to streamline an agency marred by appointee incompetence.

Whatever the intended goals, the series of reorganizations had a considerable impact on the agency careerists whose home base had been the Office of Enforcement. They were transferred as many as three different times, which meant physically moving their offices from one wing of the large Waterside Mall (which consists of two, twelve-story towers connected by two, four-story wings) to the other, reporting to different supervisors, or both. One woman reported being transferred to the Office of Hazardous Waste and then being transferred to the Office of Air for a total of two weeks before being reassigned to the Office of Hazardous Waste. She was subsequently assigned to a "special project" where she remained for the rest of Gorsuch's tenure (interview).

Careerists were separated from their colleagues, distracted from their work goals, unsure of their appointed bosses' expectations, and sometimes even unsure who their supervisors were. According to one former Enforcement official, a minimum of six months of work was lost in the confusion of all the reorganizations. Another former Enforcement attorney recalled that he and his colleagues spent the time after the reorganizations "sitting on our hands" because they were left with "nothing to do" and "all our files were in boxes somewhere."

Reorganization was not the only facet of the microlevel administrative presidency that affected career bureaucrats in Enforcement. The appointees who presided over enforcement activities applied other management techniques to this group of agency careerists.

In addition to the "hit lists" compiled "on the twelfth floor," the Office of Enforcement had a "green book" in which notes on careerists' performance were recorded. Some accounts attribute authorship of the book to General Counsel Bob Perry (a political appointee); others, to one of his appointed special assistants. One attorney I interviewed reported that he had actually seen "the infamous green book." He remembered that one entry deducted fifty points from an individual's unofficial performance rating because, in the eyes of the book's author, she had given a poor presentation. In testimony before Congress, Perry denied the existence of any such book, and the extent to which it was actually used as the basis for transferring, demoting, or firing career employees is unclear. What is clear is that knowledge of the book was widespread among careerists, as was the anxiety that the book aroused.

During this time period, Special Assistant Peter Brocolleti, a former strength-training coach for the Denver Broncos, conducted a management retreat on ethics. The retreat focused on two topics: the proper dress code for Enforcement attorneys and the proper clients of Enforcement attorneys. The message conveyed by Brocolleti was that as the president's surrogates, the appointees were the agency attorneys' clients.[16] One attorney who missed the mandatory retreat was required to write an essay discussing the EPA's clients in lieu of his attendance. He was subsequently reprimanded for writing that the public was the EPA's client.

Finally, a new appointed position of deputy assistant administrator was created below the assistant administrator and general counsel positions. This was true throughout the agency, not just in Enforcement. This position had traditionally been filled by a careerist; in fact it had traditionally been the highest career position in the agency. Consequently, "incumbent careerists were demoted to the rank of manager and reported to the new DAAs rather than to the assistant administrators" (Landy et al. 1994:248). One effect of this change was that careerists who had formerly had direct contact with the assistant administrators now dealt with a lower-level appointee instead. In general, the new hierarchy created an extra layer between the administrator's office and the program offices (Kennedy School 1985). It also limited the opportunities for high-ranking careerists to advance further up the career ladder.

In the Enforcement Division, Peter Brocolleti was elevated to this position (which did not require Senate confirmation) and used the promotion to create a deputy assistant administrator's office with his own handpicked staff. With the help of Special Assistant Bob Krautch, Brocolleti interviewed career attorneys for six or seven positions, who would serve directly under him. Three points are relevant here. First, rather unusual interview questions were asked in the selection process, including the following:

1. Are you a member of a political party or group?
2. What groups do you belong to?
3. Are you a "tree hugger"?
4. What is your partisan identification?
5. Do you belong to the Sierra Club?

Second, the group's function, while ostensibly to work on special projects, in reality was to work on projects that the appointees did not want to entrust to the regular career staff. As one career member of this inner circle noted, "work was diverted to this group" while other attorneys were left with little work to do. Third, the creation and existence of this group resulted in tension among career staff. The attorneys chosen were embarrassed to have been singled out by these unpopular appointees. And those who were not selected were excluded from the interesting work and suspicious of those who had been selected. It was both a divisive management technique and one that centralized important work under the direct and close supervision of the appointees.

THE BUREAUCRATIC RESPONSE TO THE "FIRST" REAGAN ADMINISTRATION

The management style of Reagan's appointees at the EPA, coupled with their departures from past agency policies, seems like a blueprint for bureaucratic resistance. But the bureaucratic reactions were not all the same. Instead, three patterns emerged: cooperation in the EPA at large, acquiescence in Enforcement, and three lower-level resisters.

BEHAVIOR IN THE EPA AT LARGE

Most of the respondents interviewed in the EPA at large did not engage in voice by argumentation, leaks, sabotage, whistle-blowing, collective action, or foot-dragging. Moreover, most exit occurred in Enforcement or among those affected by the reorganization of the Enforcement Division. However, there was some exit from the upper-career echelons of the EPA at large, primarily among those careerists directly affected by hit lists or transfers (see, e.g., Kennedy School 1984b; Lash et al. 1984; *National Journal* 1984).

EXIT
Turnover at the EPA was mainly the result of the administration's management techniques. These techniques entailed manipulating the rules of the 1978 Civil Service Reform Act. Careerists whose names appeared on the hit lists were demoted or transferred under the discretion of the Act. This often left the careerists with no option other than to resign if they were not in a position to relocate or if, as one observer put it, they resented having been "shuttled off into a corner with a window to stare out." None of the people I interviewed were forced out in this way. In fact, I interviewed one official who remained at the EPA despite a series of "reassignments" which were interpreted as demotions. However, a series of interviews conducted by the Kennedy School of Government included one with a careerist targeted for transfer by EPA appointees. Although he was able to buy himself some time to look for a new job (i.e., to delay the transfer), he felt that he was unable to deter the forces that had labeled him a "troublemaker" and resigned as soon as he got another job (Kennedy School 1985).

This type of turnover is important for a number of reasons. First, it shows the impact that these strategic approaches to management can have on bureaucrats. Second, it shows that these people did not "resign in protest" or because of policy disagreements. My interviews and those by the Kennedy School (1984b, 1985) indicate that if they had not been reassigned or transferred, most of these careerists would have remained at the EPA through the Reagan years.

Not all types of turnover can be attributed to the Reagan administration's strategic redeployment of personnel or to events in the Enforcement Division, however. Interviewees indicated that some of their colleagues left in late 1980 and early 1981 in anticipation of the Reagan administration. Others are reported to have left out of frustration with particular appointees and their management style, but again this occurred primarily in Enforcement. The only non-Enforcement exiter I interviewed who left during the Gorsuch period left for idiosyncratic reasons not pertaining to the Reagan administration, its policy goals, or its management style. However, it is significant to note that policy disagreement appears to have played little role in determining either the amount of or the reasons for exit.[17] Finally, a few of those interviewed for this study said that they "hunkered down" rather than leaving, based on the assumption that they would outlast the appointees. Here, unlike at the Civil Rights Division, this proved to be a prescient strategy.

VOICE BY ARGUMENTATION

The fact that Gorsuch did not like to be challenged by careerists was common knowledge among careerists and reduced their propensity to confront her. The same applied to some, but not all, of the other appointees. Overall, as one former careerist observed, "The only back-and-forth exchange on the activities of the agency was between Gorsuch and industry."

Only one person with whom I spoke engaged in voice by argumentation. He commented, "I had the feeling that I was one of the few people who were prepared to talk about what was right and wrong. She [Gorsuch] did not like it." This individual suffered reprisals for challenging the Reagan appointees. Although he was not transferred out of the Washington office, he received a number of reassignments during the Gorsuch years, each with less responsibility than the last. His colleagues believe that his career was permanently slowed if not completely derailed as a result of the path it took during those three years. Yet his only form of dissent was voice by argumentation.

One former EPA careerist recounted what he felt was a striking example of the absence of voice by argumentation. He recounted an event in which a number of EPA officials were invited to the White House for lunch. None of the five careerists present spoke up when the president recounted some of his favorite environmental anecdotes. None defended their agency or its mission in any way. None criticized the direction of the administration's environmental policy.

Another careerist, who was critical of his colleagues for their hesitance to speak out, related an incident involving the well-known case of Rita Lavelle: "I fault the career staff for Rita Lavelle's indictment. If your boss is doing something wrong, you need to advise them, point it out to them, before it gets out." In short, he believed that if careerists had been vocal rather than reticent, they could have kept Lavelle out of trouble. This in turn would have saved the agency from a tremendous embarrassment.[18] He went on to explain his colleagues' overall hesitation to use voice by argumentation, by attributing it to the appointees' management style, which caused careerists to "fear losing their job or being transferred to Oklahoma."

This civil servant was not alone in his assessment of the absence of voice. A former lobbyist and Bush appointee who has both an inside and an outside perspective believes that career managers "learned to be very cautious" during the Gorsuch era because there were "severe penalties for sticking your neck out." He added that the legacy of Reagan's appointees and their "intimidation" tactics persisted in the agency into the Bush years, resulting in the careerists' continued hesitation to speak frankly. He also thinks that careerists were reluctant to use voice because "the one thing they [the Reagan appointees] were competent at was intimidation."

LEAKING, FOOT-DRAGGING, SABOTAGE, AND COLLECTIVE ACTION

Although the interviewees denied leaking themselves, they did acknowledge that some leaking went on. For example, they related an incident in which a careerist who was present at a Gorsuch-led meeting attended by industry representatives "went public" with his knowledge of this event. Upon reflection, one interviewee suggested that Gorsuch's management style precipitated some leaks because "Gorsuch tried to make things so closed that people rebelled and leaked." She contrasted Gorsuch's approach with Ruckelshaus's more open approach, which removed the need to leak.

Most respondents, however, simply stated that they had not leaked and that leaking was not prevalent in their office or program. One was somewhat more dramatic, stating, "Some things I heard [in meetings with appointees] turned my hair white. But my professional integrity prevented me from reporting them. It's not my job to talk to reporters."

Several careerists contrasted their own reluctance to leak with the behavior of political appointees. One commented, "Leaking is usually not done by disgruntled bureaucrats; it's usually done high up on policy issues." Examples of appointee-initiated leaks abounded during the Reagan years, the result, in part, of a great deal of infighting among the appointees. In her memoir, Gorsuch recounts one such example. In that incident, John Daniel, her appointed aide, leaked information to the *New York Times* in an effort to help Gorsuch in a battle she was having with OMB's David Stockman (Burford and Greenya 1986:80–81). This pattern is similar to the one I found at the Food and Nutrition Service, where the leaking was by appointees, not career civil servants.

Respondents, including those no longer working at the EPA, were terse but pointed in their discussion of sabotage and foot-dragging. For example, with respect to sabotaging the president's program or his appointee's directives, a veteran careerist simply stated, "I don't play games." With respect to deliberately slowing down the agency's work on unpopular presidential initiatives, one insight was that "there's only so much you can do on that."

The closest thing to collective action at EPA was the time when career bureaucrats, acting in unpremeditated spontaneous concert, bought all the champagne for sale in a nearby liquor store on the morning that Gorsuch announced her resignation. In a similar incident, when the Gorsuch-era appointees began to resign, careerists had T-shirts made up listing their names, which they crossed off after each resignation. Finally, attendance at after-work softball games rose between 1981 and 1983 as civil servants sought to keep up morale and trade horror stories out of earshot of the appointees.

The one respondent who acknowledged engaging in voice by argumentation suggested that collective action might have been more effective than his lone voice, but he did not observe any during the Gorsuch era. He believed that "if more people had done it, it might have had an effect." But he did not feel that he could elicit the support of his peers and did not attempt to organize them in any way. For their part, his colleagues did not want to be associated with what they viewed as a falling star or labeled in the way they felt that he was and hence did not join or support him in his efforts.

LOYALTY

The predominant behavior among the career civil servants I interviewed at the EPA was cooperation. This cooperation stemmed from a mixture of loyalty and neglect.

Examples of loyalty abound. Some careerists exhibited considerable personal loyalty toward individual appointees. Two careerists who worked in the Superfund program under Rita Lavelle stand out in particular. One, although he described Lavelle as both "incompetent" and "pitiful," reported that he stood by her side throughout the congressional hearings at which she was ultimately cited in contempt of Congress. The other felt that "your responsibility is to your boss" and that, especially in a case such as Lavelle's in which that boss was "in over her head" and "not qualified for the job," his job was to do all he could to help her out.

Another example of loyalty was found in the individual who had been director of the Noise Pollution Office during the Carter years. He was told to abolish the office and delegate its tasks to the states as part of the administration's plan to federalize the EPA's activities. He did just that. His primary personal goal was to do it without any layoffs, and he did manage to ensure that all staff were transferred to other offices and programs, but he never betrayed the orders of the Reagan appointees in his efforts to avoid firing anyone. He was charged with abolishing the office and its work, not with eliminating jobs. Even though he believed that conducting research, monitoring, and attempting to reduce noise pollution were important and that abolishing the program "had tragic consequences," he recognized that it was not a statutory program, and thus its fate lay entirely in the hands of the executive branch. Accordingly, he complied with the administration's directive.

A third example of loyalty was reported to me by an engineer and Senior Executive Service (SES) member who was involved in the regulation of lead in gasoline, an important issue during the Reagan years (for a discussion of lead in gasoline, see Landy et al. 1994). He told a story about a colleague in the Office of Policy Analysis and Evaluation whom he considered to be something of an environmental zealot. This colleague was assigned the task of conducting the cost-benefit analysis on the lead in gasoline regulation. He did not personally favor the use of cost-benefit analysis and preferred to reduce the amount of lead allowed in gasoline regardless of cost, but he produced the analysis and sent it to OMB. OMB later presented it to bureaucrats in all the regulatory agencies as a model cost-benefit analysis. This EPA careerist not only performed the assigned task but did it in exemplary fashion.

In addition to these specific examples of loyalty, interviewees also provided broader statements regarding the behavior of their colleagues. Typical of such comments were, "We cooperated 99.9 percent of the time"; "It's hard to speak for ten thousand people, [but] at the senior level there was more cooperation than there was resistance"; "The majority were supportive and cooperative"; and the one I found most telling, "They [the appointees] thought we weren't team players and we would fight them. We aren't that way."

One careerist claimed that the higher-ranking civil servants at the EPA anticipated a change in policy direction even before Reagan took office. According to this person, the "higher-ups" (as he called career civil servants at the SES level) viewed the 1980 election as a mandate and spent the time between the election in November and Reagan's inauguration in January laying the groundwork for the anticipated policy changes based on their expectation of what Reagan would want. He argued that "the higher-ups changed their tune even before Reagan came in." To the extent that this was true, it reflects a remarkable degree of loyalty.

NEGLECT

Cooperation at the EPA also resulted from neglect. Many careerists went along with the appointees in a cooperative manner but privately were waiting for Reagan and his appointees to be gone. They expressed varying degrees of opposition to Reagan's policies but shared the feeling that not much could be done one way or the other. A number of interviewees labeled this behavior as "hunkering down." One stated, "My friends hunkered down. Their attitude was, 'This is my career. These guys [the appointees] will be gone.'" The rise in softball attendance was another indication of neglect. Career personnel viewed it as an excuse to cut back on their traditionally long work hours. In general, one manager who continued to work late noticed a marked drop-off in those putting in long hours. This was not deliberate foot-dragging or sabotage. These long work hours were not mandatory; however, in the past, EPA careerists had worked overtime out of commitment and enthusiasm. That commitment and enthusiasm waned during Gorsuch's reign at the EPA.[19]

The Office of Enforcement: A Case Within a Case

Enforcement was the office to which others pointed as the part of EPA "hardest hit" during the Gorsuch years.[20] Thus, one might expect the response of the careerists there to be different from that of their colleagues elsewhere in the agency. Yet the careerists in the Office of Enforcement did not argue, leak, blow the whistle, sabotage, drag their feet, or join together in collective action against the appointees or their policy of slowing down enforcement. The only place where real differences emerged was in the area of turnover.

EXIT

Although exact numbers are not available, the Office of Enforcement experienced significantly greater turnover than did the EPA's other divisions.[21] Some of this turnover occurred after Gorsuch had resigned, but it was attributed to her tenure. A number of Enforcement attorneys who remained at the EPA throughout Gorsuch's tenure attributed their later exit, in the mid 1980s, to "burnout" from the toll the Gorsuch years had taken. Other careerists who have remained in Enforcement reported that although they ultimately decided to stick it out, they too considered leaving the agency during Gorsuch's tenure.

Overall, the management techniques used in Enforcement, such as dress codes, retreats, training sessions, and reorganization, had the effect, intended or not, of provoking a sizable exodus from this division. The turmoil caused by the reorganizations, personal conflicts with individual appointees, the work environment, and the decline in morale caused by the retreats and training sessions (as well as the reorganizations) all contributed to exit. Moreover, as more people began to leave, morale was further reduced, causing additional careerists to consider leaving.

Strikingly absent from the reasons given for leaving the agency are mentions of policy disagreement, opposition to cutting back on enforcement, or commitment to command-and-control regulation and its attendant emphasis on enforcement. The closest indication of policy disagreement was from a supervisor who observed that "a good part of leaving was frustration that people couldn't do good work." Others were explicit that it was "*not* policy reasons" that caused them to leave.[22]

In Enforcement, frustrated attorneys preferred to switch rather than fight. But usually what they were switching from was not Reagan's policies but things like being told by a former football coach (Brocolleti) to write an essay as punishment for being absent from a training session, or having their presentations graded in a green book.

VOICE

Voice was notable at the Office of Enforcement largely for its absence. Voice was rare because people were too busy from the disruption caused by the reorganizations to have time for a response, because of their fear of spies, and because their hands were tied. One careerist explained, "On a daily basis, you did what they wanted, and if you wanted to do something, you needed their approval anyway." Others commented, "You thought your career was in danger, and you needed to keep your mouth shut"; "Exchange was inhibited, not full and frank"; "We felt in jeopardy for our lives"; "Even I hesitated, and my colleagues really headed for cover"; "Frank exchange was limited even among ourselves because the atmosphere bred paranoia."

If people did not argue, they did not leak either. One attorney claimed, in language similar to that used by attorneys in the Civil Rights Division, that "lawyers don't leak because of the confidentiality of clients." She also felt that there was not much need for leaking in the enforcement area because the drop-off in enforcement was evident from "the numbers," which were readily available to Congress, the press, and the public.

Collective action was particularly unlikely in Enforcement because of the constant turmoil in the office, with colleagues and substantive functions constantly being relocated. A unified response by Enforcement careerists was made all but impossible by the fact that they were often physically separated and thus rarely talked with one another. The closest thing to collective action had no policy implications. It occurred at an office Christmas party at which a few attorneys performed a skit in which they called Anne Burford, Anne Hereford, and whose plot was that she had to marry a cow as penance for her deeds at the EPA.

With respect to stronger forms of resistance, the interviewees told me that "there was no insubordination" and that "very few guys did acts of conscientious resistance." The possibilities for sabotage and whistle-blowing, like other acts of resistance, were also reduced by the general confusion caused by the reorganizations.

LOYALTY

Even in Enforcement, there were acts of loyalty similar to those reported elsewhere in the agency. These included the individual who, under appointee orders, withheld documents from Congress, even though he was publicly reprimanded for his action at a congressional hearing; the individual who heard appointees in congressional testimony deny the existence of the "green books" but who, when he later saw one of the green books, stood by the perjuring appointee; and the individual who developed the plan to implement the administration's goal of easing the vigor of enforcement activity. As one attorney put it, "People here will go to great lengths to accommodate themselves to new leadership. . . . Gorsuch miscalculated; she didn't harness that."

The striking difference between loyalty in the Enforcement Division and loyalty elsewhere in the agency is the anger associated with it. Career attorneys in Enforcement cooperated because they felt it was the right thing to do despite their dislike of the individuals running their office. Careerists in other parts of the EPA did not have to overcome this hurdle to the same extent. The comments from Enforcement officials have a caveat that those from careerists elsewhere in EPA did not: "There was more cooperation than they deserved"; "We hated them but acted cooperatively."

NEGLECT

Attitudes of neglect were more prevalent in the Enforcement Division than elsewhere. This was a function of the much lower morale here than in other parts of the agency. In Enforcement, the constant reorganizations, disruptions, reprimands, and disdain with which they were viewed by the appointees took a toll. As noted earlier, this often took the form of exit. But it more frequently was exhibited in low morale. Other factors, such as the fact that appointees often handled the office's important projects themselves rather than entrusting them to careerists, as well as the constant reorganizations, also contributed to neglect.

THE WHISTLE-BLOWERS

Although there was little resistance among the twenty-one high-ranking EPA careerists in my study, there was resistant behavior at the EPA. And although the interviewees who participated in my study remain anonymous, there is nothing anonymous about the group of mid-level careerists who resisted the Reagan administration and its policies at EPA. Most prominent was Hugh Kaufman, whose whistle-blowing behavior precipitated congressional investigations into the conduct of EPA assistant administrator Rita Lavelle (Johnson and Kraft 1990). Also influential was the self-proclaimed leaker William Sanjour (Sanjour 1992). In the Office of Pesticides was Dr. M. Adrian Gross, a scientist who objected to some of the registration decisions made in his office and who testified before Congress to that effect (Claybrook 1984; Lash et al. 1984). This section will briefly describe the behavior of this group (see also Benjamin 1986a; Burnham 1982a,b; Johnson 1988; Johnson and Kraft 1990; Kriz 1983; Sanjour 1992; Shabecoff 1982b, 1983a).

Kaufman and Sanjour deliberately and consciously chose not to use exit behavior for their resistance (Kriz 1983; Sanjour 1992). Although both claim that appointees tried to force them out of the agency, they rejected voluntary exit, resisted involuntary exit, and were able to maintain their employment status because of legislation that protects whistle-blowers (Sanjour 1992; Shabecoff 1983a). Both men believed that they could better effect change from the inside where, although demoted and isolated, they could keep a finger on the agency's pulse and sometimes gain access to controversial documents that they would then be in a position to leak. Adrian Gross also stayed at EPA throughout the Reagan administration.

All three dissenters started out by arguing. They raised their objections to their career and political superiors. Gross objected to rulings on selected pesticides. Kaufman objected that money earmarked for Superfund was not being spent properly or quickly enough. They wrote memoranda documenting their positions, and when their objections were not answered to their satisfaction, they went outside the agency. As Sanjour has written, "At first I fought from the inside. . . . As a result, . . . I was transferred to another position, with no duties and no staff. I became an outspoken EPA critic—a whistleblower—and have been one ever since" (Sanjour 1992:75).

When they determined that arguing was not an effective strategy, they turned to leaks and whistle-blowing. Kaufman began to collect internal agency documents, which he leaked to David Burnham of the *New York Times*. He testified on Capitol Hill, and he appeared on *60 Minutes* (Johnson 1988). Sanjour spent his time working with grassroots environmental groups, offering them ideas regarding strategies, and providing information that could be used in lawsuits (Sanjour 1992).

Both Kaufman and Sanjour had blown the whistle during previous administrations, and both have continued to do so since the Reagan administration (Hurst 1989; Sanjour 1992; Turque 1989). They objected in general to EPA's policy direction; their objections were not limited to Reagan's policies and perceived wrongdoing. It also is important to note that their careers were impacted by their behavior. Sanjour was transferred to a position with less responsibility, and Kaufman was investigated and put under surveillance, although ultimately he won a consent order from the Department of Labor that continues to protect him (Benjamin 1986a; Kriz 1983). Adrian Gross was demoted and denied further access to the data to which he was objecting (Lash et al. 1984:190). According to Jonathan Lash and colleagues' 1984 account, Gross was demoted just for voicing his objections to his appointed superiors, but his leaking may have been a factor as well.

These whistle-blowers worked individually, not collectively. They were, in the words of one interviewee, "publicity-seeking mavericks" who sought the spotlight for themselves. From this perspective, they worked alone because they did not want to share the limelight and were not team players. But they also were shunned, at least by the career civil servants I interviewed, who felt that the behavior of Kaufman and the other whistle-blowers reflected poorly on the agency's reputation. This limited the opportunities available to Kaufman and the others for collective action because their colleagues did not want to join them in their resistant activities.

ANALYSIS OF WHISTLE-BLOWERS

The behavior of the whistle-blowers at EPA demonstrates that when careerists defy their political and career superiors, blow the whistle, and leak, bureaucratic behavior can have a tremendous impact (Benjamin 1986a; Johnson and Kraft 1990). Most significantly, it affects the public and congressional agendas. Providing Congress with information initiated a process of investigation and oversight that ultimately led to the resignations of Rita Lavelle and Anne Gorsuch (Benjamin 1986a; Johnson and Kraft 1990). Indeed, without their initial leaks, the entire history of the EPA during the Reagan years might have been different.

Second, the behavior of just one person can have a tremendous effect on his or her home agency. There is no need for mass rebellion to draw attention to internal agency activity. Moreover, because one person can have such a big impact, the majority of cooperators are quickly overshadowed, and an impression of mass insurrection is created. These perceptions then color the future actions of presidents and appointees.

Third, the leakers and whistle-blowers were ostracized by their colleagues and criticized for violating bureaucratic norms. The careerists I interviewed regarded the whistle-blowers with disdain, considering Kaufman's behavior to be "beyond the pale." In addition, some believed that their careers, and those of some of their colleagues, were negatively affected by the leakers. One respondent told me that Adrian Gross, one of his subordinates, "kept trotting up to the Hill." This supervisor was among those who were frequently transferred during the Gorsuch era, and some of his colleagues believe that he was held responsible for his subordinate's behavior. Supervisors discouraged subordinates' resistance, regardless of whether or not they shared their subordinates' policy preferences.

Resisters also were criticized for hurting the agency's reputation. In fact, the careerists I interviewed were more concerned with protecting the EPA's reputation than with protesting policy change or challenging the Reagan appointees. More than one interviewee felt that Kaufman was just as responsible for "tarnishing" the EPA's image as Gorsuch and Lavelle were. Moreover, careerists attributed nothing but the basest motives to Kaufman and the others. Some viewed them as incompetent, and all those who mentioned this issue described Kaufman with words and phrases such as "disgruntled" and "in it for his own purposes." One went so far as to say that Kaufman would do anything to get on television.

Most important, however, the presence of these three whistle-blowers, along with the reports of guerilla warfare contained in O'Leary's (1995) work, provides a useful reminder about overgeneralizing from this study. It is not my intent to argue that all civil servants are responsive to all presidents and all appointees all the time. In fact, I hope that this discussion suggests that some of the compliance I found may be limited to the upper reaches of the civil service and to agency headquarters in Washington and may not trickle down to the lower levels or to the regional offices (but see Brehm and Gates 1997). In this case, however, as in the others presented in this book, the explanatory factors outlined in chapter 2 shed light on why the EPA might have exhibited this bifurcated behavior and why it might have produced both dutiful and recalcitrant employees.

As was the case at the National Highway Traffic Safety Administration and the Civil Rights Division, the EPA's historical development enables us to understand the behavior of both the three dissidents and their more obedient superiors. The careerists I interviewed believe that the EPA's historical development had a significant effect on the agency's personnel roster. Initially, the agency attracted a fair number of environmental zealots drawn to the EPA by the opportunity to work in a new and growing agency not yet captured by industry. But most of these zealots languished at EPA because zealotry was not part of the dominant agency culture, a culture grounded in the cultures of the disparate agencies that the EPA inherited when it was created in 1970. As a result, most careerists of this type had left the agency by the late 1970s. The few who remained did not advance as rapidly up the career ladder as their less ideological counterparts did. This partly accounts for the resistance at the lower levels of the agency, where the remaining strident environmentalists were located, as they would be the ones most likely to engage in resistant activities. Thus, this explains both the behavior of Kaufman and the other whistleblowers, and why this type of behavior was absent at the higher levels of EPA. The upper echelons of EPA are not populated with rabid environmentalists, and as a result, careerists at this level were more accepting of the Reagan administration's policy goals.

The "Second" Reagan Administration

Careerists at the EPA celebrated Gorsuch's departure from their agency with champagne. Her departure marked the beginning of a new era there. Some people told me that there were "two" Reagan administrations at EPA, and others went so far as to say that the Reagan administration lasted for three, not eight, years at their agency. This demarcation is chiefly attributable to the changing of the appointed guard at the EPA, which led to vastly improved appointee-career relations. This second era suggests that responsiveness can be obtained through trust and respect and that voice by argumentation can play a positive role in internal policy deliberations without threatening an agency's chain of command.

THE RUCKELSHAUS ERA

The second Reagan administration was ushered in by the appointment of William Ruckelshaus to replace Anne Gorsuch as EPA's administrator. Ruckelshaus had served as EPA's first administrator, and Reagan's choice of Ruckelshaus was viewed by many as a symbolically conciliatory gesture. Nonetheless, Ruckelshaus, who had served under Nixon and worked as a lobbyist for the Weyerhauser Corporation, could hardly be viewed as a tree-hugging liberal. But he was viewed by EPA careerists as a competent and able manager and a respected leader. This, more than Ruckelshaus's policy goals, seems to explain the careerist response to the second Reagan administration.

REAGAN'S POLICY OBJECTIVES AT EPA

When Reagan accepted Anne Gorsuch's resignation in March 1983 (she became Anne Burford the same month) and appointed William Ruckelshaus to replace her as EPA's administrator, he neither announced new policy initiatives for EPA nor renounced his earlier policy goals. In fact, in accepting Gorsuch's resignation, Reagan stated that the environmentalists would not "be happy until the White House looks like a bird's nest" (Public Papers, Reagan 1983:389). When asked about changes at the EPA under Ruckelshaus, Reagan remarked, "I'm too old to change" (Public Papers, Reagan 1983:422). But at Ruckelshaus's swearing in ceremony one month later, Reagan called for, among other things, new and vigorous action to meet the issue of acid rain "head-on" and also promised a "new beginning" in the area of environmental protection (Public Papers, Reagan 1983:734).

In evaluating Reagan's agenda, Ruckelshaus formed the distinct impression that Reagan's overriding objective was simply to keep the agency's activities out of the headlines (Kennedy School 1985). He felt that Reagan was puzzled by the events at the EPA and the controversy that they generated and that Reagan never fully appreciated the extent of the disarray caused by his appointees there (Kennedy School 1985). Ruckelshaus was, however, confident that thereafter Reagan's main goal for the EPA and environmental policy became the avoidance of adverse publicity. According to one account, "The White House seemed extremely interested in damage control" (Kennedy School 1985:14).

Although the administration did not entirely abandon its policy goals and administrative strategy at the EPA, it did abandon parts of them. One major change was the absence of clear policy direction emanating from the president himself. Reagan removed himself (or was removed by his aides) from the front lines. He also abandoned the strategy of appointing ideologically compatible loyalists to serve at EPA. Although environmentalists voiced concern over Ruckelshaus's appointment and although Ruckelshaus was relatively conservative in his approach to environmental issues, he was clearly not of the same ideological stripe as Gorsuch had been. Furthermore, as part of his agreement to return to the EPA, Ruckelshaus, unlike Gorsuch, was promised free rein in the selection of the rest of the appointed team (Kennedy School 1985). As a result, the White House lost its previous direct control over the appointments process. Finally, Ruckelshaus was given considerable discretion and leeway at the EPA. For the most part, he was free to set the agency's internal agenda. As one Bush appointee with close ties to the interest group community told me, "The White House played hands-off with Ruckelshaus."

THE ADMINISTRATIVE PRESIDENCY DURING THE RUCKELSHAUS ERA

After Ruckelshaus's appointment, the OMB was not able to secure further budget cuts at the EPA. Not only were OMB's budget figures challenged by the EPA's new administrator, but they also were rejected by Congress (Harris and Milkis 1989; Peterson 1984). But analysts differ in their assessments of the extent to which the EPA's budget was restored to its pre-1981 levels and the extent to which Ruckelshaus or OMB prevailed in setting the budget figures (Dobel 1992; Harris and Milkis 1989; Kraft and Vig 1984).

Other elements of the administrative presidency, however, continued unobstructed. The OIRA and the Vice President's Task Force on Regulatory Relief continued to review the agency's regulations and to impede their issuance. The acid-rain issue shows the continued influence of the tools for regulatory review at the president's disposal to control the bureaucracy. Ruckelshaus proposed a plan to limit emissions of sulfur dioxide as a step toward dealing with the acid-rain problem. But opposition from various quarters in the Executive Office of the President, David Stockman in particular, led him to abandon the plan (Kennedy School 1986; Landy et al. 1994). Thus, these tools of the administrative presidency continued to be utilized in spite of the changing of the guard at EPA.

Although Ruckelshaus, unlike Gorsuch, often challenged decisions made by the OIRA and the vice-president's task force, he had no real power with which to overrule them. One interviewee drew attention to the contrasting attitudes toward the OMB held by Gorsuch and Ruckelshaus. His impression of Gorsuch was that "Anne viewed OMB as the leader in regulatory reform. She was just there to implement, not to lead." On the other hand, Ruckelshaus (as well as Lee Thomas) "had a different view" which led to "many a bloodbath." But another interviewee pointed out that after a few losing and bruising battles, such as the one over acid rain, "no one really took on OMB."

RUCKELSHAUS'S POLICY GOALS AND MANAGEMENT STYLE

Ruckelshaus had three main policy objectives: to restore the agency's credibility in Congress and with the public; to restore the agency's capacity to enforce its laws and regulations; and to incorporate risk-assessment analysis into the agency's decision-making and policy-making processes (Dobel 1992). The first two goals are reminiscent of Ruckelshaus's first tenure at EPA. In the 1970s, he had tried to establish the agency's credibility, and in the 1980s he tried to restore that credibility. In both cases, he viewed enforcement activity as the means to achieve that end. One of Ruckelshaus's early acts upon his return to EPA was to hold a closed-door meeting with EPA careerists, at which he delivered what has been dubbed his "gorilla in the closet" speech (Stanfield 1984a). In it he outlined a plan to increase enforcement actions in which the EPA was to be the gorilla "behind the door" or in the closet so that the states would feel they had federal support behind them (lurking in the closet). One careerist felt that through this speech and the tone that it set, "Bill dispelled the notion that it is bad to be enforcing," which contrasted with the prevailing feeling during Gorsuch's tenure that active enforcement was frowned on. Thus Ruckelshaus immediately represented a policy change from the early Reagan years and a return to an earlier agency policy.

Using risk assessment methods, however, represented a departure in the agency's approach to decision making. This approach entails assessing the health risks posed by exposure to varying amounts of toxic chemicals and pollutants. Risk assessment also takes into account the benefits and the costs of reducing emissions. It relies heavily on the agency's scientific capacity to determine harm to health and environment caused by exposure. For example, Ruckelshaus ruled that cutting the amount of a cancer-producing pollutant in Tacoma, Washington, so that the number of cancer cases caused by the chemical was reduced but not eliminated, was an acceptable risk when contrasted with the costs of closing the plant producing the harmful chemical and losing the eight hundred jobs it provided to the community (Dobel 1992; Landy et al. 1994).

Ruckelshaus's approach to running the EPA contrasted sharply with Gorsuch's. He brought in a team of appointees, many with prior service at the EPA, who respected the capabilities of the agency's professional staff. These included Al Alm, who served as deputy administrator, and Lee Thomas, who replaced Rita Lavelle as assistant administrator for Solid Waste and Emergency Response. As one sixteen-year veteran pointed out, Ruckelshaus's team "didn't view the agency and the people in it as the enemy."

Ruckelshaus's management style featured openness and inclusion. "He demanded openness in the agency on all decisions and ensured fairness," reported one interviewee. This dovetailed with his insistence on obtaining good information and ensuring that all sides had a say in any controversy (Dobel 1992:257). One of his first actions was to write a memo, referred to as the "fishbowl memo," which set the tone for agency conduct. In it, he said that agency decisions would no longer be made in secret; that his staff would keep records of all their telephone conversations, correspondence, and daily schedules; that these would be publicly available; and that they would ensure that all interested parties (environmental and industry) would have access to the agency's decision makers. One careerist characterized the memo as sending the message "that agency policy would not be dictated by special interests and that the agency was open to everybody." This was a departure from the secrecy that had characterized the agency's decision-making processes during Gorsuch's tenure. It increased the administrator's credibility with both interest groups and agency careerists who had found that Gorsuch-era appointees "held decisions too closely to their chest."

With respect to inclusion, Ruckelshaus restored the agency's traditional operating procedures of soliciting careerists' input into decision making. "Ever since Ruckelshaus came back," said one careerist, "the atmosphere has allowed for frank discussion," discussion that was discouraged during Gorsuch's reign. Moreover, the process by which careerists provide and present information to appointees was reinstated. Careerists attended meetings on a regular basis and no longer felt that all the agency's decisions were being made on the twelfth floor. Careerists felt that channels of communication were restored and that the information they provided was being taken into account by the appointed decision makers. One careerist spoke with glee about again having the "opportunity to meet one-on-one with . . . assistant administrators," opportunities that had been taken for granted before Gorsuch's arrival.

Smaller, symbolic actions by Ruckelshaus are also telling about his approach to running the EPA. One of these was that rather than perpetuating the use of "hit lists," Ruckelshaus promoted one of the people who had been featured on those lists (Dobel 1992).

THE BUREAUCRATIC RESPONSE

How did the EPA's career civil servants react to the changing of the agency's appointed guard? Their response was overwhelmingly favorable. Only one negative comment was reported to me in twenty-one interviews, and even that was only a single specific criticism raised during an hour-and-a-half-long interview from a careerist whose overall assessment of Ruckelshaus was positive.

There was no resistance or dissent reported during this time period, no reported sabotage, whistle-blowing, or foot-dragging (collective or individual). There continued to be leaks from a few quarters, but they were attributed to a few specific individuals like Hugh Kaufman and William Sanjour whose raison d'être had become leaking (Sanjour 1992). There was no leaking by my interviewees, and they reported none among their colleagues at the higher levels of the agency where Ruckelshaus's influence and presence was most felt.

None of the exiters discussed earlier left at this time. Moreover, those who left later, after Ruckelshaus's departure, left for nonpolitical, non-morale-related reasons such as financial compensation.

Finally, voice by argumentation reemerged as a feature of life at the EPA. The access to appointed leadership and the frank and open discussion between and among careerists and appointees that had characterized the agency during the Nixon, Ford, and Carter administrations returned. Careerists in all professions, whether in program or functional offices, felt free to voice their opinions without fear of reprisal. They felt that their perspective and expertise were welcomed and valued by appointees, and therefore they no longer hesitated to exercise their voice.

The predominant behavior at the EPA under Ruckelshaus was cooperation. "After Burford left," there was "cooperation" throughout the agency. The main factor underlying this cooperation was an overwhelming loyalty to William Ruckelshaus. "People wanted to work for him" in a way that most had not wanted to work for Anne Gorsuch. The difference can be viewed as the difference between grudging cooperation and enthusiastic cooperation.

All the civil servants whom I interviewed respected Bill Ruckelshaus and reported that their colleagues shared their sentiments. According to the careerists, he came in with tremendous credibility because of his role in the Saturday night massacre during Watergate. As one noted, he had a "badge of integrity from the Saturday night massacre." The EPA careerists were devoted to him because they felt that he had "restored a sense of dignity and purpose to EPA which had been undermined to a great extent during the Gorsuch era." One careerist described the agency's atmosphere when Ruckelshaus returned as one of "euphoria"; another called it a "honeymoon"; and still another said that "Ruckelshaus was regarded as a savior."

Most civil servants described the Ruckelshaus years by comparing them with Gorsuch's reign. Said one interviewee, "The relationship [between civil servants and appointees] under Gorsuch was horrendous, suspicious, and antagonistic, and almost the complete reverse when Ruckelshaus came back." Morale was "lousy" under Gorsuch and went up "incredibly" when Ruckelshaus came back, said another. "Everything changed when Ruckelshaus came in and brought in new people," added this interviewee. In his tribute to Ruckelshaus, one careerist felt that "once Gorsuch was gone," the agency was "better managed" and "functioned better than it ever did under Carter." Another felt that "for the first term, we really felt like shit because the appointees were constantly haranguing about our competence. That changed when Burford left; those feelings were gone with Ruckelshaus." To illustrate this sentiment, shared overwhelmingly by his peers, one former career official with a propensity toward social science survey research techniques rated the relationship between careerists and the appointees on a scale of 1 to 10. He gave Gorsuch a 1.0 and Ruckelshaus an 8.0.

ANALYSIS

Why were the careerists so happy with Ruckelshaus? Was it policy agreement, return to the status quo, or something else? I believe that it was a mixture of all three.

Certainly there was policy agreement with respect to increasing enforcement activity. One would expect enforcers to want to enforce. The status quo before Reagan had been active enforcement. Thus, here there appears to be an alignment between the appointees' goals and the careerists' preference for the status quo and for more "liberal" policies regarding enforcement.

Risk assessment, on the other hand, represented a marked departure in policy. Yet not one single interviewee complained about it.[23] They appear to have accepted Ruckelshaus's policy despite reservations in some quarters. This acceptance is not surprising, for a number of reasons. First, the careerists felt that their perspective was considered by Ruckelshaus's team of appointees in agency decisions. Second, they felt that decisions were made fairly, not in secret behind closed doors on the twelfth floor, and not with disregard and disrespect for their expertise. Third, and in my view the most significant, professionals at the EPA do not believe that they have all the answers. They accept decisions made by political appointees if they believe that the decisions are made legitimately. Comments made by many interviewees were variations on "career staff recognize that we don't always know the right thing to do" and "long-standing agency policy may be wrong."

My research suggests that creating an atmosphere in which careerists feel that they are part of the process, and treating those careerists with respect even

when issuing directives to them are more important determinants of civil service behavior than policy agreement.

Careerists at the EPA respect the right of appointees to make the decisions
and to set the policy; they are aware that they often lack consensus among
themselves owing to their different professions and perspectives. Hence they
need someone else to weigh the evidence they provide and make the decision.
EPA careerists do not view themselves as ideologues or "tree huggers" but,
rather, as "balancers." Consensus building rather than left-wing environmental
policy is at the heart of their history. They prefer to be given the opportunity to
voice their opinions but lack the hubris to believe that they always know the
right answer.

Ruckelshaus's management technique did not stifle resistance. Instead, it
provided an outlet—participation—that reduced the perception that there was
a need to resist. A handful of people in the agency continued to dissent and to
leak agency deliberations to interest groups, the media, and Congress. Statements made by some of these "career dissenters" such as Hugh Kaufman and
William Sanjour indicate that they view this as their continuing mission irrespective of the administration or administrator (Kriz 1983; Sanjour 1992).
Statements made by their colleagues, however, indicate that they were regarded
as zealous, self-serving self-promoters and outside the agency's mainstream.
For the most part, the experience of EPA under Ruckelshaus was one of trust
and cooperation.

THE THOMAS ERA

William Ruckelshaus resigned shortly after Ronald Reagan's 1984 landslide re-
election. His bruising battle with David Stockman over acid rain had taken its
toll, and he felt that he could leave the EPA feeling that he had achieved his
goals of restoring the agency's credibility with the public and Congress and its
ability to function effectively.

Reagan was thus presented with another opportunity to use the administrative presidency to achieve his policy objectives through the appointment of an
ideologically committed loyalist to head the EPA. Instead, he appointed Lee
Thomas, a man who had devoted much of his career to government service, to
serve as his administrator at the EPA.

REAGAN'S POLICY GOALS AND ADMINISTRATIVE PRESIDENCY
Again, Reagan articulated few concrete proposals for the agency. And again, he
continued to apply some of the tools of the administrative presidency to the

agency while relaxing others. He called for increased funding for research on acid rain (Public Papers, Reagan 1985), and in general, the EPA's budgets continued to climb in the mid 1980s. The résumés of Thomas and the other appointees at the EPA read more like a who's who of people who had served at the EPA under Ruckelshaus in the 1970s than as evidence of the use of strategic appointments. But the OMB, the OIRA, and the vice-president's task force remained firmly in place and continued to block the EPA's initiatives (*National Journal* 1985; Stanfield 1986b).

THOMAS'S MANAGEMENT STYLE

Lee Thomas set out to maintain the course established by his predecessor Bill Ruckelshaus. On the policy side, he set out to "emphasize the continued implementation of the basic programs EPA is responsible for," maintain a strong enforcement presence, improve the agency's scientific and technical capabilities, and improve the EPA's community relations program (U.S. Senate 1985b:20–21). But it was his management style that distinguished him. As the *National Journal* noted, Thomas was more a manager than a policymaker (Stanfield 1986b). He was not a "visionary or a crusader" but, rather, was "first and foremost, a manager" (Stanfield 1986b:391). Careerists reported that his style relied heavily on input from careerists and a careful weighing of the evidence. They felt that while Thomas clearly took their input into account, he also made it clear that he was the ultimate decision maker. He was respected by careerists for the way he considered expertise but then made his own decisions.

BUREAUCRATIC BEHAVIOR

Careerist behavior generally continued on the same keel that had been established during the Ruckelshaus years. Careerists respected Thomas and tried to cooperate with him. No bureaucratic resistance, sabotage, foot-dragging, or whistle-blowing was reported. Voice by argumentation continued in the form of a frank exchange of ideas and arguments that, in turn, Thomas weighed and considered.

There was some exit—I interviewed three people who left between 1985 and 1988. But none of their reasons for leaving had anything at all to do with Lee Thomas or any of the members of his appointed team. None left because of policy disagreement, demoralization, or objections to Thomas's leadership, and none of the resignations could be construed in any way as "resignation in protest." Seasoned careerists did resign during the mid 1980s, but it was to pursue attractive, and often quite lucrative, career alternatives. One wanted a higher private-sector salary as his daughter neared college age. Another just wanted to see what the private sector was like after eighteen years in government, but financial incentives may have played a role in his decision as well. No one I interviewed left without already having a job in hand, unlike one unhappy lawyer who left during Gorsuch's tenure.

Career personnel continued to be frustrated by the OIRA and the vice-president's task force but left the job of challenging them to the appointees.

As during Ruckelshaus's reign, cooperation best characterized the agency's behavior and was directly attributed to loyalty to and respect for Lee Thomas and his ability as a manager. The EPA attorney with the penchant for utilizing survey research rated the Thomas years as an 8.5, half a point higher even than the Ruckelshaus years. Careerists continued to feel that their agency was better managed than it had ever been and that it was in the hands of a competent leader.

ANALYSIS

Overall, the same explanations apply to the Thomas years as apply to Ruckelshaus's rule at the EPA. Careerists of all professional stripes—managers, lawyers, scientists, economists—respected Lee Thomas. They viewed him as competent and as an outstanding manager. They felt that their expertise was taken into account in the decision-making process, and they accepted Thomas's authority to make the final decisions.

The extent of policy agreement between appointees and careerists varied during this time. Issues such as acid rain lingered, and old issues such as emissions trading, over which the careerists lacked consensus, reemerged. But none of this resulted in attempts to sabotage, or even resist, the appointees or the president.

Overall, Thomas's stewardship—his balanced approach, his nonideological nature, his lack of extremism, and his caution (like Ruckelshaus's)—was well suited to the preferences of EPA careerists. EPA careerists view themselves as balancers who strive for internal consensus even if that means slow decision making.

As a result of historical patterns of recruitment and promotion as well as their own personal predilections, upper-level EPA careerists are neither zealots nor ideologues. Nor are they knee-jerk budget maximizers. Instead, they take pride in their work and in their agency and respond to appointed leadership that treats them with respect and includes them in the process. But they also recognize and accept the legitimacy of appointed leadership—at least when they view that leadership as competent and fair.

Comparing the Two Reagan Administrations at EPA

This analysis focuses on four factors that contribute to our understanding of the high level of cooperation that occurred at the EPA. Two explain the cooperative behavior during the Gorsuch period. The third sheds light on cooperative behavior across appointees. And the fourth allows us to compare the contrasting experiences resulting from the tenures of Gorsuch, Ruckelshaus, and Thomas at the EPA.

The management techniques used by Reagan's appointees at EPA played a major role in helping stifle dissent. To some extent, this was achieved by removing discretion and autonomy from bureaucrats and conducting much of the agency's work "upstairs on the twelfth floor." To a great extent, it was achieved by creating an atmosphere throughout the agency, but especially in the Office of Enforcement, that altered the way EPA careerists perceived their self-interest. The hit lists, retreats, and dress codes instituted by lower-level appointees promoted a narrow view of the path to career advancement. This was the case because these lower-level appointees, although often lacking experience or expertise, held key supervisory positions in each division and office of the agency and so controlled salaries, promotions, transfers, and challenging work assignments. Thus, the path to career advancement lay in ingratiating oneself to the agency's appointees, and this was the path that many at the EPA chose to follow.

Although these management techniques removed opportunities and incentives for resistance, the absence of resistance is also explained, in part, by bureaucratic attitudes. Most careerists at EPA simply did not see a need to resist. In trying to get a sense of how they reacted to the Reagan administration, I found that whatever their home base of operations, career civil servants tended to defend their own office and point the finger elsewhere. Careerist after careerist reported that "I was lucky because Bennett was very good"; "Mobile Sources did OK; we weren't hit too hard"; "We weren't hurt so badly"; "My program was not high profile, so we were fortunate." And they added, "It was the Enforcement people who had it hard"; "It was especially bad in Enforcement"; "The leaks were in Superfund, not here." In short, the careerists reported that although the agency had been under siege for three years, their part of the agency had not been at the center of the storm.

The people I interviewed did not resist because they did not feel besieged. From their point of view, the problems lay elsewhere in the agency, outside their domain. They simply did not perceive a compelling reason to deviate from their cooperative behavior. This suggests that it takes a lot to upset career bureaucrats, at least at the upper levels of the EPA. The civil servants there were willing to endure a great deal before they were moved to protest or resign. They were open-minded about their office's policy direction and flexible in adapting to a variety of appointed managers. In short, the careerists at EPA did not react more strongly in part because they did not think that things were so bad as to require drastic action. This further suggests that if EPA appointees had been more "competent," they could have enlisted the bureaucrats to enact the policy changes that the administration desired. It also suggests that bureaucrats do not automatically regard all appointees and all policy change with hostility. And it suggests an agency culture that is flexible and not overly driven by ideology.

The role perception shared by EPA careerists also limited resistance and fostered cooperation across professions and during all three periods examined in this chapter. As the comments presented in this chapter's discussion of loyalty make clear, EPA careerists did not believe that most forms of resistance were ethical. They shared a common view regarding the role of career civil servants vis-à-vis presidential appointees. And they adhered to that view even when it meant being loyal to policies or appointees whose value or competence they questioned.

Finally, the careerists cooperated with Ruckelshaus and Thomas because they wanted to—because of the charisma, leadership skills, and integrity these men brought to their job. Comparing this time period with that of Gorsuch suggests that the career bureaucrats at EPA would probably have cooperated irrespective of the specific appointees who headed their agency. But their cooperation during Ruckelshaus's and Thomas's tenures had an enthusiasm that was missing from the first three years of the Reagan administration. Thus the critical factor was not ideology or policy goals but the appointed leadership. When EPA's three administrators are compared, it appears that although the agency's personnel behaved the same throughout the Reagan years, they did so with widely varying degrees of enthusiasm. In essence, careerists changed the tempo of their song, though not the song itself, when Anne Gorsuch resigned from their agency. Their tune went from a slow dirge (or, in the case of the Office of Enforcement, a wail) during the Gorsuch years to a whistle when Ruckelshaus and Thomas ran their agency, although their behavior remained consistently cooperative throughout the Reagan years.

As Derthick (1990) points out in her study of the Social Security Administration, it may not seem very serious if federal agencies are ill served by the workings of American government because these agencies exist to serve the political system and not vice versa. The same applies to the morale of their personnel. The purpose of our political system is not to make unelected civil servants happy. Nonetheless, this chapter indicates that there may be two roads to compliance. And if one is able to achieve the same ends with greater job satisfaction and better policy deliberation, then it is at least worth considering adopting the means (i.e., the management style) used by Ruckelshaus and Thomas rather than those used by Gorsuch and her team of strategic appointees.

Summary

Since this chapter is considerably longer than the others in this book, and since the story of what happened at the EPA is somewhat more complex than those of the other agencies, it may be useful to recap some of the main empirical and analytic points presented here.

- Careerists cooperate regardless of their attitudes toward political appointees, but appointees greatly affect careerists' job satisfaction and morale.
- Appointees can use micromanagement strategies to create an atmosphere of apprehension among careerists, which causes them to focus on protecting their careers. Or, appointees can use a more open management style. Neither management style results in resistance, as bureaucrats are cooperative under both styles. The more open style, however, does have a markedly positive effect on job satisfaction and morale, whereas the Gorsuch-style approach has the opposite effect.
- Attitudes are not necessarily translated into behavior. Even those in the Enforcement Division who hated the appointees in their section, as well as those throughout the EPA who viewed Gorsuch with hostility, did not act on their opinions.
- Despite the media's portrayal of the EPA as an agency under siege during the Reagan years, many high-ranking career civil servants did not view their plight in such dire terms. Not only did they view resistance as inappropriate, but for the most part they did not perceive their situation as calling for resistance. At least at the upper levels, the EPA seems to have a rather laissez-faire and tolerant culture, not an overly ideological or zealous one.
- The high-ranking civil servants examined here responded to the Reagan administration—during the Gorsuch years in particular—strategically rather than ideologically. They acted out of self-interest, out of concern

for their careers, which in this case meant trying to avoid activity that could be perceived as a cause for placement on the hit lists, black marks in the green books, or transfer and demotion. They did not act ideologically because they did not consider themselves ideologues. This was partly a legacy of the agency's history and culture that fosters consensus building and promotes those who try to balance environmental and industry perspectives.

- Unlike the other agencies, the EPA had a small cadre of active whistle-blowers. These whistle-blowers worked in the lower professional levels of the agency rather than in its top management ranks. They were considered mavericks and viewed with disdain by their colleagues who felt that they hurt the agency's image. In addition, they made the jobs of those who were cooperating more difficult by increasing the distrust with which appointees viewed careerists.

- The behavior of these whistle-blowers is best understood in the context of individual-level ideology and agency-level history and culture. Whistle-blowers are more likely to be zealots, and their zealotry is both a cause and an effect of their resistance. At least in the case of the EPA, environmental zealotry was likely to slow career advancement. Aborted careers, in turn, were likely to be a source of frustration and discontent. The resistant behavior of environmental extremists, then, was based on both their disapproval of the agency's policy direction and their lack of loyalty to the agency, which resulted from their dissatisfaction with their own personal career advancement.

- Finally, this case study of the EPA confirms my initial hypothesis that not all bureaucrats are alike. Their behavior and its motivations are complex. The EPA during the Reagan years reveals some of this complexity. For example, this chapter has confirmed that bureaucratic behavior is significantly conditioned by the managerial tactics of political appointees. In addition, being able to identify those persons who could be classified as zealots and those who were preoccupied with protecting their careers supports my contention that depending on how they define their self-interest, careerists may react differently to the same conditions.[24] The behavior of EPA's careerists thus calls into question rational-choice models of bureaucratic behavior which, although parsimonious, fail to capture other equally prominent motivations (but see Downs 1967). Generalizing too broadly, as rational-choice theorists are inclined to do, causes scholars to miss many of the factors that motivate civil servants, which can lead to ill-conceived prescriptions regarding how best to enlist bureaucratic compliance.

CHAPTER 7

LESSONS FROM THE REAGAN YEARS

At the outset of this book, I posed two questions: How did upper-level career civil servants react to President Ronald Reagan's attempt to redirect policy and increase presidential control over the bureaucracy, and why? Having examined the experiences of civil servants at the Food and Nutrition Service (FNS), the National Highway Traffic Safety Administration (NHTSA), the Civil Rights Division (CRD), and the Environmental Protection Agency (EPA), we are now in a position to answer these questions. Furthermore, we will consider the implications of these answers.

The answers are reassuring with respect to bureaucratic responsiveness but less so with respect to policy deliberation. And they should give pause both to defenders of bureaucracy, who fail to sufficiently acknowledge bureaucratic self-interest and caution, and to critics of bureaucracy, who see only self-interest.

How Do Real Bureaucrats Deal with Real Politicians?

The answer to the first question, how did upper-level career civil servants react to Reagan's administrative presidency, is clear. Even under the most extreme circumstances, with a president attempting to turn agency policy 180 degrees from its past, career civil servants were, for the most part, responsive to this change in elected leadership. There were few attempts to sabotage the president or derail his policies. The lesson from the Reagan years is that, at least under the conditions of the administrative presidency and at the upper echelons of federal agencies, presidents can expect a fairly high degree of responsiveness from the career bureaucrats in the executive branch.[1]

This is not to say, however, that responsiveness was the only, or the universal, response to the Reagan administration.[2] As I stated at the outset of this book, and as the exit, voice, loyalty, and neglect (EVLN) framework reveals, neither/nor (neither all responsive nor all resistant) better depicts bureaucratic behavior than does either/or (either all responsive or all resistant). As the following agency-by-agency review indicates, although compliance was the predominant response, bureaucratic behavior varied both within and across agencies. This finding may not result in a parsimonious theory or allow for the development of deductive models, but it better captures the vagaries of real bureaucrats dealing with real politicians.

The National Highway Traffic Administration

Little behavior at the National Highway Traffic Safety Administration could be classified as resistant. As a whole, NHTSA careerists exhibited little voice of any type, and minimal exit. Instead, cooperation was the prevalent behavior. Cooperation at NHTSA is best described by two remarks reported to me: "Career staff are here to do the job we're told to do. . . . It's up to the elected officials to decide what they want done" and "You kept your mouth shut and your head low to keep your job." Bureaucrats at NHTSA cooperated with the Reagan administration and did not express dissent with, or attempt to derail, its policy agenda. Moreover, most careerists behaved in a similar fashion; there were no factions at NHTSA that stood apart.

The Food and Nutrition Service

The Food and Nutrition Service also exhibited little behavior that could be classified as recalcitrant. As in the case of NHTSA, there was little exit and minimal voice in any form; leaking, whistle-blowing, voice by argumentation, collective action, and sabotage were very rare. Here, too, careerist behavior across the board was overwhelmingly compliant. In fact, career civil servants at FNS played little role in agency policymaking during this time, as many agency tasks were handled by Reagan's appointees or outside consultants. Moreover, it was these appointees and consultants who were the primary instigators of the leaking and sabotage in the agency. Once again, typical descriptions of bureaucratic behavior during the Reagan years were, "I wasn't happy but, to be frank, I'm not a zealot and I did what I was told to do;" "Folks here are straight shooters—not leakers or saboteurs;" and "Career bureaucrats realize they work for the Administration. You go through these changes and you've got to adapt to them."

THE CIVIL RIGHTS DIVISION

The Civil Rights Division differed markedly from the other cases in the behavior of its bureaucrats during the Reagan years. This difference, however, was limited to two types of behavior—exit and voice by argumentation. At CRD, as at the other agencies, leaking, sabotage, and whistle-blowing were explicitly frowned upon and rare; following the directives of political superiors was the norm. The CRD differed from the other three agencies, however, in the extent to which career attorneys challenged and argued with presidential appointees before complying with them. This agency also differed in the amount of turnover it experienced during the eight years of the Reagan administration. At CRD, behavior followed a pattern; that is, there was a "typical" CRD response to the Reagan administration. That typical response included voice by argumentation, followed by exit or the consideration of exit. But the typical response also included a high degree of responsiveness to political appointees in the postdecisional environment. This responsiveness took the form of presenting the strongest case possible to the courts, even when civil servants did not personally support the administration's position in the case.

THE ENVIRONMENTAL PROTECTION AGENCY

Two things distinguish careerist behavior in the Environmental Protection Agency. The first is the change in behavior, or at least the change in the motivations that underlay the behavior, that came with the change in appointees in 1983. The second is that not all of the careerists behaved alike. A group of "mavericks" strenuously resisted the Reagan administration and its policies. They repeatedly leaked and blew the whistle. But the remainder, and majority, of EPA careerists cooperated with all three Reagan-appointed administrators through a mixture of loyalty and neglect.

This cooperation resulted from different factors during different time periods, depending on who was in charge of the agency. During the Gorsuch era, cooperation was the result of the civil servants' ethical standards. The EPA careerists believed that their job was to "do the right thing" and that the right thing, during the Reagan years, was to obey the marching orders of the president and his appointed deputies despite any personal misgivings about the direction of the agency's policy or the caliber of the agency's leadership. Cooperation was also the result of the appointees' management techniques which made resistance difficult. During the Ruckelshaus and Thomas eras, civil servants cooperated with the administration out of respect for their appointed bosses. They also cooperated because the agency's leadership engendered good will through their own attitudes and behavior—a management style that contrasted with that employed during Gorsuch's tenure.

In sum, the research presented in this book and summarized here suggests that upper-level career civil servants are more responsive than resistant to the president and his appointed deputies. The implications of this finding will be discussed later in this chapter. For now, it is sufficient to note that these findings are consistent with much recent scholarship about democratic control of bureaucracy (see e.g., Brehm and Gates 1997; Weingast and Moran 1982, 1983; Wood 1988; Wood and Waterman 1991, 1994). It is also important to note, however, that some recent research contradicts these findings, documenting pockets of resistance in federal agencies (see e.g., Holt 1998; Mezey 1988; O'Leary 1994, 1995, 1999, forthcoming).

The next section enables us to reconcile my findings with those of other scholars working in this area. I argue that bureaucratic behavior is a function of a constellation of conditions or factors. In the cases examined in this book, this constellation of factors worked in tandem to ensure responsiveness. But in other cases, these conditions varied, resulting in different behavior.[3]

As the discussion that follows details, bureaucrats cooperate both when the administrative presidency coerces them to do so and when they are imbued with a sense of duty. They resist when professional norms or personal zealotry compel them to do so, and when they are new to an agency and have not yet been socialized into its norms.[4] And their agency's historical legacy and culture can either facilitate or discourage that resistance, depending on whether or not that agency experience emboldens or "meekens" career bureaucrats.

WHAT MOTIVATES US IN OUR CAREERS IN ORGANIZATIONS?

The second question posed at the beginning of this book was *why* do career civil servants behave the way they do: In this case, why did they react to the Reagan administration in the way they did? In chapter 2, I hypothesized that three sets of factors—operating at the individual, agency, and principal-agent levels—would all play a role in shaping bureaucratic behavior. This hypothesis was born out in each of the four agencies examined. Self-interest, role perception, agency context (especially the agency's historical legacy and professional composition), and the administrative presidency all played significant roles in determining how upper-level civil servants reacted to Ronald Reagan's presidency.

The following factor-by-factor review illuminates the role played by each of these factors. One factor, role perception, fostered cooperation. Two factors—the actions taken under the banner of the administrative presidency, and bureaucratic self-interest—discouraged resistance more than they actively promoted cooperation. And the fourth, agency context, facilitated or inhibited resistance, depending on the particular constellation of subfactors—ideology, professional composition, history, and the extent of its esprit de corps—that characterized the agency.

FOSTERING COOPERATION

ROLE PERCEPTION

The case material presented in this book has established that career civil servants are motivated, at least in part, by their role perception, and that this role perception leads them to cooperate with their appointed principals in the executive branch. As discussed in chapter 2, role perception refers to civil servants' view of their position in the political system, their sense of duty, and the code of conduct by which they are bound.[5]

Cooperation was fostered and resistance was restrained by this role perception in all four agencies studied. Careerists were unwavering in their contention that their role was to present information to political appointees, to let the appointees make the decision, and then to carry out the president's or the appointee's directives. They explicitly argued that this internal code of conduct kept them from engaging in most resistant behavior and limited their available avenues of protest. Typical of this philosophy were these two comments from careerists at EPA and FNS: "If they want policy changed and it's not outside the law and morality, you have a responsibility to assist them in implementing policies," and "Once you have explained the implications as you see them, you have got to carry out the policy to the best of your ability." Thus, for almost all the civil servants in this study, their role perception prevented them from leaking, yelling, lying, or cheating—regardless of whether or not they liked or agreed with Reagan, his appointees, or his policy goals.

Establishing role perception as a major determinant of bureaucratic behavior does not mean that politics can be separated from administration as Woodrow Wilson envisioned (Wilson 1887). The comments of the civil servants I interviewed show that they *believe* they can draw a line between presenting information to appointees and executing a presidential directive. This does not mean that they always succeed in doing so. But it does mean that they are guided and constrained in their behavior by their attempt to adhere to this standard.

Moreover, as I have argued throughout this book, bureaucratic behavior is complex and nuanced. Even the existence of this ethic does not produce uniformly compliant behavior. No one factor, role perception included, can explain all bureaucratic behavior at all times. The way that high-ranking civil servants view their relationship with political appointees and their role in the political system tempers their actions, but it is not the only condition influencing them.

However, the fact that career civil servants are self-conscious about their unelected status and act accordingly means that their motives cannot be reduced solely to economic ones. "Rational choice theorists who discount the possibility of public-spirited behavior are wrong" (DiIulio 1994:277). Rather, both scholars and politicians would be well advised to acknowledge the role played by principled motives and norms as shapers of bureaucratic behavior, to further explore their (psychological and sociological) origins, and to consider what steps can be taken to cultivate rather than deprecate these "inner checks."[6] This does not mean that presidents should abandon the administrative presidency and rely solely on civil servants' role perception. But it does mean that they should at least contemplate what can be done to encourage the latter.

Constraining Bureaucratic Resistance

Because role perception is a proactive condition, I contend that it *fosters* responsiveness. Other conditions produce responsiveness by *discouraging* other types of behavior. Still others limit resistance by making it difficult, if not impossible, to resist, for example by denying civil servants access to decision-making situations or by appropriating their resources. The way the administrative presidency was applied during the Reagan administration (particularly the use of strategic appointees and their micromanagement techniques) reduced resistance in both ways—by introducing disincentives to resistance and by removing opportunities for resistance.

THE ADMINISTRATIVE PRESIDENCY

As discussed in chapter 1, the administrative presidency employs many tools in its efforts to bring the bureaucracy to heel. It is clear from the case studies presented in chapters 3 through 6 that it was the presence of strategic political appointees that most directly colored civil servants' perceptions of the Reagan administration. Two features of Reagan's use of strategic appointments stand out as having had the most bearing on bureaucratic behavior: the large number of appointees, and their micromanagement techniques.

The large number of lower-level Schedule C appointees and special assistants appointed by the Reagan administration enabled the administration to bypass high-level career civil servants. At the CRD, FNS, and EPA, these low-level appointees provided the administration with a sufficient presence to carry out much of the work traditionally delegated to these civil servants. At the CRD, there were enough appointees to handle a large portion of the agency's case load without having to rely on career attorneys. At the EPA, regulations were drafted in the administrator's office "upstairs" rather than in the media offices with substantive jurisdiction for the policy area where regulations had traditionally been prepared. At the FNS, policymaking was centralized in an "inner sanctum" or contracted out.

The impact of the large number of appointees was magnified by the micromanagement techniques they employed. These techniques both removed opportunities for resistance and made it more difficult to resist even when opportunities were present. Examples of micromanagement techniques and appointee management style abound in the case studies we examined. Anne Gorsuch's reorganization of the Enforcement Division at the EPA serves as a prime example. Here the work of the unit was so frequently disrupted by changes in job titles and office space that careerists were unable to focus on the unit's work product, let alone mount a coordinated resistance effort.[7]

Exclusion from meetings, also particularly prevalent at EPA, removed careerists from the decision-making process. At the CRD, the court cases on the agency's docket were taken away from the careerists and prepared and argued by political appointees. At the FNS, appointees contracted out the writing of a major regulation to an outside consultant. At NHTSA, rather than vetoing proposed regulations outright, appointees perpetually remanded them to lower levels of the agency for further refinement.

Finally, management techniques such as transferring high-ranking career personnel, demoting them, and placing them on hit lists, decreased the number of opportunities for resistance.[8] This was especially common at the EPA, where troublemaking personnel were reassigned to windowless rooms in distant cities with no meaningful work assignments.

When civil servants were excluded from meetings or taken off cases, or their responsibilities were reassigned to appointees, their opportunities for resistance were cut back as well. You cannot leak information if you do not attend the meetings at which leak-worthy information is disseminated; you cannot sabotage a case if you are not the attorney representing the agency in court; and you cannot sneak through a regulation if that regulation has been rewritten, line by line, by political appointees.

In addition as we will see next, the administrative presidency changed the way that bureaucrats calculated their self-interest. It did so in two ways. First, it created an atmosphere in which civil servants were preoccupied with protecting their careers; thus they focused more on self-interest that they had in the past. Second, under Reagan's administrative presidency, self-interested behavior was compliant behavior. It did not pay to protect agency budgets, turf, or policies, but it did pay to comply with the Reagan appointees even though that meant cutting budgets and gutting programs.

Whatever one's normative view of the administrative presidency, at least during the Reagan years it was quite successful at bringing bureaucrats to heel. The principals, not the agents, ran the show during this time period (but see Brehm and Gates 1997). Thus, the administrative presidency, the deployment and management style of political appointees in particular, is a critical determinant of bureaucratic behavior and one that increased responsiveness.

SELF-INTEREST

As discussed in chapter 2, there is considerable debate among scholars regarding the extent to which political man is best characterized as economic man. By that I mean the extent to which political actors are "self-absorbed individuals promoting their own interests" (Campbell and Wilson 1995:304). In addition, rational choice scholars who study the bureaucracy argue that bureaucrats seek to shirk work and maximize their agencies' budgets. Critics of the economic or rational choice approach point to the large amount of public-spirited and principled behavior in federal agencies and elsewhere in the political system (see e.g., DiIulio 1994; Kelman 1987; Rom 1996).

This study has already established that altruism does indeed play a role in accounting for bureaucratic behavior. However, in reviewing the four cases, it is equally clear that self-interest played a role as well. As documented in the previous chapters, bureaucrats were, for the most part, compliant, even cautious and timid, during the Reagan years. Rather than defending agency policy, maximizing their budgets, or speaking truth to power, many of the career civil servants I studied "went along to get along." One of the reasons why this was the case turns out to be that it was in their self-interest to do so.

Career bureaucrats cooperated rather than resisted because they feared for their jobs, wanted to avoid the wrath of their appointed bosses, did not want to be demoted or banished, and sought to advance their careers. In other words, some of the bureaucrats in this study behaved much like Down's (1967) climbers and conservers.

In each agency, the responses of some of the civil servants interviewed reveal that they cooperated to protect their jobs.[9] We saw in each of the case studies (albeit to varying degrees) that exit was limited by the lack of job availability outside the federal government. Since many civil servants did not feel confident in their ability to find new jobs, it was very important to them to retain their current ones. Yet when they looked around them, they saw their colleagues being fired, demoted, and transferred. This was especially the case at the FNS, where two prominent members of the career Senior Executive Service (SES) were demoted, and at the EPA where Reagan appointees circulated a hit list of targeted civil servants. Careerists in these agencies became quite concerned with avoiding the fates of their colleagues who had been transferred, reassigned, demoted, or fired. They adopted behavior designed to avoid raising the ire of political appointees, drawing attention to themselves, or raising suspicion regarding their partisan or ideological loyalties. Given the prevailing political climate, this meant that careerists perceived it to be in their self-interest to distance themselves from liberalism, the Carter administration, existing agency policies, and large budget requests. As a result, these careerists were loath to voice objections to policy change or to take action to defend previous agency policy.

Another group of careerists also cooperated out of self-interest, but in their case their goal was career advancement rather than simply job security. These careerists chose to hitch their wagons to the rising stars and, at least during the early Reagan years, those stars included the likes of Ray Peck and Rita Lavelle. Thus, in spite of the fact that the goals of these appointees deviated considerably from existing agency policy and entailed shrinking the agency's role rather than expanding it, higher civil servants found it to be in their self-interest to support both budget cuts and changes in agency policy. Under the administrative presidency, career advancement went hand in hand with responsiveness.

In analyzing these findings, it becomes clear that bureaucrats complied with the Reagan appointees in their agencies in part because those appointees created a system of incentives that made it in their self-interest to do so. In other words, bureaucrats' inclination to act self-interestedly was abetted by the behavior of the political appointees. Under a different incentive system, one that rewarded speaking truth to power for example, we might have seen more public-spirited behavior than we did. Moreover, the direction that self-interested

behavior took was also a function of the incentives devised by those appointees. Under the administrative presidency, self-interest resulted in cooperation, not resistance; budget-cutting, not budget maximization; and policy
change, not policy defense. In short, the administrative presidency appealed to
bureaucrats' self-interest rather than their public spirit. It encouraged them to
focus on job security rather than principle. In fact, the blame, if there is any, for
both the extent and direction of self-interest, lies as much with the behavior of
the political appointees (i.e., the principals) as with the bureaucrats' lack of
principle. Given the situation they found themselves in, it is difficult to blame
these bureaucrats for "going along to get along."

However, it is also important not to lose sight of the fact that self-interest
was only part of the story during the Reagan years. Although some career bureaucrats acted out of self-interest some of the time, self-interest was by no
means the only determinant of bureaucratic behavior during the Reagan years.
As this chapter has already established, self-interest existed side by side with
more altruistic motivations and competed with civil servants' internal codes of
conduct. Frequently, it was the organizational context in which this competition took place that determined which motives and what type of behavior prevailed. It is to this agency setting to which we now turn.

Seeds of Resistance or Responsiveness

The research presented in this book has established that bureaucrats were primarily compliant during the Reagan years. Thus far in this chapter, I have presented three factors (role perception, the administrative presidency, and self-
interest) that help us to understand why. But, as I also noted, not all
bureaucrats were as compliant as the majority. There was some resistance in
two of the agencies I studied. Examining the internal dynamics of these agencies sheds light on this variation. Federal agencies—the organizations in which
bureaucrats work—shape bureaucrats' worldview and help us to understand
their differing reactions to the same stimulus.

AGENCY CONTEXT

Although not every member of a given agency behaved in precisely the same
manner or for exactly the same reasons, there was an overall and discernible
pattern of exit, voice, loyalty, and neglect in each agency. At the Civil Rights Division, most, though not all, career attorneys exercised voice by argumentation,
and a sizable faction, especially in the Special Litigation Section, employed the
exit response. At NHTSA, most careerists saw little need or felt ill equipped to
resist. At FNS, almost all careerists tried to tiptoe around political appointees

and went along with their decisions and actions. And at the EPA there were two dominant patterns of behavior: cooperation by the majority and resistance by a vocal minority. What is striking here is both the similarity of behavior within a given agency and the differences among the four agencies. The agency setting colored the way civil servants perceived their situation during the Reagan years and determined the range of options they considered in response. Agency history, the presence or absence of agency esprit de corps, and the agency's professional and ideological makeup, all shaped the manner in which bureaucrats in different agencies reacted to Reagan's initiatives.

These findings should not be interpreted to mean that all agencies are different. Rather, they mean that only some agencies—those with a history of success, with a great deal of internal cohesion, and with certain professional characteristics—will produce civil servants confident enough to challenge their political principals, whereas civil servants in agencies lacking in internal consensus and confidence will be much less apt to resist presidential control efforts.

Agency History

As discussed in chapter 2, civil servants learn lessons from their past, especially from their past experiences with their external environment. These experiences become a significant part of the agency's culture. Prior experiences can be positive or negative (Schein 1992), and such experiences clearly bear on the type of behavior exhibited during the Reagan years. Past experiences led careerists at CRD to exercise voice and exit, and those at FNS and NHTSA to cower. They led some at EPA to blow the whistle on their agency and others within EPA to express disdain for their colleagues' behavior.

NHTSA offers a good example of the relevance of an agency's historical legacy. NHTSA had a rocky history with respect to its dealings with its external environment. In the past, its regulations had encountered considerable resistance from Congress, the public, and the courts (Foreman 1988; Graham 1989; Kennedy School 1986b; Mashaw and Harfst 1990b; interviews). Its attempt to issue a regulation requiring automatic ignition interlock systems met with great public outrage and a subsequent legislative veto of the rule. The courts had overturned or remanded a number of NHTSA rules, including its first attempt to issue a passive restraint (air-bag) rule (Mashaw and Harfst 1990b). That court decision was only one of many negative encounters with the agency's environment during the two-decade-long debate over air bags, a debate spanning most of the agency's history. Finally, in 1981, NHTSA was "on the rebound" from its most activist administrator, Carter-appointed Joan Claybrook, who had left the agency "spent" and exhausted (interviews). These experiences produced caution at NHTSA. Civil servants were wary of doing anything that might provoke more adverse publicity for their agency. In addition, having few prior successes to tout to the Reagan appointees, their overriding goal was to avoid future failures. This agency history was one of the factors that made resistance unlikely.

A similar tale can be told at the FNS. As we saw in chapter 4, FNS policy had changed with each change in administration since its founding. It had shifted back and forth between an activist role and a narrowly defined one. It had been buffeted by presidential-congressional disputes in which the agency found itself caught in the middle. This history produced a cautious agency peopled by civil servants who lacked clear convictions regarding the "right" policy. Nothing in the agency's history had given it the prestige or confidence to resist, nor did it have a strong source of external support. At FNS, prior agency experiences were one more factor pointing in the direction of compliance.

The Civil Rights Division's history provides a sharp contrast. Entering the 1980s, CRD's history had been one of unmitigated success. CRD careerists took tremendous pride in their work and accomplishments, as well as in the fact that many had been hired to work at CRD as part of the Justice Department's "honors program." The Division entered the 1980s with an impeccable record in court. Not only did the agency rarely suffer defeat, but it had won major court victories in the areas of voting rights and school desegregation. It had also, shortly before Reagan's electoral victory, been instrumental in obtaining important legislation from Congress pertaining to the rights of institutionalized persons.

These experiences led careerists at CRD to be more loyal to the existing body of civil rights case law, the precedents that they had worked so hard to set, than to a new administration bent on overturning those precedents. CRD careerists were committed to their past victories, not because they believed in the status quo, as many scholars claim, but because they felt that the courts' support of their positions made them important to defend. In addition, the agency's previous encounters with its external environment, including the interest group community, had been positive ones, providing careerists with the confidence to challenge presidential appointees.

The EPA's history helps us sort out its two-tiered behavior. In this case, the most important facet of its history is the type of people who were initially attracted to, and hired by, the agency in the 1970s. As discussed in chapter 6, when the agency was created in 1970 it attracted a cohort of zealots drawn to the agency by its potential for advocacy for the budding environmental movement and a cadre of ambitious career civil servants who joined EPA from other federal agencies because they were drawn by the opportunities for responsibility and career advancement afforded by the young and growing agency. Over time most of the zealots left the EPA, frustrated by what was, from their perspective, the agency's lack of zealotry and its slow pace. However, some remained, although they were rarely promoted to top agency positions. At the same time, the ambitious "climbers" advanced rapidly through the organization and by 1980 many of them held important positions. The remaining zealots were responsible for the leaking and whistle-blowing at EPA, while the climbers chose the path of loyalty. Thus at EPA, the legacy of the agency's early years was its personnel. This facet of its history led to both cooperative and resistant behaviors.

In sum, one determinant of bureaucratic behavior is the agency's history. Whether these earlier experiences left a legacy of success or failure, pride or humiliation, cohesion or disengagement, needs to be factored into any equation predicting what will happen in the present or the future. Thus, the argument presented here is that an agency's historical legacy affects the way in which its current crop of civil servants will behave. Whereas some types of legacies lead to cooperative behavior vis-à-vis the president, others lead to more resistant behavior.

Agency Esprit de Corps
An agency's esprit de corps or sense of camaraderie—what Meier (1993) calls cohesion—is also part of its culture. The portrait that emerges from the interviews conducted at two of the agencies is of organizations lacking a highly developed sense of esprit. NHTSA lacked a strong esprit de corps because of the agency's organizational structure and professional divisions (Mashaw and Harfst 1990a). At FNS, the underlying cause seems to be a lack of strong leadership in the past. The agency never regained the cohesion it lost between 1968 and 1972 when it simultaneously lost policy discretion and autonomy to Congress and key agency personnel to retirement (Berry 1984). As a result, both agencies lacked the strong sense of esprit de corps needed to ignite a resistance movement.

The story at EPA is one of gradually eroding esprit. The Reagan administration took over the agency at a critical juncture in its history. EPA careerists had traditionally shared a high level of esprit de corps. Most careerists had joined the agency at the same time and for many of the same reasons and had worked closely together during the 1970s. However, by the 1980s, careerists felt that their agency had grown too large to maintain that sense of esprit. It had grown too big for shared lunches "down by the waterfront" and for shared softball games. Its size diminished the amount of cohesion possible. Thus, when the Reagan appointees joined the agency, it no longer had the type of agency cohesion necessary to foster resistance.

Once again, the CRD provides a different tale. All but one interviewee at CRD commented on the agency's strong sense of camaraderie. Careerists share a strong commitment to civil rights and civil rights law. Prior to the Reagan administration, that commitment to civil rights was further cultivated by management inside the agency. In addition, many interviewees referred to the intense bonding experiences that occur during months spent "on the road" with fellow CRD attorneys during the trial portion of cases, most of which are tried outside of Washington, primarily in the southern states. Moreover, prior to the Reagan years, CRD personnel had socialized together outside the workplace, further fostering their sense of camaraderie. This set of circumstances distinguished CRD from the other three agencies and increased its likelihood of engaging in resistance. Careerists at CRD believed in their work and had the support of their colleagues that they were "doing the right thing."

In sum, the extent to which an agency's upper echelon civil servants share or lack a sense of cohesion, camaraderie, and esprit de corps played a pivotal role in careerist behavior in all four agencies. In three agencies, it is an additional factor that reduced the likelihood of resistance. In the fourth, it supported resistance and gave civil servants the girder to engage in spirited debate with presidential appointees.

Profession

Two facets of agency profession are relevant to our understanding of bureaucratic reactions to the Reagan administration. One is the type of professionals employed within an agency. The second is the mix of professions. The manner in which these two facets of agency profession manifest themselves will become clear in our analysis of the different agencies.

The Civil Rights Division differed from other agencies on both these counts. First, it was populated exclusively by *attorneys*. Moreover, these attorneys were both trial lawyers and civil rights lawyers. Their legal training and on-the-job experience had prepared them for verbal and written combat. Recall from chapter 5 the interviewee who claimed that "one thing lawyers like to do is argue." The CRD had a cadre of professionals trained for voice by argumentation. They also possessed a credential that facilitated employment outside the agency. Secondly, CRD was populated *exclusively* by attorneys. There were no competing professions bringing different training and attitudes to the agency.

Careerists did not have to cross professional lines to join forces; all shared a common language and training. Because all careerists were attorneys, the agency did not have any internal organizational divisions based on different professions, nor did the agency have a history of policy disputes between professions. Careerists also shared their profession with the appointees in their agency, further facilitating healthy debate within professional boundaries.

None of the other agencies had these features. Each had some attorneys, but attorneys were not the majority of personnel in any of them. In the division within EPA where attorneys predominated (the Office of Enforcement), we did see some of the behaviors found at CRD—an increase in exit, in particular—albeit on a smaller scale. Other professions—such as NHTSA's engineers—were much less inclined to exercise their voice. Their view of their job was also based on their professional training. But that training led them to view their job as loyally presenting scientific evidence on which others—namely political appointees—would base their decisions.

However, it was not only the absence of lawyers that limited exit and voice in the other three cases. The other way in which these agencies differ from CRD is that each of the other agencies is best characterized as a professional melting pot. NHTSA has attorneys, economists, automotive engineers, highway safety engineers, and psychologists. FNS has nutritionists, industrial psychologists, and many generalists. And the EPA has attorneys, economists, and a wide spectrum of different types of scientists and engineers. Without a dominant or exclusive profession, professional divisions internal to these agencies have historically been replicated in organizational divisions and divisions over policy. Organizational lines based on profession have isolated professions from each other and pitted them against each other (see, e.g., Mashaw and Harfst 1990a,b). Each of these agencies has experienced organizational turf battles and professional turf battles, and none has experienced the consensus or agency identification that marks the CRD.

In short, CRD was distinguished both by the type of professional—attorneys—who populated the agency and by the dominance of one profession within the agency, rather than being characterized by internal divisions along professional lines.

The profession of agency careerists also had an effect on exit. Attorneys in all the agencies were more optimistic about alternative job prospects than were those trained in any other profession, and they were correspondingly more likely to exercise the exit option.[10]

Many insights into the way bureaucrats will respond to new circumstances can be gleaned from a review of their profession and the professional composition of their agency. The type of profession—law, science, engineering, or general management—is an important determinant of bureaucratic behavior, as is the proportion of agency members representing a given profession.[11]

Ideology

Ideological cleavages between "liberal bureaucrats" and conservative appointees are a potential source of clashes between the two groups and one that is cited frequently in the literature (Aberbach 1991; Aberbach and Rockman 1976, 1990; Maranto 1993c). In this study, however, ideology does not appear to be as important a factor in determining bureaucratic behavior as the other factors already discussed. Although it played some role at CRD and among the group of whistle-blowers identified at the EPA, career civil servants appear for the most part to leave their personal political preferences at the office door. Most of the careerists I studied did not seem to be motivated primarily by partisanship or ideology. Other factors such as self-interest and role perception better account for most of the behavior reported. In fact, many interviewees, including some of those at CRD, reported having modified their personal political views in response to changing public opinion toward the work of their agency and in response to what they perceived as an altered political climate in the nation during the 1980s.

Ideology does appear to have played at least some role at the Civil Rights Division, the agency with the strongest liberal leanings. There were no conservatives in my sample at CRD and twelve out of seventeen respondents identified themselves as liberal. Careerists at CRD defended their liberal convictions regarding civil rights policy and characterized the appointees in their agency as "right-wing ideologues." Yet at the Food and Nutrition Service, where agency personnel also characterized themselves as liberal "do gooders," ideology did not seem to impact behavior. Here, the apparent "clash of ideologies" between appointees and careerists does not appear to have precipitated resistance. The other agencies were more divided with respect to ideological, and even partisan, lines. NHTSA was evenly split between liberals and conservatives. And at EPA, although there were no Republicans and only two conservatives in my sample, careerists were evenly divided between liberal and "middle of the road," and between Democrats and Independents.

My findings thus offer a mixed picture with respect to ideology. Ideology seems to have played a role at CRD but not at FNS in spite of the liberal leanings of FNS careerists. Elsewhere, civil servants do not appear to be as liberal as indicated by previous research, a finding consistent with more recent survey research (Aberbach and Rockman 1990, 1995a).

Despite these mixed findings, I believe that ideology should be included as one of the factors that motivates bureaucrats, because it may come into play in ways that I was not able to measure. For example, the ideological composition of who exits and who enters federal agencies may have long-term effects on other features of agency culture, which in turn may impact bureaucratic behavior. However, although upper-echelon civil servants work in a highly charged political setting, I believe that, for the most part, they are less driven by ideology than previously believed.

The preceding discussion has reviewed the role played by each individual factor in motivating career bureaucrats during the Reagan years. But what does this tell us more generally about what motivates us in our careers in organizations? First, bureaucratic behavior is the result of a constellation of factors. No one factor can explain all bureaucratic behavior all the time. Bureaucrats are, on occasion, economic utility maximizers. But they are also sociological members of organizations and psychological individuals with "higher" needs and motives that lead them to act altruistically (Maslow 1943; Monroe, 1998; Pfiffner 1987, 1988). My research confirms, in the American context, Campbell and Wilson's (1995:305) contention that "the reality is that bureaucrats can be both selfish pursuers of status, agency size and salary, which rational choice writers portray, and, as their defenders maintain, the guardians of more noble concerns such as long-term national interest and confronting rulers with awkward facts."

However, the research presented in this book does suggest that the behavior of political appointees (principals) and the socializing experiences of bureaucratic agents (principles) are the key determinants of which type of behavior prevails. It is therefore important to learn more about the origins of role perception and agency context and to examine bureaucratic reactions to presidential administrations peopled by different types of appointees with different management styles.

Second, these factors interact with each other. They are interdependent, and changes in one cause changes in another. For example, the use of the administrative presidency increased the amount and the nature of self-interested behavior. Likewise, the strength or weakness of an agency's culture made the bureaucrats in that agency more or less vulnerable to the tools of the administrative presidency.

Thus, with respect to the question of what motivates us in our careers in organizations, the two points to draw from this book are that the four factors discussed are all necessary pieces to the motivational puzzle and that they operate interdependently not independently. To claim any one factor as the sole determinant of bureaucratic behavior is to do a disservice to empirical reality, to the career civil servants who people our federal agencies, and to the social sciences writ large that acknowledge the economic, psychological, and sociological components of political man.

Unfortunately, this study cannot definitively "identify those conditions that produce a bureaucracy resembling the nightmare vision of the rational choice theorists as it pursues its self-interest and those conditions that produce a bureaucracy more attuned to national or public interests" (Campbell and Wilson 1995:305). But it is my hope, and my contention, that this book has taken an important first step and pointed us down the correct path for future study.

IMPLICATIONS: REAPPRAISING RESPONSIVENESS

The research presented in this book has focused primarily on responsiveness—on assessing the extent to which, and the reasons why, the higher civil service is responsive to the president. At first glance, what I have found is reassuring for our democratic political system, in which unelected bureaucrats could otherwise wield considerable power and thwart presidents from carrying out their electoral and constitutional mandates. However, in my view, before we celebrate these findings, we need to consider the costs of attaining this degree of compliance.

Empirically, the research presented in this book demonstrates that the same constellation of factors—role perception, self-interest, the administrative presidency, and agency context—that ensure responsiveness also serve to limit voice by argumentation. In other words, the interaction of these factors proscribes the amount of dialogue that occurs between career civil servants and political appointees on policy matters. Although all the factors discussed in this book played some role in this regard, the administrative presidency had the greatest impact on bureaucratic voice. During the Reagan years, the administrative presidency not only discouraged civil servants from exercising voice but greatly curtailed their opportunities to do so. But even bureaucrats' role perception stifled their voices. This is because upper-echelon careerists, conscious of their unelected status and Reagan's mandate, did not think it was appropriate to challenge the policy directives issued by Reagan's appointees. As a result, with two notable exceptions (discussed later in this chapter), civil servants rarely voiced their opinions to their appointed bosses or entered the fray of policy debate.

The question that arises is, Does it matter? Does it matter if career civil servants fail to voice disagreement with their appointed bosses? Does it matter if they remain silent while policy is changed and programs dismantled? These questions are really variants on the question, What role do we want career civil servants to play in the American political system? Even in light of the evidence presented here, the answers to these questions are not obvious. But it seems to me that a more assertive civil service, one that is more inclined to "speak truth to power," would serve democracy well, for three reasons.[12]

First, actions such as voice by argumentation and resignation in protest draw attention to issues that might otherwise be hidden from public view. When Tim Cook resigned from the Civil Rights Division, he sent his letter of resignation to the *Washington Post* and the *New York Times* (Holt 1998). This served to make the public more aware of the issues surrounding implementation of the Civil Rights of Institutionalized Person's Act of 1980 (CRIPA) and led to congressional hearings to investigate policymaking in the Special Litigation Section of the CRD (U.S. House 1983; Holt 1998).[13]

Second, when careerists "speak truth to power," errors can be avoided. According to Barker and Wilson (1997:225), crucial errors by recent British governments "have been due in part to failures by senior civil servants to argue with sufficient vigour against policy proposals with predictably deleterious consequences." In this study, without sufficient careerist input, Ray Peck's rescission of the air-bag rule was predictably struck down by the Supreme Court, and Congress criticized Rita Lavelle for behavior that her subordinates failed to warn her about.

Third, and most important, voice by argumentation and "loyalty that argues back" enhance policy debate and deliberation. As defined by proponents of deliberative democracy, deliberation "is a reasoning process in which the participants seriously consider substantive information and arguments and seek to decide individually and to persuade each other as to what constitutes good public policy" (Bessette 1994:46; see also Guttman and Thompson 1996). In federal agencies, the locus of such information and arguments is the career civil service. Career civil servants have knowledge, professional expertise, institutional memory, and insight into policy issues that comes from experience. Therefore, if agency careerists fail to provide their appointed principals with information and arguments, both the quality of deliberation and the quality of policy decisions will suffer. As Rourke (1991a:68–69) has written,

The promotion of widespread discussion and debate preceding the execution of national policy decisions has always been looked upon as a major practical advantage as well as moral virtue of policymaking in a democratic society. Bureaucrats, like the other interested parties normally involved in the policy process, have a contribution to make to such a free-wheeling discourse on national policy, even when this contribution is no more than a cautionary tale about the possibility of failure.

To which Holt (1998:119) has added,

Our system of government is grounded in the belief that democracy is strengthened by spreading authority across governmental entities, and that a better whole will emerge from participation by each and even confrontation among parties.

In short, in my view, bureaucrats, in spite of, even because of, their professional and organizational biases, have something unique to add to the give-and-take of policymaking, and their failure to do so during the Reagan years diminished rather than enhanced both principal-agent relations and the democratic process. This is not because I prefer their policy views to those of the Reagan administration but because I believe that better policy will result when all points of view are aired and because I believe that better democracy will result if dissent is celebrated rather than stifled. Moreover, although a more deliberative process will not always resolve disagreements about policy, and although careerists will not always (and should not always) prevail, I believe that such a process will increase the mutual respect of the parties involved and enhance the legitimacy, in the eyes of both the careerists and the wider polity, of the decisions that are ultimately made.[14]

Having argued both that voice by argumentation has value and that there was too little of it during the Reagan years, the final question that must be addressed is, What can be done? Is it possible to increase voice by argumentation? Is it possible to strike a better balance between the president's need for responsiveness and the polity's need for bureaucratic expertise? The research presented in this book suggests that it is. Both the Civil Rights Division and the "second" Reagan administration at the EPA were peopled by civil servants who voiced their opinions and/or political appointees who listened. At the CRD, there was a great deal of "voice by argumentation." And Reagan's second-term EPA, under the leadership of Bill Ruckelshaus and Lee Thomas, was characterized by a great deal of free and open exchange of ideas between civil servants and appointees. What makes these two cases notable is that, as detailed in chapters 5 and 6, voice by argumentation occurred in both agencies without a corresponding decline in responsiveness. In other words, both cases demonstrate that this more active role for the career civil service can be achieved without the diminution of that equally important value, the responsiveness of unelected officials to elected ones.

Each of these agencies, therefore, offers a model if we desire more voice by argumentation. The Civil Rights Division suggests that civil servants can be imbued with an ethos that leads them to be outspoken rather than reticent. The "second-term" EPA suggests that political appointees can make reasoned argument between (even among) careerists and appointees a more central part of the decision-making process, and that appointees can create an environment in which debate rather than fear is encouraged.

What can be done to make other federal agencies more closely resemble the CRD and "second" EPA? The first step should be a greater focus on the recruitment and socialization of both career civil servants and political appointees (see, e.g., Brehm and Gates 1997). For example, civil servants need to be inculcated with a different perception of their role than they currently have, a perception more like that of CRD careerists who viewed their role as arguing predecisionally and falling into line once decisions were made. Appointees need to receive training that exposes them to the value of deliberative democracy and provides them with the management skills needed to allow deliberation without losing control. And presidents need to look for appointees who, like William Ruckelshaus and Lee Thomas, have the integrity and leadership skills to encourage deliberation inside their agencies while maintaining their loyalty to the president and his policy goals. In short, before we see an increase in civil servants who "speak truth to power," both how civil servants view their jobs (principles) and how presidents and appointees (principals) view civil servants' role will have to change.[15]

In conclusion, the factors discussed in this book, the administrative presidency in particular, both enable presidents to attain bureaucratic compliance and cause civil servants to be reticent rather than vociferous during internal agency policy deliberations. As a result, we remain confronted with the dilemma that Woodrow Wilson tried to wish away a hundred years ago. We are faced with a tradeoff between a responsive bureaucracy and one that brings its expertise to bear in policymaking. The administrative presidency resolves this tradeoff in favor of responsiveness. This book suggests, however, that there is another way out of this quandary. The case of the EPA suggests that career civil servants respond to agency leadership that promotes greater deliberation (and respect) between civil servants and political appointees. And the case of the Civil Rights Division suggests that there are circumstances in which career civil servants take an active role in voicing their opinions without crossing the (admittedly elusive) line between administration and politics.

SAMPLE INTERVIEW SCHEDULE

Reprinted below is the interview schedule used for current employees of the National Highway Traffic Safety Administration (NHTSA). The same interview schedule was used with minor modifications pertinent to each agency, for each of the other three agencies as well as for former employees of each agency (question tenses were changed). The open-ended nature of the questions allowed for spontaneous follow-up questions which are not reproduced here but are recorded in the interview transcripts.

INTERVIEW SCHEDULE: NATIONAL HIGHWAY TRAFFIC SAFETY ADMINISTRATION

Before we begin, I want to assure you that this conversation is completely confidential and that no names will be used in my study.

SECTION I: BACKGROUND INFORMATION

To start off, I would like to ask you a few questions about your background and experience in government service.

1. In what year did you join the National Highway Traffic Safety Administration?
2. What attracted you to the agency?
3. What Office or Division do you currently work in?
4. Were you here during the 1981–1988 time period as well?
   a. What office or division were you in then?
5. Are you a member of the Senior Executive Service (SES)?
   a. Is your appointment to the SES a career or noncareer appointment?

6. Is your current position a supervisory one?
7. Is your current position that of a manager or that of a scientist or technical expert serving in a non-managerial capacity?
8. What do you consider to be your primary area of expertise?
9. What is your educational background and training?
10. Do you view federal employment as a permanent career or do you expect to leave and seek employment in the private or not-for-profit sector?
    a. Why?
    b. What type of employment situation do you see yourself in?
11. Could you briefly describe the responsibilities of this office?

Section II: Agency Characteristics

Next, I have a few questions concerning how you would characterize your agency.

1. Do you think NHTSA has a clear mission, policy goals and objectives?
2. And what is that mission?
3. Did agency goals change during the Reagan years?
4. Do you think that NHTSA has a particular culture or esprit de corps?
    a. What time period are you referring to in that answer?
    b. Did that organizational culture change during the Reagan years?
5. Your agency was hard hit by budget cuts and RIFs. Did RIFs and budget cuts affect the agency's esprit?
    a. How?
    b. What happened to the people who got RIFed?
5a. What other effects did RIFs and budget cuts have on agency productivity, efficiency and policy direction?
6. How would you characterize the people who join this agency?
    a. Would you have used the same description in the 1970s and 1980s?
7. How would you describe the professional composition of NHTSA? About what percent of personnel are engineers? Attorneys? What type of engineers predominate?

Section III: Career/Appointee Relations

I am interested in the role of political appointees and in how, if at all, you viewed their role differently during the Reagan administration compared with other administrations you may have served under. The next set of questions focus on these appointed positions and on your relationship with them.

1. Overall, how would you characterize the relationship between career and appointed officials during Reagan's term of office?
   a. Some people have characterized the atmosphere in some agencies during the Reagan era as "us versus them". Do you think that description would have applied here at NHTSA?
2. Was most of the conflict and tension between career and noncareer personnel within NHTSA or was it more with OIRA, the White House or Congress?
3. Which of Reagan's appointees do you think were the most influential?
   a. Within DOT?
   b. Specifically within NHTSA?
4. How many appointees did NHTSA have during the Reagan years? How does this compare with previous administrations?
   a. Were they mostly noncareer SES or Schedule C special assistants?
5. Did you feel that the goals and priorities of the political appointees were, in general, clearly communicated to the career staff during Reagan's term of office?
   a. What were these goals?
   b. How does that compare with previous adminstrations?
   c. How were priorities communicated to career staff?
   d. How did you then convey them to *your* staff?
6. To what extent did you feel that political appointees in your department and/or agency were speaking for President Reagan and accurately reporting and conveying his wishes and policy goals?
7. In your opinion, what was the degree of partisanship among the Reagan appointees?
8. What kind of background and experience did most of the Reagan appointees in NHTSA have?
   a. Do you think that was the relevant type of background and experience to do their jobs?
   b. How does their background and experience compare with the background and experience of appointees in other administrations?
   c. Which appointees (or at least at what level {administrator, noncareer SES}) are you referring to?
9. How much turnover was there among the appointees?
   a. Is that more or less than usual?
   b. How about among careerists? What was turnover like among them?
10. To what extent were high-ranking careerists included in policy deliberations and decision-making?
    a. How does this compare with previous administrations?

11. How often did the political appointees in Transportation utilize the knowledge and expertise of the career personnel at NHTSA?
    a. Was this different than in the past?
    b. Were you satisfied with the amount?
12. To what extent did career staff have opposing views over agency direction, policy implementation or specific issues or regulations?
    a. Could you provide some examples where views differed?
    b. Were these differences discussed among careerists?
    c. How does this compare with other administrations?
    d. Did career personnel ever resign over these disagreements?
13. To what extent were career staff hesitant to express opposing views to people in appointed positions during the Reagan years?
    a. Did that change over time, that is were people less hesitant in the first or second term or under different Administrators?
14. Could you explain the channels open to career staff when there is such a disagreement?
    a. How is the final outcome determined?
15. Did appointees override, reject or overturn career recommendations or proposals?
    a. Was overturning such recommendations a common practice?
16. Did you personally have any opposing views?
    a. Did you express them?
    b. How?
    c. What was the outcome?
    d. Did you feel that your efforts had any effect?
    e. Did you ever talk with colleagues or your supervisor about this?
    f. Did you ever consider leaving NHTSA because of disagreements over policy implementation or agency direction?
17. Were leaks ever used when there were disagreements between careerists and appointees?
18. Overall, would you say that you and your colleagues and subordinates were "cooperative and responsive" or "resistant" to the Reagan administration?

Section IV: Other Branches of Government

I would now like to ask you a few questions about other branches of government with which you may have contact.

1. Could you describe this agency's relationship with OMB?
    a. Did you notice any changes in dealings between OMB and your department or agency during the Reagan years?

b. What was your perception of Peck and Steed's relationship with the OMB?

c. Did they go to bat for the agency against OMB?

2. How about the OIRA (Office of Information and Regulatory Affairs) within the OMB?

a. What kind of relationship did Peck and Steed have with OIRA?

b. Did they go to bat for the agency against OIRA?

3. Some people have said that the OIRA had a chilling effect on the issuance of new regulations during the Reagan years? Do you agree with that assessment?

4. Could you describe your agency's relationship with Congress?

a. Is the relationship friendly or hostile?

b. What committees or subcommittees do you primarily deal with?

c. Is most interaction between appointees and members, appointees and staff or careerists and staff?

5. Do you personally have much contact with Congress?

a. Could you describe that interaction?

b. Have you ever testified before Congress?

6. What kind of role do you think that Congress should play in its oversight of your agency?

a. Are you satisfied with the job that Congress does in its oversight role?

SECTION V: RESEARCH QUESTIONS

Before concluding, I would like to ask you one final question that may help me with my future research.

1. Is there anyone else who you think I should talk to, especially anyone who may have retired, resigned or been RIFed who might have a different perspective?

a. Do you know how I might get in touch with them?

That exhausts my list of questions. If you would like to add any comments, I would be very interested to hear them.

I am also going to ask you for five more minutes of your time to fill out this very brief supplementary questionnaire.

Thank you very much for taking the time to meet with me.

SAMPLE FEDERAL EMPLOYEE QUESTIONNAIRE

Reprinted below is the questionnaire used for current employees of the National Highway Traffic Safety Administration (NHTSA). The same questionnaire was used with minor modifications pertinent to each agency for each of the other three agencies (e.g., the names of the appointees were changed) as well as for former employees of each agency (e.g., question tenses were changed).

FEDERAL EMPLOYEE QUESTIONNAIRE

Thank you very much for the time that you have already devoted to the interview portion of this study. This questionnaire is an important follow-up component to my study. It is very brief and should only take five minutes to complete.

Please take this extra five minutes to answer the questions below so that I will have information that will enable me to compare different federal agencies and departments. Like the interview, all of this information will be treated confidentially.

SECTION I: GENERAL BACKGROUND

1. For which Cabinet Department did you work during the Reagan administration?

   _____

2. For which sub-department agency or office did you work during those years?

   _____

3. In what year did you join this agency?

   19_____

4. Is your appointment a career or noncareer appointment?
   [ ] Career   [ ] Noncareer

SECTION II: RELATIONSHIPS WITH AND INFLUENCE OF OTHER GOVERNMENTAL ACTORS

5. Below is a list of organizations and individuals often thought to exert influence over government agencies. After each one please indicate the extent to which that individual or organization seemed to influence important decisions in your agency during the Reagan administration.
   Using the scale provided, please indicate the amount of influence that this actor seemed to have.
   1 - No Influence
   2 - Slight Influence
   3 - Moderate Influence
   4 - A Great Deal of Influence
   X - No Basis to Judge

INFLUENCE

GROUP	NONE (1)	SLIGHT (2)	MODERATE (3)	A GREAT DEAL (4)	NO BASIS (X)
a) President Reagan	[ ]	[ ]	[ ]	[ ]	[ ]
b) White House staff	[ ]	[ ]	[ ]	[ ]	[ ]
c) OMB	[ ]	[ ]	[ ]	[ ]	[ ]
d) OIRA (Office of Information and Regulatory Affairs)	[ ]	[ ]	[ ]	[ ]	[ ]
e1) Secretary Lewis	[ ]	[ ]	[ ]	[ ]	[ ]
e2) Secretary Dole	[ ]	[ ]	[ ]	[ ]	[ ]
f1) Administrator Peck	[ ]	[ ]	[ ]	[ ]	[ ]
f2) Administrator Steed	[ ]	[ ]	[ ]	[ ]	[ ]
g) Cabinet Secretary staff	[ ]	[ ]	[ ]	[ ]	[ ]
h) Other political appointees in your agency	[ ]	[ ]	[ ]	[ ]	[ ]
i) Congress (Members and Staff)	[ ]	[ ]	[ ]	[ ]	[ ]

j) Interest Groups   [ ] [ ] [ ] [ ] [ ]
Please specify which groups >> _____

k) Career civil servants in your agency   [ ] [ ] [ ] [ ] [ ]

l1) Career SES executives in your agency   [ ] [ ] [ ] [ ] [ ]

l2) Noncareer SES executives in your agency [ ] [ ] [ ] [ ] [ ]

m) Others (please specify) _____ [ ] [ ] [ ] [ ] [ ]

6. Of those that you indicated above as having a great deal of influence, please indicate which two had the *most* influence over policy decisions in your agency during the Reagan administration.

    1. _____

    2. _____

7. Now please evaluate the same groups and individuals with respect to the Carter administration. If you were not employed at NHTSA at that time please skip this question and proceed to Section III.

INFLUENCE

GROUP	NONE (1)	SLIGHT (2)	MODERATE (3)	A GREAT DEAL (4)	NO BASIS (X)
a) President Carter	[ ]	[ ]	[ ]	[ ]	[ ]
b) White House staff	[ ]	[ ]	[ ]	[ ]	[ ]
c) OMB	[ ]	[ ]	[ ]	[ ]	[ ]
d) OIRA	[ ]	[ ]	[ ]	[ ]	[ ]
e) Secretary Adams	[ ]	[ ]	[ ]	[ ]	[ ]
f) Administrator Claybrook	[ ]	[ ]	[ ]	[ ]	[ ]
g) Cabinet Secretary staff	[ ]	[ ]	[ ]	[ ]	[ ]
h) Other political appointees in your agency	[ ]	[ ]	[ ]	[ ]	[ ]
i) Congress (Members and Staff)	[ ]	[ ]	[ ]	[ ]	[ ]
j) Interest Groups	[ ]	[ ]	[ ]	[ ]	[ ]

Please specify which groups >> _____

	NONE (1)	SLIGHT (2)	MODERATE (3)	A GREAT DEAL (4)	NO BASIS (X)
k) Career civil servants in your agency	[ ]	[ ]	[ ]	[ ]	[ ]
l1) Career SES executives in your agency	[ ]	[ ]	[ ]	[ ]	[ ]
l2) Noncareer SES executives in your agency	[ ]	[ ]	[ ]	[ ]	[ ]
m) Others (please specify) _____	[ ]	[ ]	[ ]	[ ]	[ ]

8. Of those that you indicated above as having a great deal of influence, please indicate which two had the *most* influence over policy decisions in your agency during the Carter administration.

   1. _____

   2. _____

SECTION III. PERSONAL ATTITUDES AND BELIEFS

This section contains a few questions about your personal political beliefs.

9. If you had to choose, would you rather have a smaller government providing fewer services or a larger government providing more services?
   [ ] Smaller Government   [ ] Larger Government
   [ ] Not Sure or No Opinion

10. If you had to choose, which do you think is more important at this time?
    [ ] Cut taxes   [   ] Use tax money for social programs
    [ ] Not Sure or No Opinion

11. Generally speaking, do you usually think of yourself as a Republican, a Democrat, an Independent, or what?
    [ ] Republican   [ ] Democrat   [ ] Independent
    [ ] Other   [   ] Do not think in these terms

12. Many of us do not like to pin political labels on ourselves. Our views are often too complicated to be described by a single label. But if you had to choose one word or phrase to describe your political beliefs, which of the following would you choose?
    [ ] Very Conservative   [ ] Very liberal
    [ ] Conservative   [ ] Liberal
    [ ] Somewhat Conservative   [ ] Somewhat Liberal
    [ ] Middle of the Road   [ ] None of the above

SECTION IV. ADDITIONAL COMMENTS

If you have any additional comments regarding any aspect of the interview or questionnaire, please include them here or attach an additional sheet.
Thank you for taking the time to complete this questionnaire.

NOTES

1. BUREAUCRATIC RESPONSIVENESS AND THE ADMINISTRATIVE PRESIDENCY

1. *Administrative presidency* is the term attributed to the strategy in which presidents attempt to achieve their policy goals administratively through the bureaucracy rather than legislatively through Congress, and through which they attempt to enhance their control over the actions and activities of federal agencies and their personnel (see Durant 1992; Mezey 1989; Nathan 1983a; Rubin 1985; Salamon and Abramson 1984; Sanders 1988; Waterman 1989b). A more complete definition is provided later in the chapter.

2. But see the work of a group of scholars frequently referred to as the "congressional dominance" school (e.g., McCubbins 1985; McCubbins, Noll, and Weingast 1987; McCubbins and Schwartz 1984; Weingast 1984; Weingast and Moran 1983) who believe that Congress is both better suited and the more rightful heir to control the bureaucracy. For more detailed critiques of the literature on congressional dominance, see Moe (1987, 1995); Wood and Waterman (1994); and Hammond and Knott (1996).

3. For a more complete discussion of each of these factors, see the sources cited in the text.

4. An additional goal of the administrative presidency is to give presidents a

way to avoid Congress when, as in the case of divided government, Congress is unlikely to support the president's legislation. Since the administrative presidency
brings about policy change administratively, through the bureaucracy, it does not
require new legislation or the consent of Congress.

5. Wilson (1989) employs the weapons metaphor.

6. Durant (1992), Ingraham (1991), and Hunter and Waterman (1996) also take
this microlevel, insider approach. In addition, Aberbach and Rockman (1990, 1991,
1995a) focus on changes in the ideological composition of both the career civil service and presidential appointees during this time.

7. Different scholars have used different phrases to get at the same concept—
namely, that of career civil servants actively contributing their opinions and perspective to agency decision making and policy discourse. Heclo (1977) and Pfiffner
(1987) use "loyalty that argues back"; Campbell and Wilson (1995) use Wildavsky's
(1979) phrase "speaking truth to power"; and Rourke (1992a) uses voice. See Bessette (1994) for a more detailed discussion of the virtues of deliberative democracy.

8. Motivating public employees is one of the three "big" questions identified by
Behn (1995); he calls it "the motivation question."

9. Brehm and Gates (1997) also attempt to integrate the rational choice and
public administration literatures into their analysis of bureaucratic propensities to
work, shirk, and sabotage. Their focus, however, is generally on "street-level" bureaucrats, not those employed in managerial capacities in Washington, D.C.

10. The work on internal agency dynamics and organizational culture includes
the classic work by Kaufman (1960) and more recent work by Wilson (1989), Mc-
Curdy (1993), and Khademian (1996). Friedrich (1940) and Finer (1941) initiated
discussion of a civil service ethic, although Bendix (1949) was also an early pioneer
in this regard. More recently, Pfiffner (1987, 1988), Perry and Wise (1990), and Di-
Iulio (1994) have addressed these individual level factors, and Aberbach and Rockman (1990, 1991, 1995a) have updated our understanding of the role of ideology.
Their work is treated more fully in the next chapter.

11. But see Gulick and Urwick (1937), who import scientific management into
the public sector, and Simon (1976), who critiques their approach.

12. I am indebted to Paul Light for this characterization of the Reagan years.

13. The term *hallowers* refers to bureaucratic sympathizers; *hollowers* are those
critical of bureaucracy (Golembiewski 1995). Durant (1990, 1992) uses the terms
bureauphiles and *bureauphobes* in a similar fashion.

2. A FRAMEWORK FOR ANALYSIS

1. Hirschman (1970) does not identify the neglect option, but it has been developed by Lowery and Rusbult (1986) and Withey and Cooper (1989), among others.
Hirschman (1970) also designed his categories to assess responses to "dissatisfac-

tion." Part of the concern in this study is determining the extent to which civil servants were in fact dissatisfied, and analyzing their responses to both satisfaction and dissatisfaction.

2. Niskanen (1971:38) argues that bureaucrats seek to maximize their budgets because larger budgets lead to increases in "the several variables that may enter the bureaucrat's utility function." These include salary, perquisites of office, public reputation, power, patronage, output of the bureau, ease of making changes, and ease of managing the bureau. According to Niskanen, all these variables except the last two are monotonically related to larger budgets.

Some work in this tradition modifies the budget-maximizing assumption and argues instead that bureaucrats act to maximize their *discretionary* budgets (Migue and Belanger 1974; Niskanen 1991). Other rational-choice scholars relax the maximizing part of the assumption and argue only that bureaucrats want larger budgets but not necessarily maximal budgets (Blais and Dion 1991).

3. According to Kiewiet and McCubbins (1991:5), "agents behave opportunistically pursuing their own interests," as a result of which "there is almost always some conflict between the interests of those who delegate authority (the principals) and the agents to whom they delegate it."

In this quotation and in this literature in general, the terms *principal* and *agent* are used to distinguish between those (the agents) who are hired to perform certain tasks (or to whom certain tasks are delegated) and those (the principals) who do the hiring (or delegating). As a result, these terms are used to explain a wide range of phenomena, of which the relationship between bureaucrats and elected officials is only one. Kiewiet and McCubbins (1991), for example, use them to explain the relationship between congressional parties and their members as well as between Congress and bureaucrats, and Pratt and Zeckhouser (1985) apply principal-agent theory to the business firm.

4. In Niskanen's (1991:15) words, "The incentives of bureaucrats do not lead to behavior that is fully consistent with the interests of politicians."

5. See also Brewer (1998), Crewson (1997), and Perry (1996, 1997), who are developing a theory of public-service motivation (PSM). This theory also argues that public servants are inclined to act in the public interest, even when doing so runs counter to their own self-interest (Brewer 1998).

6. The reason I have chosen to employ the term *role perception* rather than an alternative term such as *civil service ethic* or *code of conduct* is that my work builds explicitly on Pfiffner's work, and *role perception* is the term that Pfiffner (1987, 1988) uses in his discussions of this concept. See Landau (1979) for a discussion of the importance of linguistic consistency.

7. Wilson (1989:92–93) provides a more detailed response to some of the criticisms leveled against scholars who focus on culture as an explanatory variable.

8. Meier (1993) uses the term *cohesion,* Rourke (1984), *organizational esprit,* but both terms describe what is essentially the same concept.

9. I am fully aware that civil servants serve multiple principals, not just the president, and the role of these other principals is duly noted elsewhere in the text (Derthick 1990; Moe 1985b, 1987; Ringquist 1995; Wood and Waterman 1991, 1994). In the specific context of explaining bureaucratic reactions to the Reagan administration, however, it was easier to describe the roles of Congress, interest groups, and the courts in the case studies. To briefly preview, I found, first, that these actors primarily influenced agency behavior indirectly through their effect on agency history and, second, that congressional reaction to the Reagan administration manifested itself mainly in greater micromanagement of the agencies.

10. This was not possible at CRD, where all careerists (and most appointees) are attorneys. It also was not always possible with respect to former careerists, because it was easier to trace the whereabouts of attorneys than of other professionals.

11. This may introduce some bias into my sample, but given the goals of this study, which does not profess to offer a statistical portrait of behavior, this does not present an insurmountable obstacle.

12. Of the nine people I was not able to interview, only four actually declined to be interviewed. In the other cases, it was not possible to overcome scheduling conflicts, and in one case, the person died shortly before I tried to contact him. Many of those persons for whom interviews could not be arranged suggested substitutes to be interviewed in their place, and the law firm of the deceased civil rights attorney was especially helpful.

13. Size is a function of the number of high-ranking career civil servants in an agency's Washington office, particularly the number of career members of the Senior Executive Service. The Food and Nutrition Service, for example, has a large budget because many of its policies are redistributive, but it has only a small cadre of civil servants in upper management and/or policymaking positions in Washington, D.C.

14. For a more extensive discussion of elite interviewing and the use of open-ended interview questions and close-ended questionnaires, see Aberbach et al. (1975). For additional discussion of elite interviewing, see Dexter (1970) and Moyser and Wagstaffe (1987), and for a discussion of the sample selection technique used in this research, see Kingdon (1984) and Cook (1988). Przeworski and Teune (1970) and King et al. (1994) offer a general discussion of the comparative case method, and Hult (1987) and Durant (1992) provide examples of the comparative case method applied to the U.S. bureaucratic setting.

15. The chapter on the Environmental Protection Agency (EPA) has a slightly more complex organization, which is explained at the beginning of that chapter.

16. The concept of deliberative democracy in the bureaucratic context is discussed in greater detail in chapter 7. For more general discussions of the concept, see, e.g., Bessette (1980, 1994); Bohman and Regh (1997); Gutmann and Thompson (1996); and Lascher (1994, 1996).

3. NATIONAL HIGHWAY TRAFFIC SAFETY ADMINISTRATION

1. For a more detailed legislative history of NHTSA, see Mashaw and Harfst, *The Struggle for Auto Safety* (1990b).

2. This description of NHTSA depicts the agency as it existed at the time of Reagan's presidency and shortly thereafter. It does not take into account more recent changes, reorganizations, or appointees.

3. See also "Help for the Auto Industry" in *Automotive Engineering* (1981) for a detailed list of the specific rules targeted.

4. All budget figures are from the *Budget of the United States* (U.S. Office of Management and Budget 1979–1990), are actual rather than requested dollar amounts, and are rounded. It is important to note that NHTSA's budget did not decline steadily each year but, rather, went up and down over the eight Reagan years. For example, the budget was $215 million in 1983, $226 million in 1984, and $207 million in 1986. Nonetheless, the overall trend was clearly toward smaller budgets than the agency was allocated during the Carter administration.

5. Mashaw and Harfst (1990b:134–135) offer public opinion data on public opposition to the automatic ignition interlock.

6. The most recent example of NHTSA's actions being subjected to critical scrutiny by external political actors occurred in the spring of 1997 when reports of fatalities *caused by* air bags were made public. This led to congressional hearings at which NHTSA's current administrator, Ricardo Martinez, was questioned about the potential dangers of air bags (U.S. Senate 1997). Here, once again, NHTSA found itself being criticized for its advocacy of air bags. This is another example of how the complexity of the technology and the controversial nature of auto safety regulation bring NHTSA frequent criticism. Such conditions discourage risk taking and lead to caution by NHTSA careerists.

7. I did not interview any women at NHTSA.

4. THE FOOD AND NUTRITION SERVICE

1. The study was done in Mississippi by Dr. Robert Coles; the book was Nick Koltz's Pulitzer Prize–winning *Let Them Eat Promises* (1968); and the television show was a CBS documentary entitled "Hunger in America."

2. Today, the FNS's budget is about $37 billion, and participation in all three of the agency's primary programs has increased considerably (U.S. Department of Agriculture 1999).

3. The data in this chapter are drawn from interviews with twelve current and former FNS civil servants and political appointees and one person who participated in the events described in the chapter, although he was not an agency employee.

The chapter also uses the results from ten completed questionnaires. I conducted fewer interviews at this agency than at the other agencies in the study because there are fewer high-level civil servants at the FNS. But I was able to interview almost the entire population of relevant agency officials. Only one individual refused to be interviewed.

4. I conducted the interviews for this chapter in 1990.

5. Today, WIC's budget is $3.9 billion, and it serves more than 7 million people each month (U.S. Department of Agriculture 1999).

6. Careerist confidence is a component of agency context, a component that, I argue, affects bureaucratic behavior.

7. The President's Private Sector Survey on Cost Control (1984), informally known as the Grace Commission report, provided a blueprint for this plan, and rhetoric about waste, fraud, and abuse peppered Reagan's speeches. Matt and Cook (1993) concur with my assessment that reducing waste, fraud, and abuse was a high priority in the Reagan administration (see also Hoagland 1984).

8. The components and goals of the administrative presidency strategy are discussed at length in chapter 1. See also Benda and Levine (1988), Nathan (1983a), and Sanders (1988).

9. Under the Clinton administration, the assistant secretary position was retitled Undersecretary of Agriculture for Food, Nutrition and Consumer Services, and Clinton added an additional subcabinet position entitled Deputy Undersecretary for Food, Nutrition and Consumer Services (U.S. Department of Agriculture 1999). The titles used in this chapter are those in place during the Reagan years.

10. The only other appointees to receive ratings of "a great deal" of influence were Robert Leard (three "a great deal" ratings) and Bill Hoagland, the agency's first administrator (two "a great deal" ratings). One respondent also attributed the second most influence to Hoagland.

11. Despite their strategy of bypassing the expertise and input of career civil servants, appointees were unable to issue the new regulations (the reasons for this outcome are discussed elsewhere in this chapter).

12. Other tools of the administrative presidency such as the Office of Information and Regulatory Affairs (OIRA) and reorganization were not significant factors at FNS.

13. This information was provided in a personal interview, December 1990.

14. Finally, it was reported to me that "one leaker left." Since I cannot identify that person, it is not possible to analyze his or her decision to leave.

15. The name of the interviewee's office has been deleted from this quotation so that the interviewee cannot be identified.

16. A number of people provided similar accounts of the role played by Reagan administration appointees in both writing and leaking the school lunch regulations.

17. All parties involved, including the outside consultant himself and the GAO,

characterized career and consultant behavior in the same way. This incident is discussed in greater detail in the discussion of external actors.

18. Nine of ten respondents expressed this view.

19. This is similar to the argument made by Waterman (1989a) with respect to Reagan's experience at the EPA.

20. This chronology of events was reported to me in a telephone interview, October 8, 1991.

21. In an informative account of the same time period, Shep Melnick (1994) documented four additional congressional actions that limited Reagan's ability to achieve his policy goals at the FNS. The measures discussed by Melnick include a congressional resolution urging the president to protect food stamps from further cuts, increased budget appropriations, and passage of the Hunger Prevention Act in 1988 (Melnick 1994). Like the examples discussed in this chapter, these were congressional initiatives, not bureaucratic ones.

5. THE CIVIL RIGHTS DIVISION

1. Landsberg (1997:160) quotes Arthur Schlesinger Jr. as having observed, when contrasting the Civil Rights Division with the Civil Rights Commission, that "one was an agency of recommendation and the other of action."

2. All represents 100 percent. $N = 13$.

3. The remaining respondents felt that OMB had "slight" or "no" influence at their agency or that they had "no basis to judge" OMB's role—the latter, a further indication that OMB was not highly visible inside the CRD.

4. This contrasts with the interviews I recorded at the EPA in which the OIRA was credited with considerable influence and all the interviewees were more than willing to voice their opinions regarding OIRA. Survey responses regarding the OIRA clustered at the "no influence," and "no basis to judge" end of the scale. Only one respondent gave the OIRA a mark of "slight influence" and that was the highest mark it received from those who completed the questionnaire ($N = 13$).

5. An obvious exception is Clarence Thomas, an African American who headed the EEOC under Reagan.

6. The careerists' objections were ignored, and Reynolds went all the way to the Supreme Court on the side of the administration. The Supreme Court upheld the IRS's ruling, noting that the IRS had acted "in harmony with the public interest." The case caused the administration a great deal of embarrassment (Smith 1991).

7. This finding is consistent with the research reported in Holt (1998).

8. The presence of a few zealots who are willing to engage in leaking is similar to the pattern found at EPA and consistent with the typology of types of civil servants suggested by Anthony Downs in *Inside the Bureaucracy* (1967:88).

9. Holt (1998) provides a somewhat different account regarding the presence and extent of sabotage in the Special Litigation Section.

10. But see Holt (1998) for data on exit from the Special Litigation Section.

11. Other factors were personal, such as a financial incentive to take early retirement, but while these personal factors played a role, they do not fully explain the turnover during the Reagan years.

12. See Holt (1998) for a more detailed discussion of exit in the Special Litigation Section.

13. There are two different sample sizes for this agency because I conducted the interviews at two different times. The four interviewees I interviewed at the later period completed only partial questionnaires.

14. But see Holt (1998), who characterized some of the Special Litigation attorneys in her study as "assenting loyalists" and others as "apolitical," along with those who, like the careerists I interviewed, disagreed with agency policy, and whom she termed "dissenting loyalists."

15. The question asked was, "If you had to choose one word or phrase to describe your political beliefs, which of the following would you choose?"

16. The party identification question was worded, "Generally speaking, do you usually think of yourself as a Republican, a Democrat, an Independent, or what?"

17. Self-identified ideological belief does not establish policy preferences on specific issues, but I am confident that this highly educated group of respondents are constrained in their belief systems. I did not ask questions about specific policy issues because in pretests the respondents complained that multiple-choice questions were too simplistic.

18. Landsberg (1997) also points to the shared experiences of CRD attorneys under the reigns of Burke Marshall, John Doar, and Robert Owen as continuing to shape the commitment of division attorneys to their job.

19. For a more detailed discussion of the emphasis on the work ethic at the Civil Rights Division, see Landsberg (1997).

20. See Landsberg (1997) for a similar argument.

6. THE ENVIRONMENTAL PROTECTION AGENCY

1. This phrase is a play on both Charles Dickens's novel *A Tale of Two Cities* and Frederick Mosher's (1984) work *A Tale of Two Agencies,* about the OMB and the GAO. See also Harris and Milkis (1989, 1996), whose book, *The Politics of Regulatory Change,* is subtitled *A Tale of Two Agencies.*

2. Although two of the other agencies discussed in this book also experienced a changing of the appointed guard during Reagan's eight years in office, the careerists in those agencies did not view the changes in the same way as did careerists at the

EPA, nor did they perceive their agencies to have experienced two distinct administrations, as did their counterparts at the EPA.

3. Mosher (1984) uses the phrase "a tale of two agencies" in his comparative analysis of the GAO and OMB, as do Harris and Milkis (1989, 1996) in their study of the EPA and the FTC.

4. Among the scientists and engineers are biologists, chemists, other physical scientists, and civil, chemical, and environmental engineers (Hunter and Waterman 1996).

5. Harvard's Kennedy School of Government (1984a) estimates the agency's budget for fiscal year 1980 at $4.85 billion.

6. At first, it was not literally under one roof. Many programs continued to be housed in the agencies from which they had been transferred. It was not until 1973 that the agency settled into the Waterside Mall, a converted apartment complex and shopping mall in southwest Washington. The EPA ended up in this location only because the investors in this failed apartment complex were personal friends of then Vice President Spiro Agnew. Agnew bailed them out by arranging for the EPA to move into their buildings. The result is an atypical housing arrangement for a government agency in a building with two towers connected by a ground-floor shopping mall complete with supermarket, liquor store, and fast-food chains. The EPA is scheduled to relocate to the new Ronald Reagan building, but as of 1999, most of the agency's personnel still work at the Waterside Mall location. (The transferred agencies included the Federal Water Quality Administration and the Office of Pesticides, Wildlife and Fish from the Department of Interior, the National Air Pollution Control Administration, the Bureau of Water Hygiene, the Bureau of Solid Waste Management, and the Bureau of Radiological Health from HEW, and the Pesticide Regulation Division from the Department of Agriculture. See Marcus (1980b) and O'Leary (1993) for a complete list of the inherited agencies and the agencies from which they were inherited.)

7. For a detailed list of these statutes and a clear discussion of their key features, see, e.g., Bryner (1987) and O'Leary (1993).

8. These statutes included the Clean Air Act (1970) and its amendments (1977), the Federal Water Pollution Control Act (1972) and its amendments (1977), the Federal Environmental Pesticide Control Act (1972), the Federal Insecticide, Fungicide and Rodenticide Act (FIFRA) (1972), the Noise Control Act (1972), the Safe Drinking Water Act (1974), the Resource Conservation and Recovery Act (RCRA) (1976) and its amendments (1980), the Toxic Substances Control Act (1976), and the Comprehensive Environmental Response Compensation and Liability Act (Superfund) (1980).

9. Mobile sources are cars, trucks, and buses; stationary sources are industrial and municipal plants and factories. The EPA has since expanded its definition of mobile sources to include lawn mowers, tractors, and snow mobiles (Wald 1992).

10. O'Leary (1993) claims that there are more than one hundred congressional committees and subcommittees with some responsibility for oversight of the EPA.

11. Paul Light (1997) uses the phrase "watchful eye" in a slightly different context.

12. Anne Gorsuch became Anne Burford in March 1983 when she married Robert Burford and took his name. She resigned from the EPA that same month. Hence for most of the time period we are examining, she was Anne Gorsuch, and in the text I refer to her as Gorsuch. However, some interviewees and secondary sources use her current name rather than her name at the time of her tenure at EPA, and she uses Burford as the author of her memoir published in 1986 (see, e.g., Burford and Greenya 1986; Waterman 1989a,b). As a result, at times she is referred to as Burford. Any references to Anne Gorsuch, Anne Burford, or Anne Gorsuch Burford refer to the same person, Reagan's administrator for the EPA from 1981 to 1983.

13. This point is supported by Kraft and Vig (1984:430), who wrote that "unlike other presidencies in which department and agency heads might be expected to protect such cuts [budget cuts by OMB] Reagan's policy leaders welcomed the prospect of reduced budgets."

14. The Kennedy School (1984b) and the *National Journal* (1984) provide accounts of the fate of some of these bureaucrats that support this claim.

15. The word *media* refers here to the substances through which pollutants are transmitted—that is, through the air, in the water, or via waste products.

16. Since the interviewee did not attend the retreat, I do not know what the Reagan appointees' policy was with respect to the agency dress code.

17. A case prepared by the Kennedy School (1984b) includes policy disagreement as one of its explanations for the turnover at EPA, but none of the individuals it profiles expressed this view.

18. One could argue that their reticence was a form of sabotage, a conscious strategy to bring about her demise, but neither this critic nor anyone else I interviewed (and I interviewed two careerists who worked very closely with her, one of whom was no longer with the EPA at the time of the interview and was thus in a position to speak freely) gave any indication of such a strategy. In fact, the careerists around Lavelle were loyal to the end and did everything they could to defend and protect her during Congress's inquiry. But they did not speak out early in the process concerning their view of congressional intent regarding Superfund or Lavelle's potential conflicts of interests.

19. See also a Kennedy School (1985:6) case that quotes a career manager who also described a mood of neglect at EPA at this time.

20. By *Enforcement*, I am referring to those who were in the original Office of Enforcement or in the reorganized Office of Enforcement and Legal Counsel (which included many attorneys formerly in the Office of General Counsel) and anyone affected by the reorganizations of the enforcement function.

21. In her congressional testimony, Gorsuch disputed the numbers and refused to provide EPA records on this subject. The Office of Research and Development lost the greatest absolute numbers, but that office was affected by RIFs.

22. Secondary sources, however, reveal two career attorneys who did resign in protest over agency policy, one early in Gorsuch's tenure and the second shortly before she resigned (Davis 1983b; Kurtz 1983).

23. Unfortunately, I did not ask a direct question about risk assessment, as I did not become aware of its importance until after I had completed my interviews. I am relying, instead, on more general questions about the extent of policy disagreement between careerists and appointees, the issues on which there was disagreement, and careerist behavior under circumstances of disagreement. Almost all these questions were open-ended and so offered the careerists many opportunities to bring up the issue of risk assessment.

24. The apparent existence of zealots and climbers at EPA provides empirical support for the typology presented by Anthony Downs in *Inside Bureaucracy* (1967), which distinguishes among civil servants rather than treating them uniformly.

7. LESSONS FROM THE REAGAN YEARS

1. Rubin (1985) reaches a similar conclusion.

2. See also Holt (1998), Mezey (1988), and O'Leary (1994, 1995, forthcoming), who document examples of bureaucratic sabotage and guerilla warfare that caution us from over-generalizing from the findings reported in this book.

3. For example, Brehm and Gates (1997) found that principals were less influential than principles, and O'Leary (1995) found guerilla warfare in some of EPA's regional offices. These differences can be attributed to the absence of the administrative presidency and the different agency cultures between the regions and headquarters, respectively.

4. This explains Holt's (1998) findings in the Special Litigation Section of the CRD.

5. Role perception is different from public service motivation (PSM). Both, however, draw attention to civil servants' altruism and public spiritedness (see, e.g., Brewer 1998; Crewson 1997; Perry 1996, 1997; Perry and Wise 1990).

6. DiIulio (1994), Kelman (1987), Mansbridge (1990), and Perry (1997) are already taking steps in this direction.

7. Rubin (1985) provides a similar example. She discusses how the administrative presidency was used to disrupt work routines at the Office of Personnel Management (OPM).

8. All of these personnel machinations were made easier by the Civil Service Reform Act of 1978. Prior to that, presidents and appointees had less control over

salary and promotion determinations, and civil servants had greater job protection and job security. Meier (1993), Newland (1983), and Ingraham and Ban (1984) discuss the consequences of the Civil Service Reform Act and creation of the Senior Executive Service in greater detail.

9. See also Rubin (1985).

10. The industrial psychologists with Ph.D.s who conducted much of the research at the Food and Nutrition Service were similarly situated and were able to obtain employment in the academic and consulting communities.

11. Other recent research has also emphasized the importance of professional background and its impact on policy choice (Eisner 1991; Mashaw and Harfst 1990; Pruitt 1979; Sabatier et al. 1995). And as Eisner (1991) has documented, increasing the number of careerists from a given profession can alter both the agency's culture and its policy preferences.

12. Different scholars use different phrases when writing about this phenomenon. Among the phrases used, which, in my view, are roughly synonymous with voice by argumentation, are "loyalty that argues back" (Heclo 1977; Pfiffner 1987), "speaking truth to power" (Campbell and Wilson 1995; Wildavsky 1979), and "government by discussion" (Landsberg 1993, 1997). I therefore use these phrases interchangeably.

13. Resignation in protest, however, is not a panacea. As one interviewee noted, "once you have left, you lose your leverage; you can't bring about change from within."

14. Gutmann and Thompson (1996) were the first to raise the issue of mutual respect; their focus, however, was more on citizens than on intragovernmental respect.

15. Some evidence suggests that appointed principals have behaved somewhat differently during the Bush and Clinton administrations (see, e.g., Aberbach 1991, 1996). But interviews that I conducted recently with career civil servants suggest that they continue to be relatively timid and cautious when it comes to speaking truth to power.

REFERENCES

Aberbach, Joel D. 1991. The President and the Executive Branch. In *The Bush Presidency: First Appraisals*, edited by Colin Campbell and Bert Rockman. Chatham, N.J.: Chatham House.

———. 1996. The Federal Executive under Clinton. In *The Clinton Presidency: First Appraisals*, edited by Colin Campbell and Bert Rockman. Chatham, N.J.: Chatham House.

Aberbach, Joel D., James Chesney, and Bert A. Rockman. 1975. Exploring Elite Political Attitudes: Some Methodological Lessons. *Political Methodology* 2, no. 1: 1–28.

Aberbach, Joel D., Robert Putnam, and Bert A. Rockman. 1981. *Bureaucrats and Politicians in Western Democracies.* Cambridge, Mass.: Harvard University Press.

Aberbach, Joel D., and Bert A. Rockman. 1976. Clashing Beliefs Within the Executive Branch. *American Political Science Review* 70, no. 2: 466–467.

———. 1988. Mandates or Mandarins? Control and Discretion in the Modern Administrative State. *Public Administration Review* 48, no. 2: 606–612.

———. 1990. From Nixon's Problem to Reagan's Achievement: The Federal Executive Reexamined. In *Looking Back on the Reagan Presidency*, edited by Larry Berman. Baltimore: Johns Hopkins University Press.

———. 1991. Civil Service Executives: Status and Power. *Current* 331: 23–27.

———. 1995a. The Political Views of U.S. Senior Federal Executives, 1970–1992. *Journal of Politics* 57, no. 3: 838–852.

———. 1995b. The Role of Senior Civil Servants in the U.S. Paper presented at the Third National Public Management Research Conference, University of Kansas, Lawrence, October.

Abernathy, M. Glenn, Dilys Hill, and Phil Williams. 1984. *The Carter Years: The President and Policy Making.* London: Frances Pinder.

Ackerman, Bruce A., and William T. Hassler. 1981. *Clean Coal/Dirty Air.* New Haven, Conn.: Yale University Press.

Adler, Robert, and Charles Lard. 1991. Environmental Crimes: Raising the Stakes. *George Washington Law Review* 59, no. 4: 781–861.

Allison, Graham. 1971. *The Essence of Decision.* Boston: Little, Brown.

Amaker, Norman. 1988. *Civil Rights and the Reagan Administration.* Washington, D.C.: Urban Institute.

Anagnoson, J. Theodore. 1991. Administrative Goals, Environments, and Strategies. In *Home Style and Washington Work,* edited by Morris Fiorina and David Rohde. Ann Arbor: University of Michigan Press.

Anderson, Martin. 1984. The Objectives of the Reagan Administration's Social Welfare Policy. In *The Social Contract Revisited,* edited by D. Lee Bawden. Washington, D.C.: Urban Institute.

Anderson, Jack and Dale Van Atta. 1990. Reagan Minions Stalled Welfare Study. *Washington Post,* January 24.

Arnold, Douglas. 1979. *Congress and the Bureaucracy.* New Haven, Conn.: Yale University Press.

Arrow, Kenneth. 1985. The Economics of Agency. In *Principals and Agents: The Structure of Business,* edited by John W. Pratt and Richard Zeckhauser. Cambridge, Mass.: Harvard University Press.

Auto News. 1983. Peck Quits as NHTSA Chief. *Auto News,* April 25.

Ball, Howard. 1984. *Controlling Regulatory Sprawl: Presidential Strategies from Nixon to Reagan.* Westport, Conn.: Greenwood Press.

———. 1986. Racial Vote Dilution: Impact of the Reagan DOJ and the Burger Court on the Voting Rights Act. *Publius* 16, no. 4: 29–48.

Ball, Howard, and Kathanne Greene. 1985. The Reagan Justice Department. In *The Reagan Administration and Human Rights,* edited by Tinsley Yarbrough. New York: Praeger.

Ball, Howard, Dale Krane, and Thomas Lauth. 1982. *Compromised Compliance: Implementation of the 1965 Voting Rights Act.* Westport, Conn.: Greenwood Press.

Ban, Carolyn. 1987. The Crisis of Morale and Federal Senior Executives. *Public Productivity Review* Fall:31–49.

Ban, Carolyn, and Patricia Ingraham. 1990. Short-Timers: Political Appointee Mobility and Its Impact on Political-Career Relations in the Reagan Administration. *Administration and Society* 22, no. 1: 106–125.

Bardach, Eugene, and Robert Kagan, eds. 1982. *Social Regulation: Strategies for Reform.* San Francisco: Institute for Contemporary Studies.

Barker, Anthony and Graham K. Wilson. 1997. Whitehall's Disobedient Servants? Senior Officials' Potential Resistance to Ministers in British Government Departments. *British Journal of Political Science* 27 (April): 223–246.

Barry, Brian. 1974. Review Article: Exit, Voice, and Loyalty. *British Journal of Political Science* 4, no. 1: 79–107.

Bawden, D. Lee. 1984. *The Social Contract Revisited: Aims and Outcomes of President Reagan's Social Welfare Policy.* Washington, D.C.: Urban Institute.

Bawden, D. Lee, and John Palmer. 1984. Social Policy—Challenging the Welfare State. In *The Reagan Record,* edited by John Palmer and Isabell Sawhill. Washington, D.C.: Urban Institute.

Beetham, David. 1987. *Bureaucracy.* Minneapolis: University of Minnesota Press.

Behn, Robert D. 1989. Leadership Counts. *Journal of Policy Analysis and Management* 8: 494–500.

———. 1991. *Leadership Counts: Lessons for Public Managers.* Cambridge, Mass.: Harvard University Press.

———. 1995. The Big Questions of Public Management. *Public Administration Review* 55, no. 4: 313–324.

Bell, Griffin. 1982. *Taking Care of the Law.* Macon, Ga.: Mercer University Press.

Benda, Peter, and Charles Levine. 1988. The Reagan Bureaucracy: The Bequest, the Promise, and the Legacy. In *The Reagan Legacy: Promise and Performance,* edited by Charles Jones. Chatham, N.J.: Chatham House.

Bendix, Reinhard. 1949. *Higher Civil Servants in American Society.* University of Colorado Studies: Series in Sociology, vol. 1. Boulder: University of Colorado Press.

———. 1974. *Higher Civil Servants in American Society.* Westport, Conn.: Greenwood Press.

Bendor, Jonathan. 1988. Review Article: Formal Models of Bureaucracy. *British Journal of Political Science* 18, no. 3: 353–395.

———. 1990. Formal Models of Bureaucracy: A Review. In *Public Administration: The State of the Discipline,* edited by Naomi Lynn and Aaron Wildavsky. Chatham, N.J.: Chatham House.

Bendor, Jonathan, and Terry Moe. 1985. An Adaptive Model of Bureaucratic Politics. *American Political Science Review* 79, no. 3: 755–774.

Bendor, Jonathan, Serge Taylor, and Terry Moe. 1987. Stacking the Deck: Bureaucratic Missions and Policy Design. *American Political Science Review* 81, no. 3: 873–896.

Benjamin, Daniel. 1986a. The Leak That Sank Rita. *Washington Monthly* 17, no. 1: 18–19.

———. 1986b. Mutually Assured Corruption: The Justice Department and Ann Burford's EPA. *Washington Monthly* 17, no. 1: 12–21.

Benze, James. 1985. Presidential Management: The View from the Bureaucracy. *Presidential Studies Quarterly* 15, no. 4: 768–781.

————. 1987. *Presidential Power and Management Techniques: The Carter and Reagan Administrations in Historical Perspective*. Westport, Conn.: Greenwood Press.

Berman, Larry, ed. 1990. *Looking Back on the Reagan Presidency*. Baltimore: Johns Hopkins University Press.

Bernstein, Blanche. 1984. Welfare Dependency. In *The Social Contract Revisited*, edited by D. Lee Bawden. Washington, D.C.: Urban Institute.

Bernstein, Marver. 1955. *Regulating Business by Independent Commission*. Princeton, N.J.: Princeton University Press.

Berry, Jeffery M. 1984. *Feeding Hungry People*. New Brunswick, N.J.: Rutgers University Press.

————. 1989. Subgovernments, Issue Networks, and Political Conflict. In *Remaking American Politics*, edited by Richard A. Harris and Sidney Milkis. Boulder, Colo.: Westview Press.

Bessette, Joseph. 1980. Deliberative Democracy: The Majority Principle in American Democracy. In *How Democratic Is the Constitution?* edited by R. A. Goldwin and W. A. Schambra. Washington, D.C.: American Enterprise Institute.

————. 1994. *The Mild Voice of Reason: Deliberative Democracy & American National Government*. Chicago: University of Chicago Press.

Blais, Andre, and Stephane Dion, eds. 1991. *The Budget-Maximizing Bureaucrat: Appraisals and Evidence*. Pittsburgh: Pittsburgh University Press.

Bohman, James, and William Regh, eds. 1997. *Deliberative Democracy: Essays on Reason and Politics*. Cambridge, Mass.: MIT Press.

Bowers, James. 1993. Looking at OMB's Regulatory Review Through a Shared Powers Perspective. *Presidential Studies Quarterly* 23: 331–345.

Brehm, John, and Scott Gates. 1997. *Working, Shirking and Sabotage: Bureaucratic Response to a Democratic Public*. Ann Arbor: University of Michigan Press.

Brewer, Gene. 1998. Whistle Blowers in the Federal Civil Service: New Evidence of the Public Service Ethic. *Journal of Public Administration Research and Theory* 8 (July): 413–439.

Brown, Warren. 1989. NHTSA Employees Criticize Center for Auto Safety Tactics. *Washington Post*, September 21.

Brownstein, Ronald, and Nina Easton. 1982. All the President's Attorneys. *Student Lawyer* 10, no. 6: 19–26.

Bruff, Harold. 1979. Presidential Power and Administrative Lawmaking. *Yale Law Journal* 88, no. 3: 451–510.

Bryner, Gary. 1987. *Bureaucratic Discretion: Law and Policy in Federal Agencies*. New York: Pergamon Press.

Burford, Anne M., and John Greenya. 1986. *Are You Tough Enough? An Insider's View of Washington Power Politics*. New York: McGraw-Hill.

Burke, John. 1986. *Bureaucratic Responsibility*. Baltimore: Johns Hopkins University Press.

Burnham, David. 1982a. Environmental Unit Accused of Seeking to Silence a Critic. *New York Times,* December 11.

———. 1982b. Paper Chase of a Whistle-Blower. *New York Times,* October 16.

———. 1983. Tension Bubbles in the Bureaucracy. *New York Times,* March 13.

Butler, Stuart M., and Anna Kondratas. 1987. *Out of the Poverty Trap: A Conservative Strategy for Welfare Reform.* New York: Free Press.

Butler, Stuart M., Michael Sanera, and W. Bruce Weinrod, eds. 1984. *Mandate for Leadership II: Continuing the Conservative Revolution.* Washington, D.C.: Heritage Foundation.

Califano, Joseph. 1975. *A Presidential Nation.* New York: Norton.

Calvert, Randall, Matthew McCubbins, and Barry Weingast. 1989. A Theory of Political Control and Agency Discretion. *American Journal of Political Science* 33, no. 3: 588–611.

Campbell, Colin. 1986. *Managing the Presidency: Carter, Reagan and the Search for Executive Harmony.* Pittsburgh: University of Pittsburgh Press.

———. 1993. Political Executives and Their Officials. In *Political Science: The State of the Discipline,* edited by Ada Finifter. Washington, D.C.: American Political Science Association.

Campbell, Colin, and Bert A. Rockman. 1991. *The Bush Presidency: First Appraisals.* Chatham, N.J.: Chatham House.

Campbell, Colin, and Graham Wilson. 1995. *The End of Whitehall: A Comparative Perspective.* Oxford: Blackwell, 1995.

Carter, Kristin. 1989. Superfund Amendments and Reauthorization Act of 1986: Limiting Judicial Review to the Administrative Record in Cost Recovery Actions by the EPA. *Cornell Law Review* 74, no. 6: 1152–1178.

Center for Auto Safety. 1989. *Recalls Under Reagan: NHTSA's Auto Safety Recall Program.* Washington, D.C.: Center for Auto Safety.

Civil Rights Leadership Conference. 1983. *An Oath Betrayed: The Reagan Administration's Civil Rights Enforcement Record.* Washington, D.C.: Civil Rights Leadership Fund.

Claybrook, Joan. 1984. Transportation Safety. In *Retreat from Safety,* edited by Joan Claybrook. New York: Pantheon Books.

Cohen, Steven. 1984. Defusing the Toxic Time Bomb: Federal Hazardous Waste Programs. In *Environmental Policy in the 1980s: Reagan's New Agenda,* edited by Norman Vig and Michael Kraft. Washington, D.C.: Congressional Quarterly.

Cole, Richard, and David Caputo. 1979. Presidential Control of the Senior Civil Service: Assessing the Strategies of the Nixon Years. *American Political Science Review* 73, no. 2: 399–413.

Community Nutrition Institute. 1981–1991. *CNI Weekly.*

Congressional Quarterly. 1985. *Reagan: The Next Four Years.* Washington, D.C.: Congressional Quarterly Press.

Conybeare, John. 1984. Bureaucracy, Monopoly and Competition: A Critical Analysis of the Budget-Maximizing Model of Bureaucracy. *American Journal of Political Science* 28, no. 3: 479–502.

Cook, Brian. 1986. Characteristics of Administrative Decisions About Regulatory Reform: A Case Analysis. *American Politics Quarterly* 14, no. 4: 294–316.

———. 1988. *Bureaucratic Politics and Regulatory Reform: The EPA and Emissions Trading.* Westport, Conn.: Greenwood Press.

Cook, Brian, and B. Dan Wood. 1989. Principal-Agent Models of Political Control of Bureaucracy. *American Political Science Review* 83, no. 3: 965–970.

Cooper, Joseph, and William West. 1988. Presidential Power and Republican Government: The Theory and Practice of OMB Review of Agency Rules. *Journal of Politics* 50, no. 4: 864–895.

Cooper, Terry. 1990. *The Responsible Administrator: An Approach to Ethics for the Administrative Role.* San Francisco: Jossey-Bass.

Cordia, Louis. 1981. Environmental Protection Agency. In *Mandate for Leadership,* edited by Charles Heatherly. Washington, D.C.: Heritage Foundation.

Costle, Douglas. 1982. Environmental Regulation and Regulatory Reform. *Washington Law Review* 57, no. 3: 409–432.

Council on Environmental Quality. 1986. *Environmental Quality 1985: The 16th Annual Report of the Council on Environmental Quality.* Washington, D.C.: Council on Environmental Quality.

Cowen, Robert. 1990. Safeguards Needed for US Research Reports. *Christian Science Monitor,* February 20: 13.

Coxall, Bill, and Lynton Robins. 1989. *Contemporary British Politics.* London: Macmillan.

Crandall, Robert W., Howard K. Gruenspecht, Theodore Keeler, and Lester Lave. 1986. *Regulating the Automobile.* Washington, D.C.: Brookings Institution.

Crewson, Philip. 1997. Public service motivation: building empirical evidence of incidence and effect. *Journal of Public Administration Research and Theory.* 7, no. 4 (October):499–518.

Cronin, Thomas. 1975. *The State of the Presidency.* Boston: Little, Brown.

Cropper, Maureen, William Evans, Stephan Berardi, Maria Duala-Soares, and Paul Portney. 1992. The Determinants of Pesticide Regulation: A Statistical Analysis of EPA Decision Making. *Journal of Political Economy* 100, no. 1: 175–197.

Crotty, William, ed. 1991. *Political Science: Looking to the Future.* Vol. 4. Evanston, Ill.: Northwestern University Press.

Dahl, Robert. 1957. The Concept of Power. *Behavioral Science* 2 (July): 201–215.

Davies, J. Clarence. 1984. Environmental Institutions and the Reagan Administration. In *Environmental Policy in the 1980's: Reagan's New Agenda,* edited by Norman Vig and Michael Kraft. Washington, D.C.: Congressional Quarterly.

Davies, J. Clarence, and Barbara Davies. 1975. *The Politics of Pollution.* 2d ed. Indianapolis: Bobbs-Merrill.

Davis, Joseph. 1981. Anne Gorsuch: We Can Do Better With Fewer People and Dollars. *National Journal* 13, no. 43: 1900.

———. 1983a. Burford Resigns from EPA; Congress Gets Documents. *Congressional Quarterly Weekly Report* 41, no. 10: 495–498.

———. 1983b. Pressure on Burford Increases with Calls for Her Resignation. *Congressional Quarterly Weekly Report* 41, no. 9: 451.

———. 1983c. Ruckelshaus Confirmed 97–0. *Congressional Quarterly Weekly Report* 41, no. 20: 1005.

———. 1983d. Ruckelshaus EPA Nomination Approved by Senate Panel. *Congressional Quarterly Weekly Report* 41, no. 18: 877–878.

———. 1983e. Ruckelshaus Team Moving into Place at EPA. *Congressional Quarterly Weekly Report* 41, no. 45: 2391.

———. 1983f. Two Panels Advocate Increased EPA Funding. *Congressional Quarterly Weekly Report* 41, no. 9: 452.

DeMuth, Christopher, and Douglas Ginsburg. 1986. White House Review of Agency Rulemaking. *Harvard Law Review* 99, no. 5: 1075–1088.

Derthick, Martha. 1990. *Agency Under Stress.* Washington, D.C.: Brookings Institution.

Derthick, Martha, and Paul Quirk. 1985. *The Politics of Deregulation.* Washington, D.C.: Brookings Institution.

Destler, I. M. 1974. *Presidents, Bureaucrats, and Foreign Policy.* Princeton, N.J.: Princeton University Press.

Detlefsen, Robert. 1991. *Civil Rights Under Reagan.* San Francisco: Institute for Contemporary Studies.

Devine, Donald. 1991. *Reagan's Terrible Swift Sword.* Ottawa, Ill.: Jameson Books.

Dexter, Lewis Anthony. 1970. *Elite and Specialized Interviewing.* Evanston, Ill.: Northwestern University Press.

DiIulio, John. 1994. Principled Agents: The Cultural Bases of Behavior in a Federal Government Bureaucracy. *Journal of Public Administration Research and Theory* 4, no. 3: 277–318.

Dinerstein, Robert. 1984. The Absence of Justice. *Nebraska Law Review* 63, no. 4: 680–708.

Dobel, J. Patrick. 1992. William D. Ruckelshaus: Political Prudence and Public Integrity. In *Exemplary Public Administrators: Character and Leadership and Leadership in Government,* edited by Terry Cooper and N. Dale Wright. San Francisco: Jossey-Bass.

Dowd, Maureen. 1983. Superfund, Supermess. *The Nation,* February 21.

Downs, Anthony. 1957. *An Economic Theory of Democracy.* New York: Harper & Row.

———. 1967. *Inside Bureaucracy.* Boston: Little, Brown.

Dunleavy, Patrick. 1992. *Democracy, Bureaucracy, and Public Choice.* Englewood Cliffs, N.J.: Prentice-Hall.

Dunlop, Riley E. 1991. Public Opinion in the 1980s: Clear Consensus, Ambiguous Commitment. *Environment* 33, no. 8: 10–15, 32–37.

Durant, Robert. 1987. Toward Assessing the Administrative Presidency: Public Lands, the BLM and the Reagan Administration. *Public Administration Review* 47, no. 2: 180–189.

———. 1990. Beyond Fear or Favor: Appointee-Careerist Relations in the Post-Reagan Era. *Public Administration Review* 50: 319–331.

———. 1991. Fire Alarms, Garbage Cans, and the Administrative Presidency. *Administration and Society* 23, no. 1: 94–122.

———. 1992. *The Administrative Presidency Revisited: Public Lands, the BLM, and the Reagan Revolution.* Albany: State University of New York Press.

———. 1993. Hazardous Waste, Regulatory Reform, and the Reagan Revolution: The Ironies of an Activist Approach to Deactivating Bureaucracy. *Public Administration Review* 53, no. 6: 550–560.

———. 1995. Public Policy, Overhead Democracy, and the Professional State Revisited. *Administration and Society* 27, no. 2: 165–202.

Eads, George C., and Michael Fix, eds. 1984. *The Reagan Regulatory Strategy.* Washington, D.C.: Urban Institute.

Eckstein, Harry. 1975. Case Study and Theory in Political Science. In *Handbook of Political Science.* Vol. 7, edited by Fred Greenstein and Nelson Polsby. Boston: Addison-Wesley.

Eisner, Marc Allen. 1991. *Antitrust and the Triumph of Economics.* Chapel Hill: University of North Carolina Press.

Eisner, Marc Allen, and Kenneth Meier. 1990. Presidential Control Versus Bureaucratic Power: Explaining the Reagan Revolution in Antitrust. *American Journal of Political Science* 34, no. 1: 269–287.

Eisner, Marc Allen, Jeff Worsham, and Evan Ringquist. 1996. Crossing the Organizational Void: The Limits of Agency Theory in the Analysis of Regulatory Control. *Governance: An International Journal of Policy and Administration* 9, no. 4: 407–428.

Elster, Jon, ed. 1998. *Deliberative Democracy.* Cambridge Studies in the Theory of Democracy. New York: Cambridge University Press.

Etzioni, Amitai. 1964. *Modern Organizations.* Englewood Cliffs, N.J.: Prentice-Hall.

Farrell, Dan. 1983. Exit, Voice, Loyalty, and Neglect as Response to Job Dissatisfaction: A Multidimensional Scaling Study. *Academy of Management Journal* 26: 596–607.

Federal Regional Executive Directory. 1990. Washington, D.C.: Carroll.

Federal Staff Directory. 1982–1989. Mount Vernon, Va.: Congressional Staff Directory.

Federal Yellow Book. 1989. Washington, D.C.: Monitor.

Fenno, Richard F. Jr. 1973. *Congressmen in Committees.* Boston: Little, Brown.

Fesler, James. 1983. Politics, Policy and Bureaucracy at the Top. *Annals of the Academy of Political and Social Science* 466: 23–42.

Fesler, James W., and Donald F. Kettl. 1996. *The Politics of the Administrative Process.* 2d ed. Chatham, N.J.: Chatham House.

Finer, Herman. 1941. Administrative Responsibility in Democratic Government. *Public Administration Review* 7, no. 4: 335–350.

Fink, Arlene, and Jacqueline Kosecoff. 1985. *How to Conduct Surveys: A Step-by-Step Guide.* Beverly Hills, Calif.: Sage.

Fiorina, Morris P. 1977. *Congress: Keystone of the Washington Establishment.* New Haven, Conn.: Yale University Press.

Fiorina, Morris, and Roger Noll. 1978. Voters, Bureaucrats and Legislators. *Journal of Public Economics* 9, no. 2: 239–254.

Foreman, Christopher. 1988. *Signals from the Hill.* New Haven, Conn.: Yale University Press.

Fried, Charles. 1991. *Order and Law.* New York: Simon & Schuster.

Fried, Robert C. 1976. *Performance in American Bureaucracy.* Boston: Little, Brown.

Friedrich, Carl. 1940. The Nature of Administrative Responsibility. *Public Policy* 1: 3–24.

Friends of the Earth. 1982. *Ronald Reagan and the American Environment.* Mass.: Brick House.

Fuchs, Edward Paul. 1988. *Presidents, Management and Regulation.* Englewood Cliffs, N.J.: Prentice-Hall.

Gaertner, Gregory, Karen Gaertner, and Irene Deyne. 1983. Federal Agencies in the Context of Transition: A Contrast Between Democratic and Organizational Theories. *Public Administration Review* 43, no. 5: 421–432.

Galambos, Louis, ed. 1987. *The New American State: Bureaucracies and Policies Since World War II.* Baltimore: Johns Hopkins University Press.

Garand, James, and Donald Gross. 1982. Toward a Theory of Bureaucratic Compliance with Presidential Directives. *Presidential Studies Quarterly* 12, no. 2: 195–207.

Gaus, John. 1936. The Responsibility of Public Administration. In *The Frontiers of Public Administration,* edited by John Gaus, Leonard White, and Marshall Dimock. New York: Russell and Russell.

Glazer, Myron, and Penina Glazer. 1989. *The Whistleblowers.* New York: Basic Books.

Golden, Marissa Martino. 1992. Exit, Voice, Loyalty, and Neglect: Bureaucratic Responses to Presidential Control During the Reagan Administration. *Journal of Public Administration Research and Theory* 2, no. 1: 29–62.

Goldenberg, Edie. 1984. The Permanent Government in an Era of Retrenchment and Redirection. In *The Reagan Presidency and the Governing of America,* edited by Lester Salamon and Michael Lund. Washington, D.C.: Urban Institute.

Golembiewski, Robert. 1995. *Practical Public Management.* New York: Dekker.

Goodman, Marshall, and Margaret Wrightson. 1987. *Managing Regulatory Reform: The Reagan Strategy and Its Impact.* New York: Praeger.

Gordon, Michael. 1971. Civil Servants, Politicians, and Parties. *Comparative Politics* 4, no. 1: 29–58.

Gormley, William. 1989. *Taming the Bureaucracy: Muscles, Prayers and Other Strategies.* Princeton, N.J.: Princeton University Press.

Govan, Reginald, ed. 1989. *One Nation Indivisible: The Civil Rights Challenge for the 1990s.* Washington, D.C.: Citizen's Commission on Civil Rights.

Graham, Jill. 1986. Principled Organizational Dissent: A Theoretical Essay. *Research in Organizational Behavior* 8: 1–52.

Graham, John. 1989. *Auto Safety: Assessing America's Performance.* Auburn, Mass.: Auburn House.

Green, Donald, and Ian Shapiro. 1994. *Pathologies of Rational Choice Theory: A Critique of Applications in Political Science.* New Haven, Conn.: Yale University Press.

Greenstein, Fred. 1983. *The Reagan Presidency: An Early Assessment.* Baltimore: Johns Hopkins University Press.

Gruber, Judith. 1987. *Controlling Bureaucracies: Dilemmas in Democratic Governance.* Berkeley and Los Angeles: University of California Press.

Gulick, Luther, and L. Urwick, eds. 1937. *Papers on the Science of Administration.* New York: Institute of Public Administration.

Gutman, Amy, and Dennis Thompson. 1996. *Democracy and Disagreement.* Cambridge, Mass.: Harvard University Press.

Halperin, Morton. 1974. *Bureaucratic Politics and Foreign Policy.* Washington, D.C.: Brookings Institution.

Halpern, Paul. 1982. The Corvair, the Pinto and Corporate Behavior: Implications for Regulatory Reform. *Policy Studies Review* 1, no. 3: 540–545.

Hammond, Michael. 1981. The Department of Justice. In *Mandate for Leadership,* edited by Charles Heatherly. Washington, D.C.: Heritage Foundation.

Hammond, Thomas. 1986. Agenda Control, Organizational Structure, and Bureaucratic Politics. *American Journal of Political Science* 30, no. 2: 379–421.

Hammond, Thomas, and Jack H. Knott. 1996. Who Controls the Bureaucracy? Presidential Power, Congressional Dominance, Legal Constraints, and Bureaucratic Autonomy in a Model of Multi-Institutional Policy Making. *Journal of Law, Economics, and Organization* 12, no. 1: 119–166.

Harris, Richard, and Sidney Milkis. 1989. *The Politics of Regulatory Change: A Tale of Two Agencies,* 2nd ed. New York: Oxford University Press.

Hawkins, Keith, and John Thomas, eds. 1989. *Making Regulatory Policy.* Pittsburgh: University of Pittsburgh Press.

Hays, Samuel. 1987. The Politics of Environmental Administration. In *The New American State,* edited by Louis Galambos. Baltimore: Johns Hopkins University Press.

Heap, Shaun Hargreaves, Martin Hollis, Bruce Lyons, Robert Sugden, and Albert Weale. 1992. *The Theory of Choice: A Critical Guide.* Oxford: Blackwell.

Heatherly, Charles, ed. 1981. *Mandate for Leadership.* Washington, D.C.: Heritage Foundation.

Heclo, Hugh. 1977. *A Government of Strangers: Executive Politics in Washington.* Washington, D.C.: Brookings Institution.

———. 1977. *Studying the Presidency: A Report to the Ford Foundation.* New York: Ford Foundation.

———. 1984. In Search of a Role: America's Higher Civil Service. In *Bureaucrats and Policymaking,* edited by Ezra Suleiman. New York: Holmes & Meier.

Henry, William. 1982. This Ice Queen Does Not Melt. *The Nation,* January 18.

Hilts, Phillip. 1993. Why Whistle-Blowers Can Seem a Little Crazy. *New York Times,* June 13.

Hines, Michael. 1983. Administrator Who Rescinded Auto Safety Rules Resigns Suddenly. *New York Times,* April 23.

Hirschman, Albert O. 1970. *Exit, Voice and Loyalty: Responses to Decline in Firms, Organizations and States.* Cambridge, Mass.: Harvard University Press.

Hoagland, G. William. 1984. Perception and Reality in Nutrition Programs. In *Maintaining the Safety Net,* edited by John Weicher. Washington, D.C.: American Enterprise Institute.

Hoberg, George. 1990. Reaganism, Pluralism, and the Politics of Pesticide Regulation. *Policy Sciences* 23, no. 4: 257–290.

Holmstrom, Bengt, and Paul Milgram. 1991. Multitask Principal-Agent Analyses: Incentive Contracts, Asset Ownership, and Job Design. *Journal of Law, Economics, and Organization* 7, special issue: 24–52.

Holsendolph, Ernest. 1981. U-Turn for a Regulator. *New York Times,* November 1.

Holt, Karen E. 1998. *When Officials Clash: Implementation of the Civil Rights of Institutionalized Persons Act.* Westport, Conn.: Praeger.

Houck, Davis, and Amos Kiewe, eds. 1993. *Actor, Ideologue, Politician: The Public Speeches of Ronald Reagan.* Westport, Conn.: Greenwood Press.

Howe, Charles W. 1991. An Evaluation of U.S. Air and Water Policies. *Environment* 33, no. 7: 10–15, 34–36.

Huddleston, Mark. 1987. Background Paper. In *The Government's Managers: A Report of the Twentieth Century Fund Task Force on the Senior Executive Service.* New York: Priority Press Publications.

Huddleston, Mark, and William Boyer. 1996. *The Higher Civil Service in the United States: Quest for Reform.* Pittsburgh: University of Pittsburgh Press.

Hult, Karen. 1987. *Agency Merger and Bureaucratic Redesign.* Pittsburgh: University of Pittsburgh Press.

Hunter, Susan, and Richard Waterman. 1996. *Enforcing the Law: the Case of the Clean Water Acts.* Armonk, N.Y.: Sharpe.

Hurst, Blake. 1989. Wasting Away in Atchison County. *Policy Review* 50: 70–2.

Ingraham, Patricia W. 1987. Building Bridges or Burning Them? The President, the Appointees, and the Bureaucracy. *Public Administration Review* 45, no. 5: 425–435.

———. 1991. Political Direction and Policy Change in Three Federal Departments. In *The Managerial Presidency,* edited by James Pfiffner. Pacific Grove, Calif.: Brooks/Cole.

———. 1995. *The Foundation of Merit: Public Service in American Democracy.* Baltimore: Johns Hopkins University Press.

Ingraham, Patricia W., and Carolyn Ban. 1986. Models of Public Management: Are They Useful to Federal Managers in the 1980s? *Public Administration Review* 46, no. 2: 152–160.

———. 1988. Politics and Merit: Can They Meet in a Public Service Model? *Review of Public Personnel Administration* 8, no. 2: 7–19.

Ingraham, Patricia, and Carolyn Ban, eds. 1984. *Legislating Bureaucratic Change.* Albany: State University of New York Press.

Ingraham, Patricia W., James R. Thompson, and Eliot Eisenberg. 1995. Political Management Strategies and Political/Career Relationships: Where Are We Now in the Federal Government? *Public Administration Review* 55, no. 3: 263–272.

Ink, Dwight. 1982. CSA Closedown: A Myth Challenged. *Bureaucrat* 11, no. 2: 39–43.

Jaffe, Elise B. 1998. The Bureaucratic Leadership Dilemma: Agency Responsiveness and Resistance as the Locus of Coalitional Adjustment. Unpublished paper, New Haven: Yale University.

Johnson, Jeff. 1988. Hugh Kaufman: EPA Whistleblower. *Sierra* 73: 94–99.

Johnson, Roberta, and Michael Kraft. 1990. Bureaucratic Whistleblowing and Policy Change. *Western Politics Quarterly* 43, no. 4: 849–874.

Johnson, Ronald, and Gary Libecap. 1994. *The Federal Civil Service System and the Problem of Bureaucracy.* Chicago: University of Chicago Press.

Jones, Charles, ed. 1988. *The Reagan Legacy: Promise and Performance.* Chatham, N.J.: Chatham House.

Jos, Philip. 1991. The Nature and Limits of the Whistleblower's Contribution to Administrative Responsibility. *American Review of Public Administration* 21, no. 2: 105–118.

Kamieniecki, Sheldon, Robert O'Brien, and Michael Clarke, eds. 1986. *Controversies in Environmental Policy.* Albany: State University of New York Press.

Kargman, Steven. 1986. OMB Intervention in Agency Rulemaking: The Case for Broadened Record Review. *Yale Law Journal* 95, no. 8: 1789–1810.

Kato, Junko. 1998. When the Party Breaks Up: Exit and Voice Among Japanese Legislators. *American Political Science Review* 92, no. 4: 857–870.

Katzmann, Robert. 1980. *Regulatory Bureaucracy: The Federal Trade Commission and Antitrust Policy.* Cambridge, Mass.: MIT Press.

Kaufman, Herbert. 1956. Emerging Conflicts in the Doctrines of Public Administration. *American Political Science Review* 50, no. 4: 1057–1073.

———. 1960. *The Forest Ranger.* Baltimore. Johns Hopkins University Press.

———. 1981a. *The Administrative Behavior of Federal Bureau Chiefs.* Washington, D.C.: Brookings Institution.

———. 1981b. Fear of Bureaucracy: A Raging Pandemic. *Public Administration Review* 41, no. 1: 1–9.

Kelman, Herbert, and V. Lee Hamilton. 1989. *Crimes of Obedience: Toward a Social Psychology of Authority and Responsibility.* New Haven, Conn.: Yale University Press.

Kelman, Steven. 1987a. *Making Public Policy: A Hopeful View of American Government.* New York: Basic Books.

———. 1987b. Public Choice and Public Spirit. *The Public Interest* 8: 80–94.

Kennedy School of Government. 1984a. Note on the EPA Under Administrator Anne Gorsuch. Case N16-84-587. Cambridge, Mass.: Harvard College.

———. 1984b. Surviving at EPA. Case C16-84-588. Cambridge, Mass.: Harvard College.

———. 1985. Environmental Protection: Ruckelshaus Returns. Case C16-85-638. Cambridge, Mass.: Harvard College.

———. 1986. Ruckelshaus and Acid Rain. Case C16-86-658. Cambridge, Mass.: Harvard College.

———. 1986b. NHTSA and the Corporate Average Fuel Economy Standards. Case C15-86-672. Cambridge, Mass.: Harvard College.

Kenski, Henry, and Helen M. Ingraham. 1986. The Reagan Administration and Environmental Regulation. In *Controversies in Environmental Policy,* edited by Sheldon Kamieniecki, Robert O'Brien, and Michael Clarke. Albany: State University of New York Press.

Kerr, Norwood. 1990. Drafted into the War on Poverty: USDA Food and Nutrition Programs, 1961–1969. *Agricultural History* 64, no. 2: 154–166.

Kettl, Donald. 1993. Public Administration: the State of the Field. In *Political Science, the State of the Discipline,* edited by Ada Finifter. Washington, D.C.: American Political Science Association.

Khademian, Anne M. 1996. *Checking on Banks: Autonomy and Responsibility in Three Federal Agencies.* Washington, D.C.: Brookings Institution.

Kiewiet, D. Roderick, and Mathew D. McCubbins. 1991. *The Logic of Delegation: Congressional Parties and the Appropriations Process.* Chicago: University of Chicago Press.

King, Gary, Robert Keohane, and Sidney Verba. 1994. *Designing Social Inquiry: Scientific Inquiry in Qualitative Research.* Princeton, N.J.: Princeton University Press.

Kingdon, John. 1984. *Agendas, Alternatives and Public Policies.* Boston: Little, Brown.

Kirschten, Dick. 1981. Keeping the Image Clean. *National Journal* 13, no. 34: 1515.

———. 1983. Ruckelshaus May Find EPA's Problems Are Budgetary as Much as Political. *National Journal* 15, no. 13: 659–660.

Knott, Jack, and Gary Miller. 1987. *Reforming Bureaucracy: The Politics of Institutional Choice.* Englewood Cliffs, N.J.: Prentice-Hall.

Kraft, Michael, and Norman Vig. 1984. Environmental Policy in the Reagan Presidency. *Political Science Quarterly* 99, no. 3: 415–439.

Krause, George. 1996. The Institutional Dynamics of Policy Administration: Bureaucratic Influence over Securities Regulation. *American Journal of Political Science* 40, no. 4: 1083–1121.

Kriz, Margaret. 1983. Et Al: Behind the EPA's Superfuss: Whistleblower Hugh Kaufman Is the Environmental Agency's Own Private Hazard. *Student Lawyer* 12, no. 3: 49–50.

Kurtz, Howard. 1983. Since Reagan Took Office, EPA Enforcement Actions Have Fallen. *Washington Post,* March 1.

Kymlicka, B. B., and Jean Matthews, eds. 1988. *The Reagan Revolution?* Chicago: Dorsey Press.

Labaw, Patricia. 1980. *Advanced Questionnaire Design.* Cambridge, Mass.: Abt Books.

Landau, Martin. 1979. *Political Theory and Political Science: Studies in the Methodology of Political Inquiry.* Atlantic Highlands, N.J.: Humanities Press.

Landsberg, Brian K. 1993. The Role of Civil Service Attorneys and Political Appointees in Making Policy in the Civil Rights Division of the United States Department of Justice. *Journal of Law and Politics* 9: 275–289.

———. 1997. *Enforcing Civil Rights: Race Discrimination and the Department of Justice.* Lawrence, Kans.: University Press of Kansas.

Landy, Marc, Marc Roberts, and Stephen Thomas. 1994. *The Environmental Protection Agency: Asking the Wrong Questions.* New York: Oxford University Press.

Lascher, Edward L. Jr. 1994. Assessing Legislative Deliberation. Harvard University John F. Kennedy School of Government Faculty Research Working Paper Series.

———. 1996. Assessing Legislative Deliberation: A Preface to Empirical Analysis. *Legislative Studies Quarterly* 21, no. 4: 501–519.

Lash, Jonathan, Katherine Gillman, and David Sheridan. 1984. *A Season of Spoils: The Reagan Administration's Attack on the Environment.* New York: Pantheon Books.

Lauth, Thomas. 1989. Responding to Elected and Appointed Officials. In *Handbook of Public Administration,* edited by James Perry. San Francisco: Jossey-Bass.

Lawrence, Christine. 1987. Unrest at the Top of the Civil Service. *National Journal* 19, no. 15: 884–888.

Lees, John D., and Michael Turner, eds. 1988. *Reagan's First Four Years.* Manchester: University of Manchester Press.

Leone, Robert. 1984. Regulatory Relief and the Automobile Industry. In *The Reagan Regulatory Strategy,* edited by George C. Eads and Michael Fix. Washington, D.C.: Urban Institute.

Levin, Michael. 1982. Getting There: Implementing the 'Bubble' Policy. In *Social Regulation: Strategies for Reform,* edited by Eugene Bardach and Robert Kagan. San Francisco: Institute for Contemporary Studies.

Levine, Charles. 1986. The Federal Government in the Year 2000: Administrative Legacies of the Reagan Years. *Public Administration Review* 46, no. 3: 195–206.

Lewin, Leif. 1991. *Self-Interest and Public Interest in Western Politics.* New York: Oxford University Press.

Light, Paul C. 1987. When Worlds Collide: The Political-Career Nexus. In *The In-and-Outers: Presidential Appointees and Transient Government in Washington,* edited by G. C. Mackenzie. Baltimore: Johns Hopkins University Press.

———. 1997. *The Tides of Reform.* New Haven, Conn.: Yale University Press.

———. 1999. *The True Size of Government.* Washington, D.C.: The Brookings Institution.

Lindsey, Robert. 1983. Ruckelshaus' Ties Split Environmental Leaders. *New York Times,* March 26.

Lipsky, Michael. 1980. *Street-Level Bureaucracy: Dilemmas of the Individual in Public Services.* New York: Russell Sage.

Lovrich, Nicholas, and Max Neiman. 1984. *Public Choice Theory in Public Administration.* New York: Garland Press.

Lowery, David, and Caryl Rusbult. 1986. Bureaucratic Responses to Anti-Bureaucratic Administrations: Federal Employee Reactions to the Reagan Election. *Administration and Society* 18, no. 1: 45–75.

Lowi, Theodore J. 1964. American Business, Public Policy Case Studies and Political Theory. *World Politics* 16 (July): 677–715.

Luther, Gulick, and L. Urwick. 1937. *Papers on the Science of Administration.* New York: Institute of Public Administration.

Lynn, Laurence. 1984. The Reagan Administration and the Renitent Bureaucracy. In *The Reagan Presidency and the Governing of America,* edited by Lester M. Salamon and Michael S. Lund. Washington, D.C.: Urban Institute.

Lyons, William, and David Lowery. 1989. Citizen Responses to Dissatisfaction in Urban Communities: A Partial Test of a General Model. *Journal of Politics* 51, no. 4: 841–868.

Lyons, William, David Lowery, and Ruth Hoogland De Hoog. 1992. *The Politics of Dissatisfaction: Citizens, Services, and Urban Institutions.* Armonk, N.Y.: Sharpe.

Mackenzie, G. Calvin, ed. 1987. *The In-and-Outers: Presidential Appointees and Transient Government in Washington.* Baltimore: Johns Hopkins University Press.

Maitland, Leslie. 1983. House Unit to Get Subpoenaed Data. *New York Times,* February 17.

Mansbridge, Jane, ed. 1990. *Beyond Self-Interest.* Chicago: University of Chicago Press.

Maranto, Robert. 1991. Does Familiarity Breed Acceptance? Trends in Career-Noncareer Relations in the Reagan Administration. *Administration and Society* 23, no. 2: 247–266.

——. 1993a. The Administrative Strategies of Republican Presidents from Eisenhower to Reagan. *Presidential Studies Quarterly* 23, no. 4: 683–697.

——. 1993b. *Politics and Bureaucracy in the Modern Presidency. Careerists and Appointees in the Reagan Administration.* Westport, Conn.: Greenwood Press.

——. 1993c. Still Clashing after All These Years: Ideological Conflict in the Reagan Executive. *American Journal of Political Science* 37, no. 3: 681–698.

——. 1995. Comparing the Clinton, Bush and Reagan Transitions in the Bureaucracy: Views from the Bureaucrats. Paper presented at the annual meeting of the Midwest Political Science Association, Chicago, April.

Maranto, Robert, and David Schultz. 1991. *A Short History of the United States Civil Service.* Lanham, Md.: University Press of America.

March, James. 1997. Administrative Practice, Organization Theory and Political Philosophy: Ruminations on the Reflections of John Gaus. *PS* 30, no. 4: 689–698.

Marcus, Alfred. 1980a. Environmental Protection Agency. In *The Politics of Regulation,* edited by James Q. Wilson. New York: Basic Books.

——. 1980b. *Promise and Performance: Choosing and Implementing Environmental Policy.* Westport, Conn.: Greenwood Press.

Mashaw, Jerry, and David Harfst. 1987. Regulation and Legal Culture: The Case of Motor Vehicle Safety. *Yale Journal of Regulation* 4, no. 2: 257–316.

——. 1990a. Inside the National Highway Traffic Safety Administration. *University of Chicago Law Review* 57, no. 2: 443–479.

——. 1990b. *The Struggle for Auto Safety.* Cambridge, Mass.: Harvard University Press.

Maslow, A. H. 1943. A Theory of Human Motivation. *Psychological Review* 50: 370–396.

Mathmatica, Inc. 1990. *Food Stamp Participation.* Washington, D.C.: Mathmatica, Inc.

Matt, George, and Thomas Cook. 1993. The War on Fraud and Error in the Food Stamp Program. *Evaluation Review* 17, no. 1: 4–26.

Mayhew, David. 1974. *Congress: The Electoral Connection.* New Haven, Conn.: Yale University Press.

Mayo, Elton. 1945. *The Social Problems of Industrial Civilization.* Boston: Harvard School of Business.

McCubbins, Matthew D. 1985. The Legislative Design of Regulatory Structure. *American Journal of Political Science* 29, no. 4: 721–748.

McCubbins, Matthew D., Roger Noll, and Barry R. Weingast. 1987. Administrative Procedures as Instruments of Political Control. *Journal of Law, Economics, and Organization* 3, no. 2: 243–277.

McCubbins, Matthew D., and Thomas Schwartz. 1984. Congressional Oversight Overlooked: Police Patrols Versus Fire Alarms. *American Journal of Political Science* 28, no. 1: 165–179.

McCurdy, Howard. 1993. *Inside NASA: High Technology and Organizational Change in the U.S. Space Program.* Baltimore: Johns Hopkins University Press.

McGregor, Douglas. 1960. *The Human Side of Enterprise.* New York: McGraw-Hill.

Meidinger, Errol. 1989. The Development of Emissions Trading in U.S. Air Pollution Regulation. In *Making Regulatory Policy,* edited by Keith Hawkins and John Thomas. Pittsburgh: University of Pittsburgh Press.

Meier, Kenneth J. 1980. Measuring Organizational Power: Resources and Autonomy of Government Agencies. *Administration and Society* 12, no. 3: 357–375.

———. 1993. *Politics and the Bureaucracy: Policymaking in the Fourth Branch of Government.* 3d ed. Pacific Grove, Calif.: Brooks/Cole.

———. 1997. Bureaucracy and Democracy: The Case for More Bureaucracy and Less Democracy. *Public Administration Review* 57, no. 3: 193–199.

Meier, Kenneth J., and Lloyd G. Nigro. 1976. Representative Bureaucracy and Policy Preferences. *Public Administration Review* 36: 458–469.

Meiner, Roger, and Bruce Yandle, eds. 1989. *Regulation and the Reagan Era: Politics, Bureaucracy and the Public Interest.* New York: Holmes & Meier.

Meller, Norman. 1966. Executive-Legislative Conflict and Personnel Administration. *Public Personnel Review* (April 1966): 111–114.

Melnick, R. Shep. 1983. *Regulation and the Courts: The Case of the Clean Air Act.* Washington, D.C.: Brookings Institution.

———. 1994. *Between the Lines: Interpreting Welfare Rights.* Washington, D.C.: Brookings Institution.

Menzel, Donald. 1983. Redirecting the Implementation of a Law: The Reagan Administration and Coal Surface Mining Regulation. *Public Administration Review* 43, no. 5: 411–420.

Merton, Robert. 1940. Bureaucratic Structure and Personality. *Social Forces* 18, no. 4: 560–568.

———. 1968. *Social Theory and Social Structure.* New York: Free Press.

Mezey, Michael. 1989. *Congress, the President, and Public Policy.* Boulder, Colo.: Westview Press.

Mezey, Susan Gluck. 1988. *No Longer Disabled: The Federal Courts and the Politics of Social Security Disability.* Westport, Conn.: Greenwood Press.

Michaels, Judith. 1997. *The President's Call: Executive Leadership from FDR to George Bush.* Pittsburgh: University of Pittsburgh Press.

Migue, Jean-Luc, and Gerard Belanger. 1974. Towards a General Theory of Managerial Discretion. *Public Choice* 17: 24–47.

Miles, Rufus. 1978. The Origin and Meaning of Miles' Law. *Public Administration Review* 38, no. 5: 399–403.

Miller, Gary. 1992. *The Managerial Dilemma: The Political Economy of Hierarchy.* Cambridge: Cambridge University Press.

Milward, H. Brint. 1994. Implications of Contracting Out: New Roles for the Hollow State. In *New Paradigms for Government: Issues for the Changing Public Service,* edited by Patricia Ingraham, Barbara Romzek, and Associates. San Francisco: Jossey-Bass.

Moe, Terry. 1982. Regulatory Performance and Presidential Administrations. *American Journal of Political Science* 26, no. 2: 197–224.

———. 1984. The New Economics of Organization. *American Journal of Political Science* 28, no. 4: 739–777.

———. 1985a. Control and Feedback in Economic Regulation: The Case of the NLRB. *American Political Science Review* 79, no. 4: 1094–1116.

———. 1985b. The Politicized Presidency. In *New Directions in American Politics,* edited by John Chubb and Paul Peterson. Washington, D.C.: Brookings Institution.

———. 1987. An Assessment of the Positive Theory of Congressional Dominance. *Legislative Studies Quarterly* 12, no. 4: 475–520.

———. 1989. The Politics of Bureaucratic Structure. In *Can the Government Govern?* edited by John Chubb and Paul Peterson. Washington, D.C.: Brookings Institution.

———. 1995. The Presidency and the Bureaucracy: The Presidential Advantage. In *The Presidency and the Political System.* 4th ed., edited by Michael Nelson. Washington, D.C.: Congressional Quarterly.

Mohr, Lawrence. 1994. Authority in Organizations: On the Reconciliation of Democracy and Expertise. *Journal of Public Administration Research and Theory* 4, no. 1: 49–65.

Monroe, Kristen Renwick. 1998. *The Heart of Altruism: Perceptions of a Common Humanity.* Princeton, N.J.: Princeton University Press.

Morrison, Alan. 1986. OMB Interference with Agency Rulemaking: The Wrong Way to Write Regulation. *Harvard Law Review* 99, no. 5: 1059–1074.

Mosher, Frederick C. 1968. *Democracy and the Public Service.* New York: Oxford University Press.

———. 1984. *A Tale of Two Agencies: A Comparative Analysis of the General Accounting Office and the Office of Management and Budget.* Baton Rouge: Louisiana State University Press.

Mosher, Lawrence. 1980. Environmentalists Question Whether to Retreat or Stay on the Offensive. *National Journal* 12, no. 50: 2116–2121.

———. 1981a. EPA: Reversing Course. *National Journal* 13, no. 17: 743–744.

———. 1981b. Move over, Jim Watt, Anne Gorsuch Is the Latest Target of Environmentalists. *National Journal* 13, no. 43: 1899–1902.

———. 1982a. EPA Critics Agree Agency Under Gorsuch Hasn't Changed Its Spots. *National Journal* 14, no. 46: 1941–1944.

———. 1982b. More Cuts in EPA Research Threaten Its Regulatory Goals, Critics Warn. *National Journal* 14, no. 15: 635.

———. 1983. Ruckelshaus at EPA. *National Journal* 15, no. 33: 1688–1689.

———. 1985. A Clean Sweep. *National Journal* 17, no. 20: 1167–1169.

Moyser, George, and Margaret Wagstaffe. 1987. *Research Methods for Elite Studies.* London: Allen & Unwin.

Nash, Carl. 1981. Passive Restraints: A Regulator's View. In *The Scientific Basis of Health and Safety Regulation,* edited by Robert Crandall and Lester Lave. Washington, D.C.: Brookings Institution.

Nathan, Richard P. 1975. *The Plot That Failed: Nixon and the Administrative Presidency.* New York: Wiley.

———. 1976. Food Stamps and Welfare Reform. *Policy Analysis.* 2, no. 1: 61–70.

———. 1983a. *The Administrative Presidency.* New York: Wiley.

———. 1983b. The Reagan Presidency in Domestic Affairs. In *The Reagan Presidency: An Early Assessment,* edited by Fred Greenstein. Baltimore: Johns Hopkins University Press.

———. 1985. Political Administration Is Legitimate. In *The Reagan Presidency and the Governing of America,* edited by L. M. Salamon and M. S. Lund. Washington D.C.: Urban Institute.

———. 1986. Institutional Change Under Reagan. In *Perspectives on the Reagan Years,* edited by J. L. Palmer. Washington D.C.: Urban Institute.

National Journal. 1984. People: Washington's Movers and Shakers; Hit and Miss List. National Journal 16, no. 37: 1740.

———. 1985. Justice Department: A More Forceful Tone. *National Journal,* 17, no. 20: 1142–1148.

———. 1989. Transportation Department: Taking Charge of Crises. *National Journal* 21, no. 23: 1496.

National Research Council, National Academy of Sciences. 1977. *Decision Making in the Environmental Protection Agency.* Vol. 2. Washington, D.C.: National Academy of Sciences.

Neustadt, Richard E. 1960. *Presidential Power.* New York: Wiley.

———. 1990. *Presidential Power and Modern Presidents: The Politics of Leadership from Roosevelt to Reagan.* New York: Free Press.

Newland, Chester. 1983. A Mid-Term Appraisal—The Reagan Presidency. *Public Administration Review* 43 (January/February): 1–21.

New York Times. 1983. Ex-EPA Aide Says Budget Office Put Case for Industry. *New York Times,* September 28.

Niskanen, William A. Jr. 1971. *Bureaucracy and Representative Government.* Chicago: Aldine Atherton.

———. 1975. Bureaucrats and Politicians. *Journal of Law and Economics* 18, no. 3: 617–643.

———. 1991. A Reflection on Bureaucracy and Representative Government. In *The Budget-Maximizing Bureaucrat: Appraisals and Evidence,* edited by Andre Blais and Stephane Dion. Pittsburgh: University of Pittsburgh Press.

———. 1994. *Bureaucracy and Public Economics.* Brookfield: Edward Elgar.

Oldfield, Duane M. 1996. *The Right and the Righteous: The Christian Right Confronts the Republican Party.* Lanham, Md.: Rowan & Littlefield.

O'Leary, Rosemary. 1993. *Environmental Change: Federal Courts and the EPA.* Philadelphia: Temple University Press.

———. 1994. The Bureaucratic Politics Paradox: The Case of Wetlands Legislation in Nevada. *Journal of Public Administration Research and Theory* 4, no. 4: 443–467.

———. 1995. Bureaucratic Control of Environmental Bureaucracies: Exit, Voice, Loyalty, Neglect and . . . Guerilla Government? Paper presented at the Third National Public Management Research Conference, University of Kansas, Lawrence, October.

———. 1999. Bureaucratic Control of Bureaucracies: Kaufman's The Forest Ranger and Off-Road Vehicles in the Hoosier National Forest. Paper presented at the 1999 Annual Meeting of the American Political Science Association, Atlanta Hilton and Towers, September 2–5.

———. Forthcoming (2000). *Guerilla Government.* Cambridge, MA: MIT Press.

Oppenheim, A. N. 1966. *Questionnaire Design and Attitude Measurement.* New York: Basic Books.

Ott, J. S. 1989. *The Organizational Culture Perspective.* Belmont, Calif.: Dorsey Press.

Palmer, John, and Isabell Sawhill, eds. 1984. *The Reagan Record: An Assessment of America's Changing Domestic Priorities.* Washington, D.C.: Urban Institute.

Percival, Robert V. 1991. Checks Without Balance: Executive Office Oversight of the Environmental Protection Agency. *Law and Contemporary Problems* 54, no. 4: 127–204.

Percy, Stephen. 1989. *Disability, Civil Rights and Public Policy.* Tuscaloosa: University of Alabama Press.

Perry, James. 1996. Measuring Public Service Motivation: Assessment of Construct Reliability and Validity. *Journal of Public Administration Research and Theory* 6, no. 1: 5–22.

———. 1997. Antecedents of Public Service Motivation. *Journal of Public Administration Research and Theory* 7, no. 2: 181–197.

Perry, James L., ed. 1989. *Handbook of Public Administration.* San Francisco: Jossey-Bass.

Perry, James L., and Lois Recascino Wise. 1990. The Motivational Bases of Public Service. *Public Administration Review* 50 (May/June): 367–373.

Peters, B. Guy, and Donald Savoie. 1994. Civil Service Reform: Misdiagnosing the Patient. *Public Administration Review* 54, no. 5: 418–425.

Peterson, Cass. 1984. EPA's Ruckelshaus to Get Half the Budget Increase He Sought. *Washington Post*, January 27.

Pfiffner, James. 1985. Political Public Administration. *Public Administration Review* 45, no. 2: 352–356.

———. 1987. Political Appointees and Career Executives: The Democracy-Bureaucracy Nexus in the Third Century. *Public Administration Review* 47, no. 1: 57–65.

———. 1988. *The Strategic Presidency: Hitting the Ground Running*. Chicago: Dorsey Press.

Pfiffner, James, ed. 1991. *The Managerial Presidency*. Pacific Grove, Calif.: Brooks/Cole.

Pike, David. 1981. Rights Lawyers Rebel at Justice. *National Law Journal*, October 12.

Pious, Richard. 1979. *The American Presidency*. New York: Basic Books.

Plumlee, John. 1981. Lawyers as Bureaucrats: The Impact of Legal Training in the Higher Civil Service. *Public Administration Review* 41, no. 2: 220–228.

Ponder, Daniel. 1994. Reformulating Neutral Competence Theory: Expertise and Responsiveness in the Carter Administration. Paper presented at the annual meeting of the American Political Science Association, New York City, September.

Portney, Kent E., and Jeffrey M. Berry. 1993. Centralizing Regulatory Control and Interest Group Access: The Quayle Council on Competitiveness. Paper presented at the annual meeting of the American Political Science Association, Washington, D.C., September.

Pratt, John W., and Richard J. Zeckhouser, eds. 1985. *Principals and Agents: The Structure of Business*. Cambridge, Mass.: Harvard Business School Press.

President's Private Sector Survey on Cost Control. 1984. *War on Waste: A Report to the President*. Washington, D.C.: U.S. Government Printing Office.

Pruitt, Charles. 1979. People Doing What They Do Best: The Professional Engineers and NHTSA. *Public Administration Review* 39: 363–371.

Przeworski, Adam, and Henry Teune. 1970. *The Logic of Comparative Social Inquiry*. New York: Wiley.

Public Papers of the Presidents of the United States, Reagan. 1981–1988. Washington, D.C.: U.S. Government Printing Office.

Quirk, Paul. 1991. What Do We Know and How Do We Know It? Research on the Presidency. In *Political Science: Looking to the Future*. Vol. 4. Evanston, Ill.: Northwestern University Press.

Rabin, Robert L. 1989. EPA Regulation of Chlorofluorocarbons: A View of the Policy Formulation Process. In *Making Regulatory Policy*, edited by Keith Hawkins and John Thomas. Pittsburgh: University of Pittsburgh Press.

Randall, Ronald. 1979. Presidential Power Versus Bureaucratic Intransigence: The Influence of the Nixon Administration on Welfare Policy. *American Political Science Review* 73, no. 3: 795–810.

Rasmussen, Wayne, and Gladys Baker. 1972. *The Department of Agriculture*. New York: Praeger.

Rauch, Jonathan. 1984. Women and Children's Food Program is 'Off Limits' to Reagan Budget Cutbacks. *National Journal*. November 17: 2197–2199.

Reagan, Ronald. 1989. *Speaking My Mind: Selected Speeches*. Simon & Schuster.

Rector, Robert, and Michael Sanera, eds. 1984. *Steering the Elephant: How Washington Works*. New York: Universe Books.

Redford, Emette. 1969. *Democracy in the Administrative State*. New York: Oxford University Press.

Reske, Henry. 1992. Record EPA Prosecutions. *ABA Journal* 78: 25.

Reynolds, William Bradford. 1986. The Reagan Administration and Civil Rights: Winning the War Against Discrimination. *University of Illinois Law Review*, no. 4: 1001–1024.

Riley, Dennis. 1987. *Controlling the Federal Bureaucracy*. Philadelphia: Temple University Press.

Ringquist, Evan J. 1995. Political Control and Policy Impact in EPA's Office of Water Quality. *American Journal of Political Science* 39, no. 2: 336–363.

Ripley, Randall B., and Grace A. Franklin. 1991. *Congress, the Bureaucracy, and Public Policy*. 5th ed. Pacific Grove, Calif.: Brooks/Cole.

Rochefort, David. 1986. *American Social Welfare Policy*. Boulder, Colo.: Westview Press.

Rockman, Bert A. 1993. Tightening the Reins: The Federal Executive and the Management Philosophy of the Reagan Presidency. *Presidential Studies Quarterly* 23, no. 1: 103–113.

Rohr, John A. 1986. *To Run a Constitution: The Legitimacy of the Administrative State*. Lawrence: University of Kansas Press.

Rom, Mark Carl. 1996. *Public Spirit in the Thrift Tragedy*. Pittsburgh: University of Pittsburgh Press.

Romzek, Barbara. 1990. Employee Investment & Commitment: The Ties That Bind. *Public Administration Review* 50: 374–382.

———. 1992. The Dynamics of Employee Commitment. In *Agenda for Excellence*, edited by Patricia Ingraham and Donald Kettl. Chatham, N.J.: Chatham House.

Romzek, Barbara, and J. Stephen Hendricks. 1982. Organizational Involvement & Representative Bureaucracy: Can We Have It Both Ways? *American Political Science Review* 76: 75–82.

Rose, David. 1982. Twenty-Five Years Later: Where Do We Stand on Equal Employment Opportunity Enforcement? *Vanderbilt Law Review* 42, no. 4: 1122–1182.

Rose, Richard. 1988. Loyalty, Voice or Exit? Margaret Thatcher's Challenge to the Civil Service. *Jahrbuch zur Staats und Verwaltungswissenshaft* 2: 189–218.

Rosellini, Lynn, and Warren Weaver. 1982. Briefing. *New York Times,* July 3.

Rosen, Bernard. 1982. *Holding Government Bureaucracies Accountable.* New York: Praeger.

Rosenbaum, Walter. 1985. *Environmental Politics and Policy.* Washington, D.C.: Congressional Quarterly.

Ross, Stephen. 1973. The Economic Theory of Agency: The Principal's Problem. *American Economic Review Papers and Proceedings* 63, no. 2: 134–139.

Rothman, Stanley, and Robert Lichter. 1983. How Liberal Are Bureaucrats? *Regulation* 7: 16–22.

Rourke, Francis. 1981. Grappling with the Bureaucracy. In *Politics and the Oval Office: Towards Presidential Governance,* edited by Arnold Meltsner. San Francisco: Institute for Contemporary Studies.

———. 1984. *Bureaucracy, Politics and Public Policy.* 3d ed. Boston: Little, Brown.

———. 1987. Bureaucracy in the American Constitutional Order. *Political Science Quarterly* 102, no. 2: 217–232.

———. 1990. Executive Responsiveness to Presidential Policies: The Reagan Presidency. *Congress and the Presidency* 17 no. 1: 1–11.

———. 1991a. American Bureaucracy in a Changing Political Setting. *Journal of Public Administration Research and Theory* 1, no. 2: 111–1129.

———. 1991b. Presidentializing the Bureaucracy: From Kennedy to Reagan. In *The Managerial Presidency,* edited by James Pfiffner. Pacific Grove, Calif.: Brooks/Cole.

———. 1992a. Politics and Professionalism in American Bureaucracy. Paper presented at the annual meeting of the American Political Science Association, Chicago, September.

———. 1992b. Responsiveness and Neutral Competence in American Bureaucracy. *Public Administration Review* 52, no. 6: 539–546.

Rubin, Irene. 1985. *Shrinking the Federal Government: The Effect of Cutbacks on Five Federal Agencies.* New York: Longman.

Russakoff, Dale. 1990. Making Civil Rights the Exception. *Washington Post,* February 1.

Sabatier, Paul, John Loomis, and Catherine McCarthy. 1995. Hierarchical Controls, Professional Norms, Local Constituencies, and Budget Maximization: An Analysis of U.S. Forest Service Planning Decisions. *American Journal of Political Science* 39, no. 1: 204–242.

Salamon, Lester, and Alan Abramson. 1984. Governance: the Politics of Retrenchment. In *The Reagan Record,* edited by John Palmer and Isabell Sawhill. Washington, D.C.: Urban Institute.

Salamon, Lester, and Michael Lund. 1984a. Governance in the Reagan Era: An

Overview. In *The Reagan Presidency and the Governing of America,* edited by Lester Salamon and Michael Lund. Washington, D.C.: Urban Institute.

Salamon, Lester, and Michael Lund, eds. 1984b. *The Reagan Presidency and the Governing of America.* Washington, D.C.: Urban Institute.

Salamon, Lester, and Gary Wamsley. 1975. The Federal Bureaucracy: Responsive to Whom? In *People vs. Government: The Responsiveness of American Institutions,* edited by Leroy Rieselbach. Bloomington: Indiana University Press.

Saltzstein, Grace Hall. 1992. Bureaucratic Responsiveness: Conceptual Issues and Current Research. *Journal of Public Administration Research and Theory* 2, no. 1: 63–88.

Sanders, Elizabeth. 1988. The Presidency and the Bureaucratic State. In *The Presidency and the Political System,* edited by Michael Nelson. Washington, D.C.: Congressional Quarterly.

Sanera, Michael. 1984. Implementing the Mandate. In *Mandate for Leadership II,* edited by Stuart Butler, Michael Sanera, and W. Bruce Weinrod. Washington, D.C.: Heritage Foundation.

Sanjour, William. 1992. In Name Only. *Sierra* 77, no. 5: 75–76, 95–103.

Savoie, Donald. 1994. *Thatcher, Reagan, Mulroney: In Search of a New Bureaucracy.* Pittsburgh: University of Pittsburgh Press.

Schein, Edgar. 1992. *Organizational Culture and Leadership.* 2d ed. San Francisco: Jossey-Bass.

Schick, Allen. 1984. The Budget as an Instrument of Presidential Policy. In *The Reagan Presidency and the Governing of America,* edited by Lester Salamon and Michael Lund. Washington, D.C.: Urban Institute.

Scholz, John and B. Dan Wood. 1998. Controlling the IRS: Principles, Principals, and Public Administration. *American Journal of Political Science* 42, no. 1: 141–162.

Schuman, Howard, and Stanley Presser. 1981. *Questions and Answers in Attitude Surveys.* New York: Academic Press.

Schwab, Larry. 1991. *The Illusion of a Conservative Reagan Revolution.* New Brunswick, N.J.: Transaction Books.

Scott, W. Richard. 1981. *Organizations: Rational, Natural, and Open Systems.* Englewood Cliffs, N.J.: Prentice-Hall.

Seidman, Harold. 1975. *Politics, Position and Power: The Dynamics of Federal Organization.* 2d ed. New York: Oxford University Press.

Selig, Joel. 1984. The Justice Department and Racially Exclusionary Municipal Practices: Creative Ventures in Fair Housing Act Enforcement. *University of California, Davis Law Review* 17, no. 2: 445–504.

———. 1985. The Reagan Justice Department and Civil Rights: What Went Wrong. *University of Illinois Law Review,* no. 4: 785–835.

———. 1988. Affirmative Action in Employment: The Legacy of a Supreme Court Majority. *Indiana Law Journal* 63, no. 2: 301–368.

Selznick, Philip. 1949. *TVA and the Grass Roots: A Study of Politics and Organization.* Berkeley and Los Angeles: University of California Press.

———. 1957. *Leadership in Administration.* New York: Harper & Row.

Seyb, Ron. 1992. Nixon's Administrative Presidency Revisited: Aberration or Watershed? *Journal of Policy History* 4: 249–271.

Shabecoff, Philip. 1982a. House Charges Head of EPA with Contempt. *New York Times,* December 17.

———. 1982b. Resident Whistle-Blower at EPA. *New York Times,* April 14.

———. 1983a. EPA and Aide Reach Settlement Averting Hearing on Harassment. *New York Times,* February 15.

———. 1983b. EPA Nominee Meets with 26 Environmentalists. *New York Times,* April 15.

———. 1983c. Mostly, It's a Matter of Waiting for Ruckelshaus. *New York Times,* April 20.

Shanley, Robert. 1992. *Presidential Influence and Environmental Policy.* Westport, Conn.: Greenwood Press.

Shull, Steven. 1989a. *The President and Civil Rights Policy.* Westport, Conn.: Greenwood Press.

———. 1989b. Presidential Influence Versus Bureaucratic Discretion: President-Agency Relations in Civil Rights Policy. *American Review of Public Administration* 19, no. 3: 197–216.

———. 1993. *A Kinder, Gentler Racism? The Reagan-Bush Civil Rights Legacy.* Armonk, N.Y.: Sharpe.

Sigelman, Lee. 1990. The Bureaucrat as Budget-Maximizer: An Assumption Examined. *Public Budgeting & Finance* 10: 50–59.

Simon, Herbert A. 1976. *Administrative Behavior: A Study of Decision Making Processes in Administrative Organizations.* 3d ed. New York: Free Press.

———. 1997. Why Public Administration? Paper presented at the American Society of Public Administration, Philadelphia, July.

———. 1998. Why Public Administration? *Journal of Public Administration Research and Theory* 8, no. 1: 1–11.

Smith, V. Kerry, ed. 1984. *Environmental Policy Under Reagan's Executive Order.* Chapel Hill: University of North Carolina Press.

Smith, William French. 1991. *Law and Justice in the Reagan Administration: The Memoirs of an Attorney General.* Stanford, Calif.: Hoover Institution.

Spadaro, Robert. 1973. Role Perceptions of Politicians vis-à-vis Public Administrators: Parameters for Public Policy. *Western Political Quarterly* 26 (December 1973): 717–725.

Stanfield, Rochelle. 1984a. Ruckelshaus Casts EPA as "Gorilla" in States' Enforcement Closet. *National Journal,* 16, no. 21: 1034–1038.

———. 1984b. Ruckelshaus and Clark Seek to Blunt Environmental Lobby's Political Swords. *National Journal* 16, no. 26: 1256–1260.

———. 1985. Public Support Has Never Wavered on Environment. *National Journal* 17, no. 2: 113–114.

———. 1986a. The Elusive Bubble. *National Journal* 18, no. 14: 820–822.

———. 1986b. EPA Administrator Lee Thomas Is More a Manager Than a Policy Maker. *National Journal* 18, no. 7: 391–395.

Starr, Judson. 1991. Turbulent Times at Justice and the EPA: The Origins of Environmental Prosecutions and the Work That Remains. *George Washington Law Review* 59, no. 4: 900–915.

Stehr, Steven. 1997. Top Bureaucrats and the Distribution of Influence in Reagan's Executive Branch. *Public Administration Review* 57 (January/February): 75–82.

Stein, Robert. 1990. The Budgetary Effects of Municipal Service Contracting: A Principal-Agent Explanation. *American Journal of Political Science* 34, no. 2: 471–502.

Stewart, Joseph, and Jane Cromartie. 1982. Partisan Presidential Change and Regulatory Policy: The Case of the FTC and Deceptive Practices Enforcement. *Presidential Studies Quarterly* 12, no. 4: 568–574.

Stretton, Howard, and Lionel Orchard. 1994. *Public Goods, Public Enterprise, Public Choice: Theoretical Foundations of the Contemporary Attack on Government.* New York: St. Martin's Press.

Strock, James. 1990. EPA After 20 Years. *Trial* 26, no. 8: 916–937.

———. 1991. Environmental Criminal Enforcement: Priorities for the 1990s. *George Washington Law Review* 59, no. 4: 916–937.

Swain, Frank. 1981. The Department of Transportation. In *Mandate for Leadership*, edited by Charles Heatherly. Washington, D.C.: Heritage Foundation.

Swartzman, Daniel, Richard Liroff, and Kevin Croke, eds. 1982. *Cost-Benefit Analysis and Environmental Regulations: Politics, Ethics, and Methods.* Washington, D.C.: Conservation Foundation.

Sylvester, Kathleen. 1983. The Reagan Rights Record. *National Law Journal*, July 18.

Taylor, Frederick. 1911. *The Principles of Scientific Management.* New York: Harper Bros.

Taylor, Stuart. 1983. EPA Inquiries Center on Four Issues. *New York Times*, March 13.

Thompson, Dennis. 1985. The Possibility of Administrative Ethics. *Public Administration Review* 45, no. 5: 555–561.

Thornton, Jeannye, and Clemens Work. 1983. Highway-Safety Agency Hits a Rough Road. *U.S. News & World Report* 94, no. 17: 68.

Tietenberg, T. H. 1992. *Innovation in Environmental Policy.* Brookfield: Edward Elgar.

Tobin, Richard. 1984. Revising the Clean Air Act. In *Environmental Policy in the 1980s: Reagan's New Agenda*, edited by Norman Vig and Michael Kraft. Washington, D.C.: Congressional Quarterly.

Tolchin, Susan, and Martin Tolchin. 1983. *Dismantling America: The Rush to Deregulate.* Boston: Houghton Mifflin.

Trattner, John. 1988. *The Prune Book.* Lanham, Md.: Madison Books.

Trice, Harrison, and Janice Beyer. 1993. *The Cultures of Work Organizations.* Englewood Cliffs, N.J.: Prentice-Hall.

Tullock, Gordon. 1965. *The Politics of Bureaucracy.* Washington, D.C.: Public Affairs.

Turque, Bill. 1989. Nebraska's New Favorite Son. *Newsweek* 114: 21.

Twentieth Century Fund. 1987. *The Government's Managers.* New York: Priority.

U.S. Commission on Civil Rights. 1981, 1983. *Civil Rights Update.* Washington, D.C.: U.S. Government Printing Office.

———. 1987. *Federal Enforcement of Equal Employment Requirements.* Washington, D.C.: U.S. Government Printing Office.

U.S. Congress. 1990. Joint House Select Committee on Hunger and Senate Committee on Agriculture, Nutrition and Forestry. *National WIC Evaluation: Reporting and Follow-up Issues.* 101st Cong., 2d sess., January 24.

U.S. Department of Agriculture. 1995a. *Nutrition Program Facts.*

———. 1995b. *Permanent Positions by Grade and Staff Year Summary.*

———. 1995c. Food, Nutrition and Consumer Services. *Fact Sheet.*

———. 1999. Food, Nutrition and Consumer Services. *Home Page.* http://www.fns.usda.gov/fncs/.

U.S. Department of Justice. 1979. *Legal Activities 1979.* Washington, D.C.: U.S. Department of Justice.

———. 1983. *New Directions 1981–1983: A Report to Employees from William French Smith.* Washington, D.C.: U.S. Government Printing Office.

———. 1985. *Challenge, Change and Achievement: The Department of Justice, 1981–1985: A Report to Employees from William French Smith.* Washington, D.C.: U.S. Government Printing Office.

———. 1982, 1983. *Annual Report of the Attorney General.* Washington, D.C.: U.S. Government Printing Office.

U.S. Department of Justice. Civil Rights Division. 1988. *Enforcing the Law.* Washington, D.C.: Department of Justice.

U.S. Department of Transportation. National Highway Traffic Safety Administration. 1982. *Sixteenth Annual Report.* Washington, D.C.: U.S. Government Printing Office.

———. 1983. *Motor Vehicle Safety 1982.* Washington, D.C.: U.S. Government Printing Office.

U.S. General Accounting Office. 1978. *Report of the Comptroller General of the U.S. on Federal Regulatory Activities.* Washington, D.C.: General Accounting Office.

———. 1985. *Overview and Perspectives on the Food Stamp Program.* Washington, D.C.: General Accounting Office.

———. 1986. *Food Stamp Program: Accuracy of Quality Control Error Rates.* Washington, D.C.: General Accounting Office.

———. 1989. *Food Assistance: The National WIC Evaluation: Reporting and Follow-up Issues.* Washington, D.C.: General Accounting Office.

U.S. House. 1981a. Committee on the Judiciary. Subcommittee on Civil and Constitutional Rights. *Authorization Request for the Civil Rights Division.* 97th Cong., 1st sess., March 11, April 1.

———. 1981b. Committee on Education and Labor. Subcommittee on Elementary, Secondary and Vocational Education. *Oversight Hearings on Meal Pattern Changes in the School Lunch Program.* 97th Cong., 1st sess., September 17–18.

———. 1981c. Committee on Energy and Commerce. Subcommittee on Oversight and Investigation. *Role of OMB in Regulation.* 97th Cong., 1st sess., June 18.

———. 1981d. Committee on Energy and Commerce. Subcommittee on Telecommunications, Consumer Protection and Finance. *Motor Vehicle Safety Issues.* 97th Cong., 1st sess., June 4, July 29.

———. 1981e. Committee on Energy and Commerce. Subcommittee on Telecommunications, Consumer Protection and Finance. *National Highway Traffic Safety Administration Authorization and Oversight.* 97th Cong., 1st sess., February 25.

———. 1982a. Committee on the Judiciary. *Authorization Request for the Civil Rights Division.* 97th Cong., 2d sess., March 4, March 23, March 25, April 5.

———. 1982b. Committee on Agriculture. Subcommittee on Department Operation. *EPA Pesticide Regulatory Program Study.* 97th Cong., 2d sess., December 17.

———. 1982c. Committee on Education and Labor. Subcommittee on Elementary, Secondary and Vocational Education. *Oversight Hearings on the Administration's 1983 Budget Proposals for Child Nutrition.* 97th Cong., 2d sess., March 22.

———. 1983. Committee on the Judiciary. *Hearings on the Civil Rights of Institutionalized Persons Act.* 98th Cong., 1st sess., December 7.

———. 1985a. Committee on Energy and Commerce. Subcommittee on Oversight and Investigations. *EPA's Asbestos Regulations.* 99th Cong., 1st sess., April 16.

———. 1985b. Committee on the Judiciary. Subcommittee on Civil and Constitutional Rights. *Oversight and Authorization Hearing for the Civil Rights Division of the U.S. Department of Justice.* 99th Cong., 1st sess., April 3, 16, 17.

———. 1985c. Committee on Education and Labor. Subcommittee on Elementary, Secondary and Vocational Education. *Hearing to Extend Five Expiring Child Nutrition Programs.* 99th Cong., 1st sess., April 2.

———. 1986a. Committee on the Judiciary. *Authorization Request for the Civil Rights Division.* 99th Cong., 2d sess., April 17.

———. 1986b. Committee on Energy and Commerce. Subcommittee on Surface Transportation. *Budget Hearing.* 99th Cong., 2d sess., February 19.

———. 1986c. Committee on Energy and Commerce. Subcommittee on Oversight and Investigations. *Review of EPA Regulations.* 99th Cong., 2d sess., May 8.

U.S. Office of Management and Budget. 1978–1990. *Budget of the United States.* Washington, D.C.: U.S. Government Printing Office.

U.S. Presidential Task Force on Regulatory Relief. 1981. *Year End Summary of the*

Administration's Regulatory Relief Program. Washington, D.C.: Office of the Vice-President.

———. 1982. *Reagan Administration Achievements on Regulatory Relief.* Washington, D.C.: Office of the Vice-President.

———. 1983. *Reagan Administration Activities.* Washington, D.C.: Office of the Vice-President.

U.S. Senate. 1981a. Committee on Agriculture, Nutrition and Forestry. *Proposed Reauthorization of the Food and Agriculture Act.* 97th Cong., 1st sess., March 16, April 2, 16.

———. 1981b. Committee on Commerce, Science and Transportation. *Confirmation Hearing of Raymond Peck.* 97th Cong., 1st sess., April 1.

———. 1981c. Committee on Environment and Public Works. *Nominations of Anne Gorsuch and John Hernandez.* 97th Cong., 1st sess., May 1, 4.

———. 1981d. Committee on Agriculture, Nutrition and Forestry. *Nomination of Mary Jarratt to Be Assistant Secretary for Food and Consumer Services.* 97th Cong., 1st sess., May 13.

———. 1981e. Committee on the Judiciary. *Confirmation Hearing of William Bradford Reynolds.* 97th Cong., 1st sess., June 24, July 17.

———. 1983a. Committee on Environment and Public Works. *Nomination of William D. Ruckelshaus.* 98th Cong., 1st sess., May 3, 4, 5.

———. 1983b. Committee on Commerce, Science and Transportation. *Nominations: Department of Transportation and Civil Aeronautics Board. Nomination to Be Administrator, National Highway Traffic Safety Administration.* 98th Cong., 1st sess., September 16, 19; October 26; November 3, 7, 10.

———. 1985a. Committees on Appropriations and Labor and Human Resources. *Joint Hearings on the Care of Institutionalized Mentally Disabled Persons.* 99th Cong., 1st sess., April 1–3.

———. 1985b. Committee on Environment and Public Works. *Nomination of Lee Thomas.* 99th Cong., 1st sess., February 6.

———. 1985c. Committee on the Judiciary. *Nomination of William Bradford Reynolds to be Associate Attorney General of the United States.* 99th Cong., 1st sess., June 4, 5, 18.

———. 1986. Committee on Commerce, Science and Transportation. *Oversight of the National Highway Traffic Safety Administration and the Office of Motor Carriers.* 99th Cong., 2d sess., December 11.

———. 1987a. Committee on the Judiciary. *Authorization Legislation and Oversight of the U.S. Department of Justice.* 100th Cong., 1st sess., March 10.

———. 1987b. Committee on Agriculture, Nutrition and Forestry. *WIC Program.* 100th Cong., 1st sess., June 11.

———. 1989. Committee on the Judiciary. *Department of Justice Authorization and Oversight.* 101st Cong., 1st sess., May 2.

———. 1997. Committee on Commerce, Science and Transportation. *Hearing on Air Bag Safety.* 105th Cong., 2d sess., January 9, April 29.

U.S. Task Force of the Vice President. 1981. *Actions to Help the U.S. Auto Industry.* Washington, D.C.: U.S. Government Printing Office.

U.S. Vice-Presidential Task Force on Regulatory Relief. 1981. *Year End Summary of the Administration's Regulatory Relief Program.* Washington, D.C.: Office of the Vice-President.

Vig, Norman, and Michael Kraft. 1984a. Environmental Policy from the Seventies to the Eighties. In *Environmental Policy in the 1980s: Reagan's New Agenda,* edited by Norman Vig and Michael Kraft. Washington, D.C.: Congressional Quarterly.

———, eds. 1984b. *Environmental Policy in the 1980s: Reagan's New Agenda.* Washington, D.C.: Congressional Quarterly.

Volcker, Paul. 1990. *Leadership for America: Rebuilding the Public Service. The Report of the National Commission on the Public Service.* Lexington, Mass.: Lexington Books.

Wald, Matthew. 1992. Lawn Mower is New Target in War Against Air Pollution. *New York Times* August 6: 1.

Warshaw, Shirley Anne. 1995. White House Control of Domestic Policy Making: The Reagan Years. *Public Administration Review* 55, no. 3: 247–252.

———. 1996. *Powersharing: White House–Cabinet Relations in the Modern Presidency.* Albany: State University of New York Press.

Warwick, Donald. 1975. *A Theory of Bureaucracy: Politics, Personality and Organization in the State Department.* Cambridge, Mass.: Harvard University Press.

Washington Council of Lawyers. 1982. *Reagan Civil Rights. The First Twenty Months.* Washington, D.C.: Washington Council of Lawyers.

Waterman, Richard. 1989a. Environmental Policy from the Seventies to the Eighties. In *Environmental Policy in the 1980s: Reagan's New Agenda,* edited by Norman Vig and Michael Kraft. Washington, D.C.: Congressional Quarterly.

———. 1989b. *Presidential Influence and the Administrative State.* Knoxville: University of Tennessee Press.

Waterman, Richard, and Kenneth Meier. 1998. Principal-Agent Models: An Expansion. *Journal of Public Administration Research and Theory* 8, no. 2: 173–202.

Waterman, Richard, Robert Wright, and Amelia Rouse. 1994. The Other Side of Political Control of the Bureaucracy: Agents' Perceptions of Influence and Control. Paper presented at the annual meeting of the American Political Science Association, New York City, September.

Weber, Max. 1946. Bureaucracy. In *From Max Weber: Essays in Sociology,* edited by H. H. Gerth and C. Wright Mills. New York: Oxford University Press.

Weekly Compilation of Presidential Documents, Reagan. 1981. Washington, D.C.: U.S. Government Printing Office.

Weingast, Barry. 1984. The Congressional-Bureaucratic System: A Principal-Agent Perspective with Applications to the SEC. *Public Choice* 44, no. 1: 147–191.

Weingast, Barry, and Mark Moran. 1982. The Myth of the Run Away Bureaucracy. *Regulation* 6 (May/June): 22–8.

———. 1983. Bureaucratic Discretion or Congressional Control? Regulatory Policymaking by the Federal Trade Commission. *Journal of Political Economy* 91, no. 5: 765–800.

Weinraub, Judith. 1992. The Tiger in the Consumers' Tank: Joan Claybrook, Roaring About Campaign Funding. *Washington Post,* May 5.

Weisband, Edward, and Thomas Franck. 1975. *Resignation in Protest.* New York: Grossman.

West, William. 1995. *Controlling the Bureaucracy: Institutional Constraints in Theory and Practice.* Armonk, N.Y.: Sharpe.

West, William, and Joseph Cooper. 1985. The Rise of Administrative Clearance. In *The Presidency and Public Policymaking,* edited by George Edwards, Steven Shull, and Norman Thomas. Pittsburgh: University of Pittsburgh Press.

Whitaker, John C. 1976. *Striking a Balance: Environment and Natural Resources Policy in the Nixon-Ford Years.* Washington, D.C.: American Enterprise Institute.

Wholey, Joseph. 1984. Executive Agency Retrenchment. In *Federal Budget Policy in the 1980's,* edited by Gregory Mills and John Palmer. Washington, D.C.: Urban Institute.

Wildavsky, Aaron B. 1979. *Speaking Truth to Power: The Art and Craft of Policy Analysis.* Boston: Little, Brown.

———. 1984. *The Politics of the Budgetary Process.* 4th ed. Boston: Little, Brown.

———. 1992. *The New Politics of the Budgetary Process.* 2d ed. New York: Harper-Collins.

Wilsford, David. 1984. Exit and Voice: Strategies for Change in Bureaucratic-Legislative Policymaking. *Policy Studies Journal* 12, no. 3: 431–445.

Wilson, Graham K. 1977. Are Department Secretaries Really a President's Natural Enemies? *British Journal of Political Science* 7 (July): 2723–2799.

Wilson, James Q. 1967. The Bureaucracy Problem. *The Public Interest,* no. 6: 3–9.

———. 1989. *Bureaucracy: What Government Agencies Do and Why They Do It.* New York: Basic Books.

Wilson, Patricia. 1994. Power, Politics, and Other Reasons Why Senior Executives Leave the Federal Government. *Public Administration Review* 54, no. 1: 12–19.

Wilson, Woodrow. 1887. The Study of Administration. *Political Science Quarterly* 2, no. 2: 197–222.

Wines, Michael. 1982a. Administration Says It Merely Seeks a Better Way to Enforce Civil Rights. *National Journal* 14, no. 13: 536–541.

———. 1982b. Automobile Bumper Standard Crumples as Cost-Benefit Analysis Falls Short. *National Journal* 14, no. 4: 145–149.

———. 1983. Reagan Plan to Relieve Auto Industry Gets Mixed Grades. *National Journal* 15, no. 30: 1532–1537.

Withey, Michael, and William Cooper. 1989. Predicting Exit, Voice, Loyalty and Neglect. *Administrative Science Quarterly* 34, no. 4: 521–539.

Woll, Peter. 1977. *American Bureaucracy.* 2d ed. New York: Norton.

Wolters, Raymond. 1996. Right Turn: William Bradford Reynolds, the Reagan Administration, and Black Civil Rights. New Brunswick, NJ: Transaction Publishers.

Wood, B. Dan. 1988. Principals, Bureaucrats, and Responsiveness in Clean Air Enforcement. *American Political Science Review* 82, no. 1: 213–234.

Wood, B. Dan, and James Anderson. 1991. The Politics (or Nonpolitics) of U.S. Antitrust Regulation. Paper presented at the annual meeting of the Midwest Political Science Association, Chicago, April.

Wood, B. Dan, and Richard Waterman. 1991. The Dynamics of Political Control of the Bureaucracy. *American Political Science Review* 85, no. 3: 801–828.

———. 1994. *Bureaucratic Dynamics: The Role of Bureaucracy in a Democracy.* Boulder, Colo.: Westview Press.

Worsham, Jeff, Marc Allen Eisner, and Evan J. Ringquist. 1997. Assessing the Assumptions: A Critical Analysis of Agency Theory. *Administration & Society* 28, no. 4: 419–440.

Yarbrough, Tinsley, ed. 1985. *The Reagan Administration and Human Rights.* New York: Praeger.

Yates, Douglas. 1982. *Bureaucratic Democracy: The Search for Democracy and Efficiency in American Government.* Cambridge, Mass.: Harvard University Press.

INDEX

Aberbach, Joel D., 10, 18, 26

acid rain, 113, 138, 139, 144, 145, 146

administrative presidency: defined
  183n1; described, 5–8; Reagan's use
  of, 2–3, 5, 6, 8–10, 13, 14, 32–33, 158;
  resistance and, 3, 156–58;
  responsiveness and, 1–15, 154,
  170–72; tools of, 5–8, 14–15, 23, 24,
  29, 30–32, 156–58

Administrative Procedure Act, 119

AFDC. *See* Aid to Families with
  Dependent Children

affirmative action, 85, 92

agency context: 13, 25, 29, 160–167;
  bureaucratic behavior and, 20, 22,
  25–30, 59–60, 110, 155, 160–61; at
  CRD, 82–84; at EPA, 110–15; at
  NHTSA, 40, 54–58; responsiveness
  and, 13, 168

agency culture: 27–28; bureaucratic
  behavior and, 25, 59, 148, 161; at

CRD, 107; at EPA, 110, 137, 150; at
  FNS, 63; ideology and, 167; at
  NHTSA, 40; resistance and, 29, 149

agency history: 27–28; bureaucratic
  behavior and, 110, 161–63; at CRD,
  101, 104, 161, 162; at EPA, 111–15, 137,
  150, 161, 162, 163; at FNS, 62–65, 79,
  161, 162; at NHTSA, 41–43, 51, 56–58,
  161–62; resistance and, 56–58, 104

Agriculture, U.S. Department of
  (USDA), 62, 75

Aid to Families with Dependent
  Children (AFDC), 66

air-bag regulations: 27, 56–57, 161, 169;
  under Claybrook, 42; under Peck,
  40, 43, 45–46, 47, 50

Alm, Al, 140

altruism: 13, 20, 21, 22, 158, 160, 167; at
  FNS, 62–63. *See also* public spirit;
  role perception

Amaker, Norman, 84

Power, Conflict, and Democracy:
American Politics Into the Twenty-first Century